Chicken Soup for the Soul.

Angels Among Us

Chicken Soup for the Soul: Angels Among Us
101 Inspirational Stories of Miracles, Faith, and Answered Prayers
Jack Canfield, Mark Victor Hansen, Amy Newmark

Front cover photo courtesy of Getty Images/Richard Newstead, Lifesize. Back cover and interior photo courtesy of Photos.com/Musat (© Christian Musat), and Photos.com. *Cover and Interior Design & Layout by Pneuma Books, LLC*

Distributed to the booktrade by Simon & Schuster. SAN: 200-2442

Publisher's Cataloging-in-Publication Data
(Prepared by The Donohue Group)

Chicken soup for the soul : angels among us : 101 inspirational stories of
  miracles, faith, and answered prayers / [compiled by] Jack Canfield, Mark
  Victor Hansen, [and] Amy Newmark.

     p. ; cm.

  ISBN: 978-1-61159-906-0

  1. Angels--Literary collections. 2. Angels--Anecdotes. 3. Spiritualism--Literary
collections. 4. Spiritualism--Anecdotes. 5. Miracles--Literary collections. 6. Miracles-
-Anecdotes. 7. Anecdotes. I. Canfield, Jack, 1944- II. Hansen, Mark Victor. III.
Newmark, Amy. IV. Title: Angels among us

PN6071.A65 C45 2013
810.8/02/37   2012951784

PRINTED IN THE UNITED STATES OF AMERICA
on acid∞free paper

22 21 20 19 18 17 16 15 14 13   01 02 03 04 05 06 07 08 09 10

Chicken Soup
for the Soul.

Angels
Among Us

101 Inspirational Stories of
Miracles, Faith, and
Answered Prayers

Jack Canfield
Mark Victor Hansen
Amy Newmark

Chicken Soup for the Soul Publishing, LLC
Cos Cob, CT

Contents

❶

~Miraculous Intervention~

❷

~Divine Messengers~

❸
~Answered Prayers~

❹
~Angels in Disguise~

❺
~Faith in Action~

❻

~Angelic Visitors~

❼

~Healing Touches~

8

~Love from Beyond~

9

~Angel Guides~

❿
~Angel Protection~

Angels Among Us

Among Us

Miraculous Intervention

Neighborhood Watch

Angels are never too distant to hear you.
~Author Unknown

I t was summer and I was twelve. My friend and I had been walking the neighborhood. It was around dusk, or shortly after, because it was the coolest time to be outside. There were plenty of street lights so we never felt in any danger. We were doing what twelve-year-old girls do, chatting, singing, being silly, and just enjoying one another's company.

On this particular night, we got this eerie feeling that we were being watched. About a block from our street, not wanting to appear afraid, we kept our pace steady, not hurrying.

"We should be back on our street in a few minutes," I said.

"Yes, our brothers are still outside, riding their bikes," said my friend. This was our way of communicating to our potential watcher that we were safer than we might look.

The next night, while her parents were out, someone tried to break into a bathroom window of my friend's house. Her two older brothers frightened him away.

I saw the lights from the police car when they pulled up to my friend's house down the street, but I didn't learn what had happened until the next day.

"Do you think this was the person watching us yesterday?" I asked.

"I bet it was," she whispered. "Someone was watching to see when the car was gone before they tried to break in."

This man may or may not have been the person who was watching us. In fact we had no proof that anyone was watching us at all, just a gut feeling. Still I feared that he would try to come for me next.

We had many discussions about it over the next week. This was high drama for twelve-year-olds. We were not afraid during the day. It was the nights that we feared. Well, I feared them. My friend had a house full of people at all times. I only had two younger brothers and a mom. My dad was in Vietnam.

We did not have central air, just a window unit in the kitchen. At night, unless it was abnormally hot, we turned it off and opened the windows. I began to keep my windows closed and locked, my curtains pulled. I also pulled the covers up to my chin, a ridiculous safety ploy, but one every child understands. I would lie there, unable to sleep, imagining that someone was watching and waiting.

When I did fall asleep, I would wake up several times a night, usually sweating heavily from the closed windows, the covers, and the fear. I remember reciting a kind of rhyming prayer that I had learned as a very small child: "Four corners to my bed. Four angels 'round my head. One to keep me. One to pray. Two to guide me through each day." I did not want to close my eyes, but fatigue always won out.

One evening, my brothers, my mom and I went to visit with a family down the street. We enjoyed a meal and then played pinochle for a while. Having not slept much, I was the first to grow tired and decided to walk home.

It wasn't long before I noticed that a car was following me down the street. I was right on the curb and the car was not passing. It was keeping pace with me. I didn't want to go back since that was the direction of the car, and I didn't want to run, yet. When I arrived at the bottom of my driveway, I was sure the car would drive past. I was wrong. It followed me up the driveway. As I approached the front door, I heard a car door open and shut behind me.

In our neighborhood, doors were seldom locked unless everyone was settled in for the night. We had been gone and ours were not locked. All of our lights were off. The house, inside and outside, was totally dark. Part of me was afraid to enter the house. Part of me felt an urgency to do so, quickly.

About that time, our next-door neighbor, a Green Beret, pulled into his drive on his motorcycle. It was impossible not to notice him since his motorcycle was pretty loud. He pulled his beret on as he hopped off his bike and waved.

I guess the sight of him must have scared off the driver. I heard the car door open and shut again. I turned just in time to see a dark car pulling out of my driveway. Thankfully, I also saw the rest of my family making their way down the street toward home. I waited on the front porch so we could enter the house together.

"Who was that in the driveway?" my mother asked me.

"I don't know," I replied, "but they followed me home."

"I don't think so, honey. Why would they follow you?" she asked. "They were probably just at the wrong house."

I told her the whole story. The feeling someone was watching us. Our take on the break-in down the street. Now this. It was clear that she thought I was letting my imagination run wild.

I added, "Mr. M. pulled up on his motorcycle and scared them away."

My mom gave me the strangest look. "You know that Mr. M. is in Vietnam with Daddy," she said. Yes, I did know that, but I was so relieved to see him pull into his driveway that I had forgotten. "He must be back," I said. "He even waved to me."

"No, honey, he's not back."

I was not convinced. I had seen him. My mother had to walk me next door to talk with his wife who confirmed that he was still overseas.

That night, after praying and repeating my angel rhyme in my head, I thought about Mr. M. He was there. I saw him and I heard his motorcycle, and so did the person who was following me. Suddenly, I noticed a light at the end of my bed. At first I thought it was an optical illusion, the angle of the streetlight through my curtains. I just lay still and watched it, wondering. A sense of calm slowly flowed through me.

I knew, just as sure as I knew anything in this world, that I was being visited by an angel. God had sent this messenger to me to let me know He was watching over me. Maybe that had been who I had mistaken for Mr. M.

All my fear dissipated. I tossed the covers off, got up and opened the windows to the small, but welcome, breeze. Back in bed, I looked at the foot of my bed. The light was still there, a soft glowing shape. It was the best night's sleep I had in days. No other incidents disturbed those carefree summer days.

~Debbie Acklin

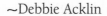

Rx for the Road

Nature has no mercy at all. Nature says,
"I'm going to snow. If you have on a bikini and no snowshoes,
that's tough. I am going to snow anyway."
~Maya Angelou

Dad's voice came across the phone line, frantic, "I'm out of my medication." Since Dad had gotten older, I tried to remind him not to let his prescriptions run out. Yet here we were again, in a crunch. I pushed the curtain away from my window and looked outside. Snow had been piling up since early that morning and now my car was covered with at least six inches of white powder. I took a deep breath and thought for a moment. "Don't worry, Dad," I said. "I'll call the pharmacy and pick up the refill."

"Just be careful," he reminded. "It looks like it's getting slippery out there."

It wasn't getting slippery—it already was slippery. I stood at the window an extra minute after we finished the call and watched as cars inched along, their tires barely getting any traction on the road. I wasn't looking forward to this drive, even though it was only a mile and a half to Dad's house, with the pharmacy directly on the way. I dressed for the elements, then grabbed my car keys. As I walked down my front steps, I could hear emergency sirens blaring on the main road. An accident. I tossed my car keys back into the house, then pulled my scarf a little snugger around my neck. I'd better walk this errand.

In more pleasant weather, I had made this walk with some frequency. I enjoyed the exercise and the opportunity to connect with some neighbors along the way. But today, under these conditions, I was not looking forward to the experience. By the time I reached the pharmacy though, I was grateful that I had walked. Cars were having trouble moving forward, backing up, and stopping.

I looked up into the gray sky as I started my final leg of the trip and sent up a silent prayer of gratitude that I was moving along safely, and soon I discovered I actually was enjoying the whole situation. The brisk air was just chilled enough to be invigorating and I found myself reveling in the sights and smells of a fresh snowfall. In fact, I hadn't enjoyed, really enjoyed, a snowstorm like this since I was a child.

Then, just as I was pondering these thoughts, I felt a hand grab me at the elbow and give me a sharp tug. I stumbled several feet onto a neighbor's lawn only to see a car careening up the curb. The vehicle finally came to rest in the exact place where I had been walking. Stunned, I dusted myself off, then turned around to thank whomever it was who had pulled me from danger. Yet, no one was there nor were there any tracks other than mine in the snow. As I started on my way again, I offered up another silent prayer of gratitude—this time for the angel sent to watch over me and keep me safe in the snow.

~Monica A. Andermann

A White Feather

The guardian angels of life fly so high as to be beyond our sight,
but they are always looking down upon us.
~Jean Paul Richter

I t was about ten o'clock on a Saturday morning. Having changed my baby daughter Holly, aged eight months, I decided to take a trip to the shops to get something for our lunch. We lived in a small village at the time and although it was only a ten-minute drive to get to the local shops, the drive was via several narrow lanes. I had lived in the village all my life, so I knew the road like the back of my hand.

I strapped Holly into her car seat and we set off for the short journey, listening to her favourite nursery rhymes CD. We arrived at the local shops, went into the bakery and the post office, and then I strapped Holly back into the car and we set off for home.

The lanes in the village were never designed for heavy goods vehicles and yet truck drivers still insisted on using them as a short cut to get to the main road. Over the years I had signed many petitions that had been drawn up by other villagers, but the council still allowed them to use the narrow roads. So I was always careful navigating the lanes, in particular one very tight bend that was almost an S shape and just a little wider than one car. If another vehicle were coming the other way, one of them would have to reverse up the lane a few yards to allow the other to pass.

As we headed home and approached the S-bend, I put my foot

gently on the brake just in case a car was coming the other way. As I drove round the bend, there heading straight toward us was a huge red truck. At the speed he was going, there was no way he would ever hit his brakes in time to stop and he was heading directly for our car.

I really believed that the truck was going to plough straight into us, so in a split second I hit my brakes, unbuckled my seat belt and threw myself over Holly. At least if I took the impact, she might survive. They say your life flashes before you, but that's not what happened to me. All that went through my mind was, "Right, this is my time then." My darling dad had a saying when he was alive: "When the white feather touches you on your head, then it is your time to go." All I remember thinking is, "I hope this doesn't hurt too much and I pray that my baby survives."

In those few seconds, I closed my eyes and prepared myself for what was coming, telling Holly how much I loved her. I could hear the truck rumbling loudly towards us as I shielded my little girl.

Suddenly everything went completely silent. So silent that I thought the impact must have happened and I was already dead, being transported to heaven or wherever it is we go next. There was no noise whatsoever. After what seemed like ages, I gingerly opened my eyes. I was still lying across Holly, I was still in my car, and the road was completely quiet. No traffic, no truck coming towards us, nothing. It was as if a huge hand had picked up my car, moved it out of the way and placed it back down on the road again. I looked in the rearview mirror and there was no sign of the red truck. It had simply vanished into thin air.

Shakily I drove home. There wasn't another car on the road for the whole journey. When I got Holly out of her car seat, there in her seat was a small white feather.

I keep the feather in my car as a reminder that angels were looking after us that day, almost ten years ago, and I thank them every day for looking after us when we travel anywhere.

~Deborah Durbin

Divine Driver

Never drive faster than your guardian angel can fly.
~Author Unknown

It was such gorgeous weather that mid-June day thirteen years ago. My friend Kristen and I gathered some friends to go to the beach. Kristen, Karen, Eric and I met and piled into my new, cherry-red Mazda Protégé. I was so excited to drive my new wheels to the beach. Windows down, beach gear in the trunk, the smell of sunscreen wafting through the car, we hopped on the highway, toward the beaches of Rhode Island. None of us had any obligations for the day, so it was the start of a relaxing summer day in our young carefree lives.

As we got closer to the beaches, we noticed an increase in traffic.

"Oh no, I forgot about the Air Show this weekend! The traffic is going to be horrible," I lamented.

I was referring to the annual Quonset Air Show, hosted by the Rhode Island National Guard. With amazing aerial displays and family-oriented activities, the show is very popular and draws a huge crowd. That crowd uses the freeway to get there, the same freeway that everyone uses to get to the beaches. Therefore, traffic that weekend is even more congested than usual.

"I should have gone another way," I muttered.

"But it looks like the cars are only clogging up the show exit," Kristen pointed out.

As we got closer to the Air Show exit on the right, we realized that Kristen was correct. I was able to keep my reasonably fast speed because the traffic affected only that exit. I kept my foot on the gas and kept cruising along in the right lane.

Until…

What was that car doing? It was stopped in the line of traffic at the exit, but started to pull out in front of me. There was no way it could accelerate fast enough! We were going to crash! I slammed on my brakes. I couldn't stop in time. We were going to crash!

The smell of brakes burning; everything was in slow motion; the other car was getting closer; someone in my car was screaming….

We veered into the left lane. But a car was there! We were going to sideswipe that car now! I screamed.

I was shaking. We were in the breakdown lane. I was a little confused. We were safe. We didn't get into an accident. We were okay! There was silence in the car, a long silence. We all had to process what almost happened.

The car that caused this whole thing drove by slowly, its occupants looking at us. I wasn't sure if the looks on their faces were apologetic, confused, indifferent, or just ignorant to their mistake. I didn't care. I was just happy to sit there, in silence.

Then, "That was the best driving I have ever seen!" Eric exclaimed from the back seat.

It pulled us out of our silence and our thoughts. Kristen breathed a sigh of relief. "I thought we were done there!"

"I can't believe those people did that!" Karen said.

Eric just restated, "That was the best driving I have ever seen!"

I couldn't say anything. I needed to figure how to explain what had happened: It wasn't me driving the car.

I hit the brakes, but after that I didn't do anything else — except scream. When our car veered to the left lane, I didn't steer it. The car next to us in the left lane somehow moved out of the way just in time, but it wasn't me who perfectly timed the maneuver. It wasn't me who calmly steered the car back into the right lane when the coast was clear and then calmly moved to the breakdown lane. It was not me. Someone or something had intervened.

When we finally got back on the road and drove to the beach, I still hadn't found the words to describe what had happened. Instead I enjoyed the beautiful beach day with my friends with a newfound respect for life. But most of all, I marveled at who or what helped me that day.

I didn't tell the others in the car about the divine intervention until many weeks later. I couldn't think of any other way to say it except, "It wasn't me driving that car."

Today, I still talk about that event with anyone who will listen. I state it as a fact. I would swear to it in court. There is no doubt in my mind. An angelic being saved my friends and me from a terrible accident that day.

I always think about that day. I think about it every time I witness something beautiful, or have a good laugh, or hug my husband. I think about it more now after having my two beautiful children. When I think about the angel that helped me, I easily find the words to whisper, "Thank you. Thank you always."

~Melissa G. Christensen

The Boy at the Pool

"If you can believe, all things are possible to him who believes."
~Mark 9:23

I t was a typical blistering hot Georgia summer, and like every other kid in the state I wanted to go swimming. The nearest pool was in the apartment complex six blocks away. I passed it every day on my walk home from school. My steps would slow as I walked past the fenced enclosure and I'd listen with envy to the cool splashes and squeals of delight coming from the lucky kids that lived there.

The closest I was going to get was with our green backyard hose hooked to the garden sprinkler! It just wasn't the same.

One hot Friday afternoon as I passed the pool, the plan began to formulate. I pulled my sister Joan aside and said, "Hey, what if we just put our swimsuits on under our clothes tomorrow and ask Mama if we can walk to the drugstore for an ice cream cone? We could just go in the gate like all the other kids and we can swim and play in the water a little while, slip our shorts back on and the sun will dry our hair while we walk home. Want to?"

Joan was six. She looked up to me as the older, wiser one and nodded in total agreement. If I suggested it, it must be fine and somehow that seemed almost like getting Mama's permission. So the plan was set and the next afternoon we were going swimming.

Saturday afternoon, just as planned, we asked if we could walk to the drugstore and get ice cream. When Mama agreed, we ran in and slipped on our swimsuits under our shorts and headed out the door. That was when the first obstacle was thrown into the plan. Mama was standing at the back door with my four-year-old sister.

"Andrea, come and get Renee and let her walk with you. She is crying because you are leaving her."

It was going to be hard enough to get Joan to stay quiet—Renee would never understand she wasn't supposed to tell, and she didn't have a swimsuit on. I went back grudgingly, got her by the hand and headed down the driveway once more.

As soon as we were out of earshot I turned to Renee and said, "We are going to go play at a pool a few minutes and if you promise not to tell, we'll let you go swimming too—promise?" She nodded—delighted to be included like a big girl. "You can just swim in your shorts. That's how you do it in the sprinkler at home."

When we got to the pool the second obstacle appeared—the pool was closed and the gate to the surrounding fence padlocked. Again, I should have stopped but I had come this far and the pool was beckoning, so I climbed over the gate. Joan helped push Renee up to me.

We pulled off our shorts, laid them on a nearby lounge chair, and carefully stepped into the cool blue water. It was heaven.

We splashed and played, and I was careful not to let my sisters out of the three-foot section of the pool. After about fifteen minutes I decided that we should get out and start drying off. As I turned around to gather everyone's clothes I heard a loud "splash." Renee was nowhere in sight. I frantically searched the pool and saw the top of her head just under the water—directly underneath the diving board in the nine-foot deep section of the pool!

I wish I could say my bravery and concern for her made me jump in to save her, but the truth is I could not go home and tell Mama I took her baby and let her drown. So without thinking I sailed right in after her, never considering the fact that now neither of us could get out because I could not swim any better than she could.

Groping around underwater, my hand finally made contact with her. I latched on and pulled her up to the top of the water so she could get a breath. Of course as I did, and both my hands were pushing her upward, I held my breath as I went under.

When it felt my lungs were going to explode, I fought to get to the top as she sunk back into the water. I held onto her with one hand, knowing if I let her go she might sink to the bottom and I might not be able to reach her again.

As I went to the top for a breath I reached upward for the diving board—my only hope was to grab onto something stable so I could pull us out—but it was inches from my reach. I barely knew how to tread water and that was made more difficult with only one free hand. I sunk back down into the water and pushed her upward for a breath.

I remember thinking "God, help us—we are going to drown." As she came back down in the water I knew my strength was giving out and this would probably be my last chance to try to reach that diving board. I gathered all my strength to try to reach the end of the diving board, but again fell short.

As my outstretched arm failed to make contact and was sinking back down, I suddenly felt someone holding me up by my wrist. In shock I looked up into the face of a little boy no older than I was.

Not a word was exchanged. He did not seem upset or in a panic. He was just calmly lying on the diving board leaning forward, both of his hands wrapped tightly around my wrist. He didn't try to pull us out. He simply pulled my hand the few inches I needed in order to reach the diving board.

Once I had hold of something solid I was able to pull up and get to the side of the pool. I struggled and finally got us out, and holding tight to my sister, we fell back on the warm concrete terrified and exhausted. Suddenly I remembered the boy. I looked for him but he was gone. All three of us had seen him, yet no one had seen him come in or leave... and the gate was still locked!

My sister and I are alive today because of this mysterious little boy. I always felt, and even more so looking back on it today, that the only logical explanation was divine intervention.

~Andrea Peebles

Proof Positive

Angels are direct creations of God, each one a unique Master's piece.
~Eileen Elias Freeman,
The Angels' Little Instruction Book

On Friday, February 9, 2001, an angel talked to me. I had not believed in angels. I was pragmatic, fifty-three years old, and happily married for thirty-two years. I made decisions based on my five senses.

Around noon, I was driving my Jeep alone at sixty miles per hour on Highway 65, a four-lane expressway. All of a sudden, a male voice shouted to me from the front passenger seat "SLOW TO 35." Even though nobody else was in my Jeep, I looked around to see who said it. I knew the voice was real, but from someone or something I could not see.

I tried to figure out what to do. How could this be happening? My sixth sense kicked in. My mind told me "This sounds important." My intuition told me to do what it said. I immediately slowed to thirty-five miles per hour. Within seconds, a car sped past me and stopped at a traffic signal that was hundreds of feet ahead and showing green.

"That is crazy," I said to myself. "Why are they stopping at a green light?"

Then to my surprise, as I approached that green light, that car turned into my lane.

I slammed on my brakes, but kept skidding right into the side of the car and landed on top of the hood. Both vehicles were demolished. I was shaken, but not injured.

When the California Highway Patrol arrived, I told the officer what happened. He said, "Mister, if you were going sixty, you would most certainly be dead. I see this all the time."

At that moment, everything came into focus. I realized that the voice and my willingness to follow the message saved my life and the life of the other driver. Who was that voice and why me? What would I tell people about this? Would they call me crazy? Should I keep this to myself? Was my encounter with an angel? I knew that I had to find out.

For the next three years I consulted with all kinds of professionals who might know whose voice it was, yet with no tangible results. Then one night as my wife Carol and I slept, we were woken at 1:30 a.m. by our bed shaking violently from side to side and all the lights going on and off. This lasted for about a minute.

We were startled and scared, but could not find anyone in our house, or any reason for these events. As I was starting to go back to sleep, with my eyes closed but still awake, a bright light came into the center of my vision. This light instantly turned into a picture of an incredibly large and beautiful angel standing in profile.

I saw huge wings that towered over his head. I knew it would be impossible to describe the intricate detail of his body, wings, and feathers to others. Then the angel turned its head and looked directly at me. The figure rapidly transformed into this same angel, but on a horse with warrior clothing, a shield, and a sword.

As quickly as it had come, it disappeared. I realized that I had experienced a "vision." This vision was so unforgettable that I could not sleep the rest of the night, wondering who it was, why I got to see this vision... so many questions.

The next morning, I felt this intense message to go to a nearby bookstore to look for angel books. As I got to the metaphysical section, I took the very first angel book off the shelf and turned to a random page in the middle of the book. And there He was—plain as day. It was an illustration of an angel on his horse with his shield and sword. The book identified this angel as Archangel Michael.

It was clear to me that I was led to this store to find my answer. I finally got the confirmation of the angel in the vision.

Three years later in May 2008, the confirmation process continued on a trip to Sedona, Arizona. We had become interested in labyrinths, so when we found one at the St. Andrew's Episcopal Church there, we decided to walk it. This one was painted on the large concrete parking lot surface modeled to match the one in Chartres, France. As we walked it, I noticed that the clouds were building rapidly overhead. I looked up and, incredibly, this angel came to me again in the form of a cloud—the same image on his horse with a sword. We could not believe our eyes! Carol and I were so excited. It was surreal. How could clouds do this?

Fortunately, I had my camera and I hurriedly took photos of Archangel Michael in this cloud before it disappeared. Now I had my proof!

Over the years following these events, I have had over 200 visions. Visions of people, animals, and symbols, but never another angel.

Yes, I was saved by an angel. So you might wonder what this all means. The last eleven years have changed everything for me. I have discovered the world of the angels, and I have felt their caring messages being sent almost daily through whispers in my ear, messages in my mind, cloud images, songs, and meditations. All of us can tap into such messages with consistent meditations and patience.

~Tom Lumbrazo

Don't Mess with Us

For He spoke, and it was done;
He commanded, and it stood fast.
~Psalm 33:9

Gazing at the hostile faces surrounding his car he knew he had made a bad choice. My son had driven to an isolated area beside the railroad tracks where he knew there were sometimes parties. He'd been there before so he took a chance that he would find some of his friends there.

He did find a party, but as he walked toward it he saw unfamiliar, hostile faces. The one acquaintance he found there made it clear that he should leave or suffer the consequences. Alcohol and drugs equal danger in any situation, and he decided to leave.

As he hurried back to his car he heard footsteps behind him. A group of guys had followed him.

He locked himself in his car and felt better until his car would not start. The guys who had followed him now surrounded his car, taunting him.

Just then an oversized pickup truck appeared from nowhere. The truck parked but the engine and lights remained on. Two enormous men stepped out and the crowd could see the two shotguns hanging on the gun rack inside the cab of the truck. The men looked over the situation, and the threatening kids moved back into the shadows, watching.

One of the men stood guard while the other bent down and spoke to my son.

"Do you need some help?" he said.

"I'm trying to get my car started."

"Try again," he said.

He stood back and watched while my son turned the key once again. After a moment the engine caught and roared to life.

"Thanks, I'm good now."

"Okay," the massive man said. As he left the other man followed.

They made no comment about the party and didn't tell the kids to go home; they walked with purpose straight to their truck.

My son watched them climb into their truck, then turned his attention to getting out of there. When the car was facing the road he was surprised that the truck was nowhere in sight. There wasn't even a dust trail. The truck was gone. He raced ahead trying to catch sight of the missing vehicle, a futile attempt.

When my shaken son arrived home he asked me to sit and talk with him. I know our kids don't always tell us what they have been doing, especially if they know we would not approve, but he wanted to tell me the entire account of his unnerving night.

As I listened to him reveal the details of the evening I trembled with the realization I could have been receiving a late night call from the hospital or the morgue, instead of sitting across the table from my healthy son hearing this amazing story. My son shared his wonder about the appearance of the truck and how it had ended up in that remote location. There wasn't a well-traveled road leading there. Where had these guys come from? Why had his car started after they arrived and where had they gone when they left? There weren't any side roads they could have driven down; they had simply disappeared.

The men hadn't seemed concerned about the party going on with underage drinking and drugs, they seemed to have only one goal—to protect my son.

When the story was all told I let out the breath I had been holding and smiled in relief. I knew those men were angels sent by God in answer to my continual prayers of protection for my children. If I had any doubts concerning the effectiveness of prayers, those doubts dissolved that night.

I knew my next words might raise my son's eyebrows but he needed to hear this.

"I have to tell you this; those two men were angels."

He surprised me by answering, "Mom, I know they were. Those were awfully big men and the truck came out of nowhere and vanished once I was safe."

We sat in quiet awe of God's all-knowing presence and experienced gratitude for His fearsome angels who came to my son's aid in a mighty big pickup truck.

~Diane Marie Shaw

Angel at the Market

How beautiful a day can be
When kindness touches it!
~George Elliston

"I'm going over to Highway Market. Want to come?" I welcomed this invitation, as there were few recreational choices within walking distance of our college campus. Being students, we were all broke, but bargains were to be had a couple of hundred yards up the road. On one occasion, I had returned to the dorm with a ten-pound bag of bananas. They were only pennies a pound! It hadn't occurred to me that I couldn't eat so many bananas before they turned black and I ended up giving most of them away. Still, with this kind of treasure in mind, my friend Michael and I set off for the store, a few dollars burning holes in our pockets.

The small lobby was particularly crowded as we entered the front door. It was full of people ascending to the store on the next level. We opted for the ramp between the two sets of stairs. It was a cross between an escalator and the people movers you see in airports—in the early 1980s, it was way ahead of its time. It had polished stainless steel walls with a hard rubber railing and a rubber-coated tread that moved you up the slope.

As we began to move forward, I noticed that there were two or three children playing on the ramp. They would ride it to the top and then race down the stairs to ride it up again. More than once, they ran the wrong way down the ramp, pushing past customers to get to the bottom.

Just as we neared the top, one of the children directly in front of us slipped and fell. He was wearing loose socks and, as he slid off the tread onto the metal grate, one of his socks was pulled into the gap where the tread disappeared into the floor. Immediately, the teeth of a hidden gear grabbed the sock and the boy began to scream.

Someone quickly hit the large red "kill" switch at the top of the slope and shut the machine down. This, however, did nothing to relieve the pressure on the boy's ankle. As we crouched to try to help, a panicked shopper began to wrench at the child's leg, making the whole situation worse and the screams louder. The boy's leg was swelling badly, ugly red and puffy.

A young man in a store apron quickly blocked off the bottom of the ramp with a plastic barrier to keep people from crowding in for a closer look. This left Michael and me the only ones on the ramp between the barrier and the child.

Urgently, someone shouted, "Help, we need a knife to cut him free." I always carried a pocketknife and began to rummage through my pockets for it. Seldom did I go anywhere without it but on this occasion, when we needed it most, I had left it on my nightstand in my dorm room.

What happened next is still clear in my mind even after more than thirty years. Michael and I were standing almost shoulder-to-shoulder. The end where the boy lay was blocked. Yet a woman appeared in front of us on the ramp. She hadn't come past us and she hadn't climbed over the sidewalls or the boy to get to where she stood. Neither did we see her appear. She was suddenly just there in front of us. She was wearing a parka, which struck me as odd because it wasn't very cold outside.

The woman immediately turned, looked Michael in the eye and said, "Michael, give me your knife." Until that moment, Mike hadn't realized that he had a knife with him. He dipped his hand into his pocket and came out with an old folding pocketknife. He opened it and handed it over.

Quickly, the woman crouched down and sawed through the sock, releasing the boy. By that time his mother had arrived and she hugged him as she and the boy both cried. We were relieved to see the skin on the boy's leg had not been broken and the leg was returning to normal size and color.

It took only a few seconds for Michael and me to realize that the woman who had so dramatically intervened in the situation was gone. Again, she hadn't passed by us and there was no space for her to have pushed past the kneeling mother and her child, still blocking our exit. We were stunned. Where had she come from? How had she known Michael's name, let alone that he had a knife in his pocket that he hadn't realized he was carrying?

Over the next few years at school, we discussed the incident many times, yet we never came up with a rational explanation. Neither of us could even describe what she looked like other than the coat. While all the other details of the event were clear in my mind, the woman's face was fuzzy, a blur.

From time to time, the subject of meeting angels comes up in Bible discussions or in the popular media. It always makes me think of that day at the market when it seems we had direct intervention from God in a time of need. I believe that on that day Michael and I met an angel.

~John P. Walker

What I Know for Sure

Be anxious for nothing, but in everything by prayer and supplication,
with thanksgiving, let your requests be made known to God.
~Philippians 4:6

I t was a frigid night in the winter of 1982 when I found myself in a situation that easily could have ended my life. I was on my way back to the small town of Chester, where I had landed my first teaching job, after spending a weekend with my fiancé, Don, in Columbus, Ohio.

My 1973 pea green Ford Gran Torino, nicknamed "The Yacht" by my brothers, was not the most reliable car, and it had a reputation for dying at the most inopportune moments. Under these circumstances, traveling by myself at night in a rural area in the dead of winter, with a temperature hovering twenty degrees below zero before the wind chill wasn't the smartest thing I had ever done. But there are a lot of crazy things we do for love.

I was five or ten miles from home, traveling south on Route 7, when my engine started sputtering. I pulled over to the side of the road as the engine emitted its last cough and then completely died. Having dealt with this situation before—in daylight—I was prepared, albeit still scared.

I tried to remain calm as I retrieved my ice scraper and flashlight from the glove box, got out of the car, lifted the hood, and found the choke. I lifted the flap and stuck the ice scraper into the opening, a routine I had done too many times before.

I tried starting the car. Rr-r-r-r. No luck as I pumped the gas and turned the key. "Remain calm. Take a deep breath," I told myself as cars went barreling by on the dark divided highway. "You'll be all right. Just try again," I continued in my head in a voice that pretended more confidence than I felt.

I climbed out of my car again, readjusted the ice scraper with gloved fingers that were already feeling stiff from the cold, got back in the car, and tried again. No luck. I felt the panic beginning to rise.

One more time. Out of the car I leapt, a little too anxiously, locking the door behind me by force of habit. In that terrifying instant, I realized that the key was still in the ignition and the lights were on. My mind filled with the horrifying possibilities facing me:

1) No one would stop to help me, fearing that I was setting them up for a robbery or an assault.

2) I would freeze to death by morning.

3) I would get hit by a car.

4) If I waved someone down, they might be a rapist or murderer or kidnapper just waiting for an opportunity.

5) It would take hours or days for a law enforcement officer to come by on this lonely stretch of road.

In the few seconds that all of these scenarios played in my mind, I made a decision. An impulsive one, but one that seemed to be my only choice given the dire circumstances. I waved—tentatively—towards the oncoming traffic, not knowing what risk I might be taking.

Almost immediately a car pulled alongside me. The window of the passenger side rolled partway down to reveal a female passenger and a male driver, both middle-aged.

"Do you need some help?" they asked. "Can we take you somewhere?"

"Oh, yes, thank you," I replied with a voice that must have displayed both relief and trepidation. "My car has broken down and won't start again. I have friends, the Eichingers, in Tuppers Plains. If you can just get me to their house, I would be grateful."

On the short trip to the Eichingers, we chatted a bit. The driver shared that he was a pastor of a small church in the area and his passenger was his wife. I explained who I was, where I was coming from, and where I had been heading. When we arrived at my friends' house, I thanked the couple profusely for their timely assistance and made a mental note to send them a thank you note for taking a chance with their own safety to ensure mine.

Soon afterwards I began asking the locals for the whereabouts of this church that my rescuers had mentioned, but to my surprise, no one had heard of it. Odd. I looked in the phone book under churches. Nope! No church by that name was listed there either.

Now perhaps this church really did exist but was too small to be listed in the phone book, or had such a sparse congregation that most people in the area just hadn't heard of it, but to me, it really didn't matter. I now knew for sure the truth that my mother and those Catholic school nuns had been trying to teach me all of my growing up years: there are angels watching over me. And I had met them in the flesh.

~Sherry A. Bentley

Hands on My Shoulders

He spake well who said that graves are the footprints of angels.
~Henry Wadsworth Longfellow

I was just an ordinary nine-year-old kid enjoying my summer vacation. My family and I lived in a small town called Lakewood. I was walking to my friend's house about two blocks from my home, and thinking about my grandmother; she had passed away a few years earlier.

My grandmother was a small, silver-haired lady with glasses and a warm, pleasant smile. She had a gracious spirit and always spoke in a calm and peaceful tone. I always felt loved, safe and secure around her. I saw my mother cry for the first time when my grandmother died.

As I walked, I suddenly became aware of all the sounds around me — people talking, cars going by, and birds chirping. I also smelled the honeysuckles in the air; they were in full bloom. I turned onto the block of my friend's house. As I approached his driveway I felt a strange gust of wind. Not from side to side, but from the top of my head to the bottom of my feet. It seemed as if someone had overtaken me. I stopped just before my friend's driveway. I felt a sense of calmness and peace, and a heightened awareness. I could not move or hear anything around me, but I could see everything. It felt like someone had covered me with wings. Then I felt as if someone placed their hands on my shoulders and pulled me back slowly three steps.

A moment later a car backed out of the driveway right in front of me. I had barely stopped short of walking into the car's path. I realized that the driver would not have seen me if I had continued walking, and this was long before cars had beeping warning indicators for the driver when they backed up. As the car backed onto the street and pulled forward, I felt the hands on my shoulders lift and a gust of wind—this time from my feet to the top of my head. I could move freely again. I turned around to see the person who saved my life, and saw no one.

I ran home to tell my mother what had happened to me. When I told her the entire story, she was relieved I didn't get hurt. My mother told me that God had dispatched an angel to save my life. She held me and kissed me, and cried with tears of joy.

All through my life, I have felt the presence of God. I believe the angel who came to me that day was my grandmother, dispatched by God to save my life. I will never forget the feelings of peace, joy and love that were at the heart of my experience.

~Reverend Anthony D. Powell

Chapter 2

Angels Among Us

Divine Messengers

On the Wings of a Dove

Remember, Angels are both God's messengers and God's message,
witness to eternity in time, to the presence of the divine amidst the ordinary.
Every moment of every day is riddled by their traces.
~F. Forrester Church

"Follow me, but be quiet," my mother instructed as she woke me from sleep. Still disoriented in the early morning hours, I followed Mom into her bedroom without question. She stopped at her window and pointed toward a hedge that stood within arm's reach of the house.

My mother worshipped nature. She found beauty in the curve of a leaf or in the way a raindrop glistened off a blade of grass as the sun set. She often pointed out such sights to me. But waking me to look at a bush? Really? It was barely sunup. I harrumphed and started to shuffle back to the coziness of my bed.

Mom caught my arm and pulled me back. "Look," she whispered. "A dove." And there it sat, a beautiful, plump, pure white dove like none I had ever seen before. The sight of it was truly awe-inspiring.

"Wow," I said. "Cool."

"This dove has been sitting here and crying since sunrise. Did you hear it?" Mom asked.

Actually, I had heard crying coming from the direction of Mom's bedroom. In fact, during the past few weeks such sounds were almost a nightly event. My grandmother Oma, elderly and ill, had taken another poor turn. My mother had recently received word that

Oma had been re-admitted to the hospital. Earlier that summer, my mother had been called to Oma's side when she had experienced another health crisis. Mom had been struggling with the question of whether to visit her mother again. The trip was long—twenty-four hours door-to-door—and I knew Mom had been hemming and hawing about this decision for days. She wanted to be with her mother as she made her transition, yet questioned whether this was the right time. Deep inside too, she hoped that Oma would somehow rally again.

Mom and I gazed at the dove. He sat peacefully for a long while, watching us back with his dark, round eyes. Then quietly, calmly, he lifted from the hedge and flew away. Mom and I looked at each other, shrugged our shoulders, then silently made our way to the kitchen for a mind-clearing cup of tea. As my mother poured the water, I spoke first. "That was weird."

"No," she said. "That was a message."

"A message? What kind of message?"

Mom answered soberly, "That dove came to tell me that Oma is gone."

"Oh, c'mon. I'm sure she's fine," I answered quickly. "Besides, that kind of stuff doesn't really happen."

"Oh, yes it does," my mother insisted. "Yes it does."

I just blinked and took another sip of tea. It was too early in the morning to try to figure any of this out, I decided. A dove was a dove and that was all. I sat a bit longer, then returned to my bedroom to get some more sleep. No sooner had I closed the door when I heard the phone ring. I stood frozen as I overheard the news; Oma had passed away that morning, peacefully.

I had never given much credence to the Sunday school fluff about angels being sent from the heavens to alter situations or offer comfort. To me, the whole notion of a well-timed visit from a white-feathered presence seemed nothing more than a convenient fairy tale. Until then. That morning, thanks to a visit from a dove, I witnessed my mother's grief transform into a calm acceptance of the inevitable. And I felt the same peace within me, too. Oma's struggle was over; she had moved on peacefully just as the dove had. Just as we would.

~Monica A. Andermann

Who Was that Man?

He had a face like a benediction.
~Miguel De Cervantes

The temperature in downtown Toronto at noon on Thursday, November 20, 1980 was a chilly four degrees Celsius (39F) and a wet snow was falling as I walked northward on the east side of Yonge Street at 11:55 a.m. Why would I recall such mundane information on a particular date more than three decades ago? Partly because my life changed that day, and I remember it like it was yesterday.

I was working as editor of a high-profile corporate magazine for an international company. I should have been happy in my career, but I was miserable. I felt unfulfilled because my dream was to be a full-time freelance writer, working out of my home, but I did not have the courage to escape from my secure corporate job. I had the love and encouragement of my schoolteacher wife, Kris, but even that wasn't enough to strengthen my resolve to pursue my life's ambition.

On this particularly wintry day I decided to walk the short distance from the King Street office building where I worked, in the heart of Canada's business capital, to enjoy the quiet solitude of the noon-hour Mass at St. Michael's Roman Catholic Cathedral on nearby Church Street.

The sidewalks on this bleak and nippy day were teeming with noonday shoppers and workers on their lunch break. There was also the usual number of panhandlers standing on street corners along this stretch of Yonge Street, known as "the longest street in the world." As I neared Richmond Street I was lost in my troubled thoughts when a tall, slim, bearded young man thrust something into my hand. I didn't miss a stride. Yet, in my haste, I noticed that he was rather shabbily dressed and wore a long, dark-colored raincoat that seemed much too flimsy to ward off the November chill. Our eyes met for the briefest of moments and he smiled at me. He neither asked for money nor spoke, but he did hand me something.

I thought no more of this stranger and I soon reached the cathedral just in time for the Mass. The then-150-year-old church in downtown Toronto had served as an oasis for me in the past. During the service I prayed for guidance, strength and the courage to change my career and follow my dream of being a freelance writer. Yet, when the Mass ended, I was no more certain of my future than when I had arrived forty-five minutes earlier.

I stood on the steps of the church and prepared to return to the office when I reached into my pockets for my gloves. My right hand came upon the tiny booklet that had been handed to me by the stranger. For the first time, I saw that it was a miniature, red-covered, thirty-two-page "Personal Bible" measuring a mere two by two-and-a-half inches. I opened the paper booklet to the first page, and my eyes widened as I read aloud the words of John 14:27 that filled the entire page: "Let not your heart be troubled, neither let it be afraid." The verse rang in my ears like the tolling of a bell, and I realized it was tolling for me.

Without hesitation, I ran down the stairs and retraced my steps along Yonge Street to Richmond, but the man who'd given me the little holy booklet was no longer there.

I returned to my office feeling like I had been relieved of a heavy burden. I gathered some personal belongings from my desk, picked up my briefcase and informed my boss that I would not be returning. He was very understanding. He was well aware of my unhappiness in my job.

The next morning I made a cold call to *The Toronto Star* and was connected to Mike Walton, an editor at the paper who is now deceased. I told him that I had a story idea that might interest him. I said I'd like to write a feature article for *The Star* titled "101 Free Activities for Winter." He said if I could pull it off, he'd pay me $175 for the story and he'd publish it in the new year. I was true to my word and he was true to his: My article appeared on a full page in the country's largest newspaper on Sunday, January 11, 1981.

I was a bona fide freelance writer!

Today, I am an award-winning book author, and several hundred of my newspaper and magazine articles have been published in over sixty-five publications in Canada, the U.S. and Europe.

I have worked out of my home office for over thirty years and I continue to follow my dream.

As I write this, I am looking at that little red "Personal Bible" that is always on my writing desk. I often ask myself, in wonderment: "Who was that man at the corner of Yonge and Richmond Streets on that fateful day in 1980?"

~Dennis McCloskey

A Tim Hortons Angel

All God's angels come to us disguised.
~James Russell Lowell

O
ur minds were reeling. We had just met with the
oncologist at the hospital. Cancer. It was definite.
Surgery was imminent. There seemed so much to
digest, so many questions, so many unknowns. As
my husband and I contemplated what lay before us we decided we
needed some time before we faced our family. We tried desperately
to fathom what God's divine plan might be. How could He allow this
to happen? How could I have cancer?

"Why don't we get some lunch?" my husband suggested.
"Timmies?"

I agreed. A Tim Hortons coffee shop in the big city where no one
knew us sounded like a good place to go. We could grab some lunch,
talk, and prepare ourselves before we met with our family. We drove
down the busy city street and pulled into the entrance of the first Tim
Hortons we saw.

I looked for an empty table while my husband got the order.
There was a vacant spot by a window. As I headed for the table, I
caught the eye of a grayish-haired woman, probably in her early sixties, seated in the corner. She smiled and nodded at me. I returned
the greeting.

I sat down and gazed out the window. I thought about my cancer diagnosis and my impending surgery. The tears swelled. My husband sat down with the food and gave thanks.

No sooner had we said Amen then the woman came over to me and placed a hand gently on my shoulder. I looked at her.

"I have something I think you need right now," the stranger said.

She pulled a green piece of paper from her jacket pocket. She smiled and I felt a strange warmness.

I quietly took the paper from her outstretched hand.

Both my husband and I read the four-stanza poem on the paper. Our eyes brimmed as we read the final lines:

I asked for happiness for you,
In all things great and small,
But it was for His loving care,
I prayed the most of all…

I turned around to thank her for her incredible timing. I wanted to thank her for sensing my sadness and for being so compassionate. I wanted to tell her about my cancer. But she was gone. I searched the sea of faces at the counter. I looked at the doorway. She was nowhere to be found.

God worked in a magnificent way that day. He placed a perfect stranger in our path to let us know that all would be well and that we were assured of His loving care. God's love washed over us in that moment and we felt the glorious peace that passes all understanding.

"An angel?" I said to my husband through tear-filled eyes.

"A Tim Hortons angel." He smiled, and took a sip of his double-double.

~Glynis M. Belec

The Right Track

When my spirit was overwhelmed within me, then You knew my path.
~Psalm 142:3

As the sun rose on another hot summer day, I crawled out of bed after a fitful sleep in hopes of pounding the pavement and relieving some stress. I couldn't decide what to do after the closing of the company where I'd handled the marketing for eight years. I'd loved every minute of it and had given it my all. Now, I felt lost.

There was no question about whether I had to work, just how to proceed. Should I work for someone else with 24/7 dedication like I'd done in previous positions? Should I start my own company instead? Would my creative abilities and writing skills set me apart from the competition as they had in the past? Would clients put their faith in me? Could I make it financially?

Doubts plagued me.

I hurried across the parking lot in the south Georgia humidity to the tree-canopied portion of the walking trail in the county park. Buzzing cicadas, rustling leaves, and the scent of damp earth bombarded my senses.

The majesty of the sounds, textures, smells, and beauty of nature usually soothed my soul, but not today.

I rushed past spiky palmettos, delicate ferns, and wild grapevines on the sun-dappled path. Magnolia leaves shimmered in the sunlight. A bird squawked and flitted from the ground to a branch in the trees, barely heard over the persistent croaking of tree frogs.

The moss-draped live oaks closed in on me. The cacophony of sounds jangled my nerves.

"Stop," I cried. "Just stop."

I wiped sweat from my brow with the back of my hand.

"What's the use?"

I turned around, backtracking toward my car. Footsteps from behind startled me.

A stranger's voice asked, "Are you familiar with 1 Peter 5:7?"

"I'm not sure," I answered, looking back over my shoulder at a tall, slender man.

He smiled at me.

"Cast all your anxiety on him because he cares about you," he said.

I returned his smile, but chills ran up my spine. Where had he come from?

As we continued to walk, he spoke of God's love.

"God has a plan for us," he said, "but sometimes we're scared and don't listen to him."

I thought of how my instincts had been pushing me toward starting my own company, and how I'd hesitated because of fear.

"He's with you every step of the way," he assured me. "Keep moving, and he'll guide you in the right direction. He hears you when you ask for help."

I had prayed for help before I got out of bed. Was this guy my sign God had heard my plea?

During our walk, he quoted scripture and talked of the importance of using our talents for God's purpose.

"We're all given talents," he reminded me. "Some great, some small. No matter what, we glorify God when we use them to further his kingdom."

We moved to the right to allow room for oncoming runners.

"God is interested in the passion we have for whatever gifts he has given us," he said with sincerity.

"Are you a preacher?" I asked.

"No, I just go where God leads me."

He prayed for me, and then he disappeared through an opening in the trees.

For the first time in a long while, I felt a bounce in my step. Starting my own company would allow me to use my talents and to follow God's lead. Excitement rushed through me. I put one foot in front of the other and breathed a great sigh of relief, confident I was on the right track.

~Debra Ayers Brown

Star Struck

*May God grant you always... A sunbeam to warm you, a moonbeam to
charm you, a sheltering angel so nothing can harm you. Laughter to cheer
you. Faithful friends near you. And whenever you pray, Heaven to hear you.*
~Irish Blessing

Years ago, a group of friends and I decided to take a drive
along Los Angeles's busy freeways to visit the Griffith
Park Observatory. Located on the southern slope of Mt.
Hollywood, we'd heard the view of the city was spectacular,
and the structure itself, in 1930s Art Deco style, astounding. The
walls, built of thick concrete just after the 1933 Long Beach earth-
quake, had survived many tremors since, and stand strong to this
day.

We planned to enjoy all the springtime beauty the area offered,
with cool mornings and sunny, warm afternoons. During those few
months, the gray of winter fades to a memory and the scorch of summer is still a hazy dream. Flowers bloom. Life feels good.

We arrived mid-morning and spent time enjoying the
Astronomers Monument, which was erected in honor of those schol-
ars who dedicated their lives to furthering our understanding of the
stars and planets. We read the list of names, a few familiar from our
school days, most new to us.

Listening to my friends' carefree chatter, I felt like an imposter,
my smile a thin mask.

Over the past few weeks, I had become more and more

anxious about my health. Sometimes, a mild pain radiated up my neck—nothing terrible, but enough to concern me. As a registered nurse, I recognized the symptoms. My heart was failing.

The thought of visiting a doctor and having my suspicions confirmed left me paralyzed with fear.

Today was worse. The hairs on the back of my neck stood on end. I was being watched; I sensed it. I hesitated. Crowds filled the observatory—maybe I was overreacting to the bustle. I scanned the faces, unable to see anyone I knew.

That's when I noticed him, just an ordinary-looking fellow, staring at me. Probably in his mid-thirties, he wore jeans and a chambray shirt. He looked like the photo you'd spot when checking the dictionary's definition for the word non-descript. His brown hair and face would fit right alongside.

We stopped to inspect the central rotunda, leaning over a half-wall to watch the 240-pound brass ball of the Foucault Pendulum swing in perpetual motion. The ceiling delighted us, a vast mural depicting Atlas, the Four Winds and other key characters of celestial mythology. I felt a soft nudge, and moved to excuse myself. There he stood again, the man from the observatory.

He nodded knowingly, sending a shiver up my spine.

There was something about him, something I couldn't place. The air around him seemed to move, almost like heat waves at the beach. A glow. An aura, perhaps? I didn't know. I wasn't schooled in that sort of thing.

I smiled at him, nodding in acknowledgement.

He didn't return my smile, didn't blink. He simply gazed at me.

At the gift shop a few of us picked up a small trinket for a loved one, or a postcard to remind us of this special day. I chose a pair of earrings for my daughter, shimmery and bright.

He stood near the door watching me.

Lunchtime rolled around and we discovered the Café at the End of the Universe. One of our group wondered aloud as to whether the name referred to a location or a time yet to come.

A burst of laughter and speculative conversation followed, as we shared a taste of this or a sip of that. From the corner of my eye, I saw the shirt, the jeans. I didn't turn my head. I didn't want to know for certain it was him.

Our group visited the laser light show, an attraction mixing music and beams of bright colors as they formed constellations and abstract shapes. An awe-inspiring performance, but as it ended, I noticed the stranger, eyes still focused on me. I turned away quickly.

"Look—over by the door. There he is again." I gestured for my friend to sneak a peek in the direction of the man.

"Where?" She squinted, her head pointed straight at him. "I don't see him—maybe he left."

Frustration tinged my voice. "He's right there—hasn't moved an inch. He's almost smiling at me now. Please don't try to say I'm imagining him." Fear mounted in me. Was I being stalked? I tucked the thought away, determined to enjoy this time with my companions, to relax in the gentle warmth of the sun.

As our excursion neared its end, I glanced to the left, at the wall of a building, devoid of gates or doors of any sort. The man leaned against it, looking at me. This time I stared back, determined to show a bravery I didn't feel. Hidden in pockets, my hands trembled.

A calm smile and deep compassion shone on his face as we locked eyes for what felt like minutes, but probably lasted only seconds. Then—I don't know how to explain it—it was as though a burst of conversation swept from his mind to mine.

"Everything's going to be all right."

I felt an intense warmth head to toe, as though embraced in a spiritual hug from the inside out.

"There's work ahead."

I took a deep breath, maintaining the eye contact, listening.

He continued to smile with his eyes. "I'll be watching."

I nodded slowly, softly. I understood. And felt safe.

A friend tugged on my arm, pulling me toward another monument. I turned my head back for a glimpse of the man, but he was gone. I scanned the building once more, searching for openings he could have exited through. There were none.

I shook my head. I knew I'd seen him. And he'd seen me. I was certain he was real. I still felt his warmth.

We headed for home, my mind filled with questions about the man, and the message I'd somehow received. Reason fought against intuition. He was just an ordinary guy. Or was he?

In the months to come, I overcame my fears and visited the doctor. I underwent three cardiac catheterization operations, and a successful triple-bypass surgery. Through them all, I knew I'd be all right.

Years have passed since that day. But the peace he projected has remained with me. God sent me comfort in a way I needed, in a form I could understand and trust — an ordinary-looking man. He gave me the courage and the confidence to take care of my health problems.

My angel.

And even though I can't see him, I know he's still watching. I know things are going to be all right.

How can I be so sure?

Because there's still work for me to do. He told me so.

~Nancy Zeider

The Vandal and the Angel

Angels are not merely forms of extraterrestrial intelligence. They are forms of extra-cosmic intelligence.
~Mortimer J. Adler

The brick felt unnatural in my hand. Its rough edges and extra weight felt nothing like the softballs I had thrown many times. But I was angry—angrier than I had ever been. My face was red, my heart was pounding, tears tumbled down my face, and all I could think about was throwing the brick as hard as I could through my landlord's living room window.

Located on the side of the house, the window and I were obscured by several tall shrubs. Additionally, I had arrived home early from work, so there weren't that many people home yet. I looked around just in case. All clear. Then I arranged the brick in my hand like it was a softball and reared back. When I was about to use all the strength I had to send that brick through my landlord's window, I heard a man's voice. I jumped and turned around quickly.

He asked, "What are you doing?" His voice was calm but loud enough to get my attention.

I turned around and about ten feet from me stood a rotund man with thinning gray hair and a soft, pinkish face. He wore a gray polyester suit with a white shirt and a yellow and burgundy striped tie. I wondered if he was a salesman. I also wondered where he had come from. My plan for revenge spoiled for the day, I lowered the brick.

"What are you doing?" he asked again, still calm. "Are you okay?"

I managed to sputter my story through my tears. "My landlord rented his garden apartment to me." I pointed at my little apartment at the back of the house. "My landlord lives there," I said, gesturing to the right with my eyes toward the window I had planned to smash. "Well, he lived there," I continued, "until he fell in love with a woman and moved to Tuscaloosa. He didn't even tell me."

"You had feelings for him?" the man asked.

"No! He moved and had all the utilities cut off. I have been without hot water for five days now."

"Do you have his new number?"

This man liked to ask lots of questions, which should have aggravated me further, but somehow I was beginning to feel less angry. The brick still rested in my loose grip.

"I do. I've called him several times a day for several days now. He keeps telling me that he's in love and that he's been so caught up in everything that he hasn't had time to call the utility companies for me." I shook my head. Someone who was twenty years older than me should know better.

"And what am I going to do with a new landlord?" I asked the man. "He could raise my rent or have lots of wild parties or be violent or all kinds of horrible things."

The man in the gray suit continued to stand in the same place. I thought he might be afraid of a crazy twenty-something girl with a brick and an attitude.

"From what I've heard, your new landlord doesn't have much to live up to," the man said.

I nodded and said, "That's true."

"Perhaps you should be more forgiving and more hopeful, especially when it comes to people. Imagine how you would act if the man of your dreams swept you off your feet."

I laughed. "Well, I don't know if that will happen any time soon. But I guess if it did, I would become a little forgetful myself."

The Vandal and the Angel : Divine Messengers   49

"Would you feel better if you broke your landlord's window?" he asked.

I looked down at the grass and a line of ants that were passing by my tennis shoes. Suddenly, I felt ashamed. I was smarter and kinder than the girl who stood before him.

"No," I said. "I would still be angry. And then I'd feel guilty too."

"I'm glad you didn't break the window. Next time you speak to him, really listen and try to put yourself in his place. And whether he is right or wrong, forgive him," he said.

"One last thing," he said. "Remember to forgive yourself. Everyone has a bad day or a bad week." At that, he smiled at the brick in my hand.

"You're right," I said as I walked to the edge of the house to put the brick where I found it.

I continued, "Thank you for listening."

I turned around expecting some version of "You're welcome," but the pudgy man was gone. I hadn't heard him leave. I walked to the front of the house where I found no people or any cars except for mine. He had slipped away in a hurry, and I began to wonder who or what this man really was.

The few people with whom I have shared this story say the man must have been an angel. There really was no explanation other than he took off really fast in his car, but I would have heard it. He certainly wouldn't run in a polyester suit on a hot September afternoon in Alabama. He certainly didn't look like a runner. He wasn't a salesman. If he was, he would have carried literature or samples with him. The man who saved my landlord's window and, more importantly my dignity and conscience, must have been an angel.

I was visited by an angel in the body of a large man in a gray polyester suit. I'll always be grateful to him and to God for sending him to me. If I had smashed my landlord's window, I might not have been caught but I would have carried the weight of my actions, far heavier than any brick, for a lifetime.

Forgiving others and myself has been one of the most valuable lessons I have ever learned. Granted, it's a lesson that I constantly have to review, but the peace I gain as a result of forgiveness is more than worth it. And if I am ever visited by a nondescript man who looks like a salesman and who is very wise, I'll keep an eye on him. I would love to spend more time talking to an angel.

~Dana J. Barnett

A Wild Messenger

If angels rarely appear, it's because we all too often
mistake the medium for the Message.
~Eileen Elias Freeman,
The Angels' Little Instruction Book

I do not recall why I went to the door and opened it. It must have been on a weekend because I was home during the day, not at work. I do know it was early in September of 1995, and the summer was finally giving way to the cooler air of the fall.

Perhaps I was going outside to get the mail, or I had heard something near the house and was going to see what it was. I can't remember. But I do vividly recall that when I opened the door I had a very big shock! There on the deck rail about three feet in front of me sat a small owl with large eyes. Our eyes locked, and for the next five or six seconds we both froze like statues. Then very quickly, this small owl turned around on the rail, unfolded his wings, and flew away!

I didn't leave the house. I was so astonished that I went back inside and sat down. I could not believe what just happened. First of all, that is the only time I have seen an owl where I live and I have been in this house for twenty-six years. I have cats that enjoy bird watching through the windows, so I do pay attention to the many types of birds that frequent this rather densely populated area. That's why I was bewildered, shocked really, that such an unusual bird would set itself on the railing right outside my door in the middle of the day.

I told several people about this encounter, not just because it was out of the ordinary, but the sensation I was left with stayed with me for a couple of days. The feeling was very much like one of those dreams that is so strong, so engaging, that it sticks with you all day long.

Shortly after this experience, some friends, family and I went on vacation to Canyonlands National Park in Utah. I had forgotten the owl incident. Our trip to the outdoors was wonderful but nothing out of the ordinary happened. We arrived home the first week in October, and on October 6th my father passed away at home unexpectedly. Just that day, my father had gone to the camping trailer to put away some items used on the trip. His passing was difficult for all of us. Several weeks later, I finally began to get back to some of my usual routines, one of which is reading.

I had borrowed several books from the library, one of which my sister had recommended about Native American Indians, a topic we both enjoy reading and learning about. Although I do not recall which book it was, I was flooded with the same sensation and visual memory that I had during my owl encounter. The book talked about how birds, especially owls, can be messengers, often letting us know that someone in our lives is close to crossing over. It felt like someone poured something cool over me, hairs on my arms stood on end, and in my mind's eye I was looking straight into those owl's eyes all over again.

This lasted just a second or two, but it was then I knew exactly why I had been paid a visit from the owl. Soon after, I spoke to my sister. I told her that I believed the owl was a messenger, to let me know someone was close to leaving the planet. We both had most likely read about the Native American belief that birds and animals can be messengers, much like angels, bringing us information when we need it. But neither of us had put the two together until I read about it weeks later.

I feel comforted and blessed that somewhere, someone sent a beautiful owl my way in the tradition of a most honored people. And thank goodness they got me to read a certain book so I would get it.

Which shows whoever synchronizes these things knew I would need help putting two and two together!

~Cindy V. Rodberg

All Shapes and Sizes

*Watching a peaceful death of a human being reminds us of a falling star;
one of a million lights in a vast sky that flares up for a brief moment only to
disappear into the endless night forever.*
~Elisabeth Kübler-Ross

I watched as Dad's strength faded before my very eyes. He was in a hospice house as Alzheimer's disease continued its relentless assault on his brain. After more than five years of its debilitating effects, the progressive malady finally managed to rob him of his desire for food and water. Without those vital necessities, my brothers and I knew Dad's time with us was coming to an end. His six-foot-two body weighed less than 140 pounds.

I left Dad's room around 10 p.m. that March evening and headed home, exhausted. My forty-ninth birthday was coming in three days, but there was no cause for celebration. The only thing that kept going through my mind during the drive was how lucky I was to have had Dad around for forty-nine years.

I fell into bed and immediately went fast to sleep. Around 1 a.m. I was awakened by a noise coming from my kitchen. The sound aroused my suspicions enough to get me out of bed to investigate. I grabbed the baseball bat that I kept by the bedroom door as I cautiously crept toward the kitchen. However, I found nothing out of the ordinary, only my cat playing with a plastic bag. She was usually asleep at the foot of my bed at that hour, so I wondered why she was up. I checked all the doors and windows and decided my imagination was running away with me since I was so tired, and the noise obviously had been made by the cat.

I fell back into bed, but sleep wouldn't come. My mind kept replaying the doctor's words when he said the end was very near, so I decided to go back to the hospice house and wait out the night in Dad's room.

I arrived around 2:30 a.m. to find Dad sitting upright in bed as I slipped quietly into his room. He smiled when he saw me, and I fought back tears because he had not recognized me in more than two years. However, there appeared to be a glimmer of recognition as I walked to the side of the bed and he reached for my hand, his blue eyes twinkling. I felt my throat tighten.

"How ya doing, Dad?" I asked, even though I wasn't expecting an answer because he had not spoken an intelligible word in over a year.

His smile grew bigger as he motioned for me to sit in the chair beside his bed, another feat from his plaque-ridden brain that caught me off guard. I sat down and he continued to hold my hand as he motioned to the ceiling with his other hand, pointing for me to look up. I did as he asked, but I saw nothing. He kept pointing.

"What do you see?" I asked.

"Mama," he replied, again pointing and wanting me to see her, too.

Hearing the clarity of his voice in that one-word answer both shocked and surprised me since all his words had been locked inside his head for so long, thanks to the ugliness of Alzheimer's.

I couldn't see anything on the ceiling, but I wish I could have because he obviously was looking into the face of his mother, who died in an accident when Dad was only six years old. That accident also claimed his father's life.

I believe a thin veil separates us from heaven, and at that point the veil was lifted. He saw his mother just the way he remembered her that November morning of 1923 as she waved goodbye from the car window. Less than two hours later, he and his siblings were orphaned when a Southern Railway train slammed into the side of their vehicle in Pelzer, South Carolina.

For another hour Dad pointed upward, smiling and nodding for me to look up. It saddened me to think that I couldn't share in the wonderment he saw as he gazed upward, but I was delighted to participate in his enjoyment of the moment. I was amazed at his burst of energy, even though he never spoke another word. I could tell he was revisiting a happy time in his life, perhaps a time where he was a carefree lad running barefoot through the meadows or catching tadpoles at the old farm pond. It was the time before his six-year-old world shattered and he and his brothers and sister had to learn to fend for themselves and depend on each other for survival.

Soon exhaustion overtook him and, still clutching my hand in his, he leaned back against his pillow and closed his eyes. He never opened them again. I held his hand until after the sun came up, reminiscing about happier days we had shared. The doctor on duty said he had lapsed into a coma. As I watched his chest rise and fall and his breathing become labored, I whispered into his ear that it was all right if he was ready to go. He breathed his last breath around four o'clock that afternoon. He was buried on my birthday three days later.

Even though these events took place thirteen years ago, that night is a precious memory that's still fresh in my mind. One thing that sticks out is how exhaustion had overtaken me that evening, yet the cat, which normally slept with me, had woken me from a deep sleep with that plastic bag. If that had not happened I could not have shared those wonderful final moments of Dad's life with him.

I firmly believe angels take on many forms and come in all shapes and sizes. They don't always come to us in a mist wearing wings and halos, and they don't always spell out their mission. Sometimes we have to observe and listen and be open to receiving their messages. I believe my cat was commissioned that night as Dad's angel, summoning me to his room.

Because of those special last moments, I know Dad is in a safe, loving place today where he has no symptoms of Alzheimer's. I am also certain in my heart that he has reunited with "Mama," and that thought alone gives me much to smile about.

~Carol Huff

Encouraging Words

I believe we are free, within limits, and yet there is an unseen hand, a guiding
angel, that somehow, like a submerged propeller, drives us on.
~Rabindranath Tagore

" saw her. I talked to her. I put antifreeze in her car, for Heaven's sake!" It may have indeed been for Heaven's sake the day our Pastor encountered her. Pastor B., as we have called him for years, is one of the most down-to-earth, realistic and reliable men in all of St. Louis. If he tells us something, we believe it; which is why we had to believe that his "angel story" was true.

He, his wife and their two daughters were on a long drive back east for Christmas. They had pulled off the interstate to fill up with gas and the family had gone in the convenience mart to purchase snacks while Pastor B. was left out in the falling snow to service the car. As he walked to the front to scrape the windshield, he saw an older car at the next pump with the hood up. Noticing it was an elderly woman, he walked over to see if she needed help. She told him she was trying to find the place to pour in the windshield wiper fluid. Of course Pastor B. had a supply in his own car and had her ready to leave in no time.

This elderly gray-haired lady had no way of knowing our pastor was going through a tough time and had an important decision to make. He had shared with us many times how he needed prayer just to get the clear "go ahead, or not" from God. Being a man of wisdom and discernment, he never made split-second, reckless decisions about anything—much less about our potential million-dollar expansion program to reach thousands of needy folks in the community.

As he closed the hood for her, he headed back to his own car to put the half-full container of windshield fluid away. The snow was now really coming down and he was totally unprepared for what happened. With the strength of a man, the old woman whirled him back around and gripped him squarely by the shoulders, drawing him to her, face to face. With steel gray eyes, looking straight into his soul, she slowly and simply said, "Get ready for what God has ready for you." Taking this perhaps as a "sign" Pastor B. said, "Would you wait here just a second while I get my wife so she can hear that too?" He turned to run into the mart to get his wife and daughters, but they were already coming out the door. "Girls come here! I want you to hear what this lady…"

In just a split second, he turned back around to point out the sweet elderly lady he had just helped, but was simultaneously hearing from his family, "What lady? Dad, are you okay?" Not only was there no lady, there was no car, and no tire tracks on the fresh snow leading out to the interstate. There were no other cars at all. Pastor B., still holding the half-filled wiper fluid jug, ran over to see if there was a wet place where it had poured into her car, and looked closely again for any sign of tire tracks. Nothing. Pastor B. said he had always thought he would know an angel when he saw one. Now he wasn't sure what he saw. However, he was very sure of what he had heard; and he thanked God, right then, right there, with his family wondering if his brain had frozen!

Several months later, the expansion nearing completion, over two thousand members of all ages, races, and backgrounds came together in the two Sunday morning services. We too have learned to live in great expectation that angels can appear any time, any place, and in the least expected way.

~Dr. Debra Peppers

The Missionary

Prayer is the principal means of opening oneself to the power and love of God that is already there, in the depths of reality.
~Bishop James Albert Pike

High on the plateau overlooking the Sahara desert in Nigeria is the city of Jos. During the dry season it's a baking arid tabletop, prone to violent dust storms and merciless droughts. For a boy from the cool wet climes of the Pacific Northwest, it was as different from home as could be.

I had arrived at Lagos International Airport in January, suffering from a severe sinus infection and punchy from lack of sleep. My first adventure, being forced to leave the airport before my host showed up, was luckily brief and ended happily when I was discovered wandering in the lobby of a nearby hotel.

In the three months that had passed since then, I had discovered what it meant to be in the mission field, alone. Previous evangelistic excursions to Mexico and Europe had been in groups of ten to twenty of my best friends, sort of a ministry holiday. To be sure, we worked hard, but at the end of each day there was the camaraderie of friends to look forward to. In the desert, I was surrounded by strangers. The work as a tutor was difficult, much more so than the physical labor of clearing land and building houses. I spent my days walking a fine line between the teachers that I worked with, who desired my assistance is maintaining discipline, and the parents of the children I tutored, and lived with, who were sure that the issues at hand were the fault of the teachers.

This, combined with severe homesickness and a terrifying bout of malaria, had left me nearly despondent, convinced that I had failed myself, my church, and my God.

One Saturday, I rose early, hoping to avoid the heat of the day. Taking a bottle of water and my pocket Bible, I walked to the outskirts of town and began to follow a long rusty railroad track into the desert. I walked for an hour or two, humming a worship song and looking for a likely spot to stop and read. Alone with only my thoughts, I began, again, to question the whole trip. What was I accomplishing? Who was I helping? How was I ever going to explain this to the body of believers who had sent me out, with their money and their prayers, to make a difference halfway around the world?

The temperature began to rise, and I stopped to sip from my water bottle. Far ahead, across the flat, barren sands of the plateau, I could see a small dot through the rippling heat waves. From where I stood it looked like a person, someone walking towards me, following the same tracks back toward the city.

Soon I could see him plainly, a man, dark and thin, carrying a bundle of kindling on his shoulder, dressed in faded jeans and a tattered white dress shirt. Shambling toward me, his feet were protected from the burning desert floor by thin, weathered sandals. My first reaction was fear; that is how low my faith had come to be. As the man grew closer I could see that he was elderly, at least seventy, though the years of depravation and harsh surroundings made him look much older by the standards of my own pampered country.

As he approached me he raised a hand in greeting and I suddenly smiled and did the same. At my smile, the stranger broke into a long flowing monologue in his native tongue, none of which I was familiar with. His broad white teeth gleamed in the desert sun as he gestured to himself and then to the desert behind him. I shook my head, still smiling, and used the handful of Yoruba that I knew to explain that I couldn't speak his language. His smile grew even broader and he continued to chatter happily. Reaching for my water bottle, I unscrewed the plastic cap and offered it to the stranger, whose grin became even wider as he took it and drank.

Then, pulling on a leather cord that hung across his neck and down his back, he retrieved a battered skin water bag and offered it to me. I undid the wooden stopper and sipped the warm dusty water, tasting the tanned leather of the bag as I did.

We watched each other for a moment, unable to make ourselves understood. Then the old man reached into the breast pocket of his worn shirt and pulled out a scrap of paper, which he offered to me. He pressed the page into my hand, tapping my chest and pointing skyward. Then, touching his fingertips to his forehead, he continued his trek towards town. I stood there a moment, feeling the sun burning through the back of my shirt and sweat trickling down my face.

I opened my hand and found a small, much folded track, written in English, which outlined the plan of salvation. The page showed in simple pictures man's sin, Christ on the cross, and his bridging the gap between God and us. I knew the track well; I had handed out hundreds like it in other far off countries. Looking at the dusty, time-worn, track, I felt tears coming to my eyes. This was it. This is what I had forgotten.

In all of the meetings and lesson plans and disagreements and fear, I had forgotten what had put me on a plane, my arm still bruised and sore from a battery of innoculations, and brought me to this completely unfamiliar place. I had forgotten why I had left my family and friends, my home and livelihood. It was all laid out for me again on the scrap of paper.

This man, this missionary, who I had met by chance along the railroad tracks in the desert, he had understood what I had forgotten, that the message is what's most important! Finding the opportunity to share the plan of salvation, regardless of race, position, or even language, was what mattered. I turned to thank him, to see if I could help him with his load of sticks, but he was gone. Across the wide, empty, expanse of desert that lay between myself and the edge of the city, there was nothing but the dusty railroad tracks and blowing white sand. I retuned to Jos that afternoon with a new sense of purpose. I might not accomplish what I was sent to do, I might even fail miserably at it, but I could take advantage of every opportunity to share the message through my words and my actions.

Looking back on the months I spent in Nigeria, I think of all the things that I learned—what true poverty looks like, what real perseverance is and what it can accomplish, and how our God, in his infinite love and wisdom, can use any opportunity, overcome any barrier, to remind us how simple his calling really is. The missionary who changed my life did it with only a smile and a wrinkled piece of paper.

~Perry P. Perkins

Angels Among Us

Answered Prayers

Seeing Red

A good man's prayers will from the deepest dungeon climb heavens' height,
and bring a blessing down.
~Joanna Baillie

I grabbed my lined jacket, stepped into the garage and slipped on my rubber boots. The old dog looked up at me as if to say, "Do I really have to go with you? It's miserable outside."

I gave her a pat. "Okay, old girl, I'll let you off this time." I headed to the corrals. Walking was awkward. Previous mud impressions from my boots were filling with snow and freezing. I shook my head in disbelief. This was May.

Earlier, Red had shown signs of calving. Our small herd was gentle and easy to handle, except for old Red. No matter what we did for her, she was never friendly.

Approaching the corral, I noticed Red wasn't outside. I rattled the chain on the gate while calling so that I wouldn't startle her. I reached the doorway of the small calving shelter and kept talking while my eyes adjusted to the dim light inside. "How are you doing?" I asked, focusing on her form near the back of the shelter.

"Oh," I exclaimed." You've had it already. Is everything all right?" I didn't step inside. I wasn't about to get trapped in the building with a new mother. As I shifted for a better look, my eye caught a swift movement from Red. Wham! I felt myself being driven into the doorframe. When my feet hit the ground again, I spun around to get away. Whack! I was hit from behind and went flying, arms flailing. One arm caught my new glasses. They jumped off my face. Frantically I tried to grab them as I descended towards the ground. I missed, landing with the glasses somewhere under my chest.

Slowly I raised myself onto my hands and knees. Bang! I was knocked flat again. I was shocked. I figured that because I wasn't near her newborn, Red would leave me alone. Not so—she was enraged! Each time I tried to get up, she hit me from behind. I became a cow-powered plow as she pushed me around the corral making a trail through the snow, mud and manure. Eventually I stopped, wedged between the shelter and water trough.

Red stood on my back with one front hoof and pawed at me with the other. Now I was her human trampoline. I threw a gloved hand over my neck for protection. Whenever I raised my head, Red slammed it with hers. "Stop it, please stop it! Help!" I cried. I wished the dog had come along. She might have distracted the cow long enough for me to get up. I thought of my family. Would they find me here trampled to death? I felt Red's hot breath on the back of my head and heard her irate grunts as she fought to destroy me. What a way to die, I thought, face down in manure!

Suddenly I bolted my head up, realizing I hadn't called on the only one who could help me. "Lord, help me!" I called. Once again I felt my face dig into the muck from another head butt.

Abruptly, Red stopped, turned, and ran to the far side of the corral. I raised my head and stared at her. Her flaming eyes focused not on me, but on something above me. I followed her gaze. I didn't see anything, but she certainly did.

Slowly I rose, keeping one eye pinned on the cow while also trying to see what she was staring at. Motionless, she seemed hyp-notized. I took two steps. She remained rigid. Her glazed eyes were frightful. Would she let me out? I stumbled towards the railed fence. Red never budged. Her eyes glanced briefly as I moved, but then again fixated just above me.

I felt someone unseen on each side of me supporting me by my arms and coaxing me along. I vaguely remember reaching the fence. Doubled over and holding my sides, I turned towards the house, then stopped and eyed the haystack. Maybe I should rest a bit first. Something, or someone, urged me to keep going. I trudged towards the house, leaning on my helpers for support. I knew instinctively that God had sent his angels to minister to me. I was not afraid.

As I stepped inside the house, the angels released me. I hobbled into the kitchen and reached for the phone. Pain seared my ribs and chest. My breathing was rapid and labored. How much internal damage was there?

At the hospital, staff and onlookers stared at my dung-saturated clothing. "I had a fight with a cow and the cow won," I told the nurse.

I was whisked to the X-ray department. After completing the X-rays, the technician spoke: "I'll be right back."

Returning he uttered, "Okay, we get to go for another ride." An ultrasound was next on the agenda. "Your doctor will be right with you," he stated as we returned to the emergency room. His aloofness told me something was wrong.

The doctor entered. I had three broken ribs and perhaps a few cracked ones. The sternum was intact, but I was quite bruised front and back and had several cuts on the back of my neck where the cow's hooves pawed me. There did not appear to be any spinal damage. Had I not shifted my body just before the cow hit me, a direct blow on the sternum could have been fatal. My heavy jacket and the soft wet ground had probably saved me from more serious damage.

"While everything appears to be okay internally, we are concerned about possible damage, particularly to the spleen. We'll keep you overnight for observation. If the spleen is damaged we may have to do emergency surgery," the doctor warned.

I prayed. I didn't have time for surgery. It was spring seeding time. Doctors and nurses kept checking me through the night. Over and over the attack played in my mind. Had I imagined divine intervention? No, the fear in Red's eyes as she stared at that apparition was as real as my pain. No, I wouldn't have made it out of there and back to the house unaided. Angels had rescued me. I had felt their touch. Everything would be okay.

In the morning my husband arrived with my weirdly bent glasses and news that mother and calf were fine. I was cleared for discharge.

It took time for the ribs and bruising to heal. It took more time for me to have the courage to walk among the herd again, but a summer filled with tasty steaks and hamburgers courtesy of Red aided the healing process. Part of her was even dehydrated and sent to friends in Siberia. Siberia—a fitting place for her I thought.

Often farmers are killed in angry cow attacks because there is no escape, no one to intervene. Praise God for divine intervention! Thank God for sending his angels to rescue me. "Are not all angels ministering spirits, sent to serve those who will inherit salvation?" (Hebrews 1:14 NIV)

~Irene R. Bastian

A Hand from Above

For every mountain there is a miracle.
~Robert H. Schuller

All my life I've believed in angels. When I first heard about them as a little child I believed there existed beings who were sent by God to help people in their time of need. I believed there were people who had been saved by angels, pulled from a fire, guided through the wilderness, or just comforted in their time of loss or need. But I never thought an angel would come to me and literally give me a hand when I needed it the most.

I was a climber in my youth. I loved the great outdoors, hiking through unexplored terrain, camping out and enjoying the beauty that nature had to offer. Most of all I loved being up high, high enough to look out over this landscape God had created and marvel at the beauty and the wonder that is this world.

Climbing was something I started when I was in college, when a friend of mine who was a climber volunteered to teach me. At first, I would slip and stumble more than I would get a firm grip on the hill I was trying to climb. But over time I came to understand the texture of every rock surface, the patience and strength needed to spend all day traversing the face of a mountain. And I came to feel the wonder at being a small being in such a grand place as the mountains that I explored.

I switched from climbing with ropes to free climbing, where

it's just you and the bare rock. It took me more time to learn how to accomplish that, but soon I was inching my way across the faces of many of the climbing community's favorite mountains. I was young and strong and adventurous, and I thought there was no mountain I couldn't conquer.

And so it was that I did a foolish thing. I decided to climb on my own on a very difficult rock face that many world-class climbers had found too treacherous to summit. Even worse, I didn't tell anyone where I was going. Oh, they knew the general part of the wilderness I was headed for, but not that I was going to do anything as dumb and dangerous as what I set out to do.

So there I was, three hundred feet up the face of my chosen mountain, dangling from a corner of rock that jutted out over the landscape, when I realized that I didn't have any strength left in me. My legs were exhausted. My fingers and hands were cramped and my arms were trembling. I was getting ready to fall.

I began to pray. At first I prayed that God would give me the strength to reach a place where I could rest and regain my strength, but soon enough I realized there was not going to be any time for that. My fingers were beginning to slip. I looked down and saw the ground very far below me, and for the first time in my life I thought I was going to die.

My prayers became something more earnest. I prayed to God and asked him to save me. I told him I knew I was going to fall and prayed he would catch me. Then it happened. My fingers lost their hold on the rock and I felt my tired body drop. My legs brushed the side of the mountain but were too weak to do anything. I closed my eyes and waited for the impact.

All of a sudden I felt two hands wrap themselves around my waist. I felt them gently squeeze me. I was being lifted up. I couldn't believe it, but I was being lifted to a place higher up than I had been dangling from. I heard a whisper in my ear at that moment and a rush of warm, gentle air. The voice said, "Don't be afraid. I have you in my arms."

I didn't have time to ask any questions. I looked up and saw a ledge above me and felt myself being taken to it. The squeeze around my waist tightened, and suddenly I felt strength pour into my arms and legs. I reached up and took hold of an outcropping and set my feet on the ledge. The gentle hands that had been holding me released me, and I stood safely on the rock.

Then I looked down to see who or what had saved me, but there was no one there. I heard the rush of warm air again go past me. In that moment I knew that God had answered my prayers. He'd sent an angel down as I was falling to catch me and to set me back safely on the mountain. He'd saved me from my own foolish pride.

As soon as my strength returned I made my way down the mountain. I did climb again after that, but never so foolishly. I am forever grateful for the second chance I got on that mountain, and for the loving arms of an angel who lent me a hand when I needed it the most.

~John P. Buentello

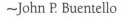

My Dream Babysitter

Pay attention to your dreams—
God's angels often speak directly to our hearts when we are asleep.
~Eileen Elias Freeman,
The Angels' Little Instruction Book

I had just become a divorced mother of two young children. I remember the fog of those days; this new title I had acquired, the sadness and anger, the feeling of being lost and not knowing what to do next. A counselor I had been seeing suggested I go to college to upgrade my skills, as I'd been out of the workforce for six years. She thought it might be a good experience for me to not only study something I loved, but to help recover emotionally from the divorce. I thought the idea was ridiculous.

But I began the process anyway. In May of that year, I went through the motions of admissions, testing, meeting with a financial aid officer, thinking in the back of my mind that this was never going to happen, nor did I care. I had always loved to learn, so I wasn't afraid of failing. Instead, I was afraid of how I was going to do this: attend college full-time, work part-time in the evenings and on weekends, raise two young children who had been my whole world for six years. Daycare was out of the question because they were familiar with home, with one-on-one attention, and I didn't want that to change, especially now. The world I had known for years was gone.

"Who am I kidding?" I thought. "I just wrecked their lives, along with my own, so what difference does it make if I go to college or not?"

I believed all the years they had been at home, loved dearly and cared for by two parents, would slowly go down the drain. I was certain they would end up as statistics on some latest case study of children of divorced parents who fall through the cracks and become juvenile delinquents, and then adult criminals who remain in prison for the rest of their lives. What made me think I could successfully get through college during such a time of upheaval? I don't ever recall a time I had felt like such a failure.

I passed the pre-entrance exams, and I even got through the financial aid meetings with grants for non-traditional students, code for "older" students going to college for the first time. And, boy, was that intimidating: the thought of attending college with a bunch of eighteen-year-olds fresh out of high school, and me, the divorced, older woman with a couple of kids. It scared the daylights out of me.

But what I couldn't find was someone to watch over my babies. I knew, no matter how well the pre-college pieces fell into place, I wasn't going anywhere without adequate care for my children. I went through that whole process just for kicks, knowing full well this wasn't going to happen.

I was desperate for a life changer—and not the divorced kind. I began to pray. I had gone to church all my life, but my faith was built on ritual and tradition, going through the motions, living my life pretty comfortably, believing my faith was solid, that I was doing all the right things. But that summer I began to pray hard. I began to ask God, if this was His will, to fling open all the doors, have all the pieces fall in place, and show me clearly that I was on the right path. Oh, and find me the ideal babysitter.

The weeks passed by as everything about college fell into place except finding a babysitter. It just wasn't happening. I called everyone I knew, looked into all the local daycare centers, still nothing.

One night, after praying and crying myself to sleep again, I had a dream. I was in a huge department store with my kids, each of them fussing and crying as I tried to get all of us through the store, pushing a large cart that was so heavy I could barely move it.

I set the cart aside for a moment to sit down with my kids as shoppers walked by. Suddenly, an older woman walked up and sat down beside me. I noticed a pin of some kind on her shirt. She looked right at me and asked, "Do you know what those children need?"

I looked at her, too tired to argue, or say much for that matter except, "What?"

"They need a Butterfinger candy bar." And she proceeded to pull two from her purse, handing one each to my son and daughter. Immediately, they sat down on her lap and stopped crying, eating their Butterfinger candy bars, heads resting on her shoulders. They seemed so peaceful with her.

I was amazed. Then she asked me, "Can you drive me home? I'm a widow and I don't drive."

I agreed to drive her home. She told me where she lived, and when we pulled into her driveway I noticed old railroad ties lining her driveway and steps leading up to her doorway. I put the car in park and asked if I could help her to the door.

"No, I'm fine. Now you take those babies (who had fallen asleep in the back seat) and go home and get some rest. I am going to take care of you and your children." Suddenly, she was gone.

When I awoke the next morning, I felt such a calm sense of peace. I just lay there, basking in that new feeling.

Months went by, and summer ended. College was starting in two weeks and I still had no one to watch my children. I remembered the prayer.

"God, I don't know if you're listening, but I remember that dream a few months ago, and I'm trying to be patient and trust that angel who came to me. I know you're busy with way more important things, but we're coming up on two weeks now before college starts, and I really need to hear from you."

One week before college began, a friend gave me the number of an older woman who used to babysit. She was a widow who lived in town.

I called her, and after we spoke for a bit, she asked me if I could come to her house to pick her up so she could meet my children.

"I don't drive, you see, I'm a widow." She gave me directions to her home. Could it be?

I pulled into a driveway lined with railroad ties and steps leading to a door. I had goose bumps. The door opened, and there she was, giving me a hug, saying, "It's so nice to meet you. I can't wait to meet your children."

As we drove to my home, I noticed an angel pin right there on the pocket of her shirt.

~Patricia Beaumont

Angels Have Charge Over Me

The angels are the dispensers and administrators of the divine beneficence toward us; they regard our safety, undertake our defense, direct our ways, and exercise a constant solicitude that no evil befall us.
~John Calvin

To retire up north in the woods on a lake was something my husband and I dreamed about for years. So when we heard of a resort selling its cottages as condominiums in October of 1995, we seized the opportunity to rent one with an option to buy. One week later, after moving to Lake George in Rhinelander, Wisconsin, 200 miles from family and friends, my husband died of a heart attack.

The evening following my husband's funeral, sitting among dozens of unpacked boxes, reality set in. I was totally alone. After forty years of having someone to talk to, to hold me, and to say goodnight to, I was alone.

How would I survive the loneliness? Worse yet, I had been afraid of the dark since I was eight years old. I wondered how I would get through the nights. I ran through the house locking all the doors and windows. I even braced the doors with chairs under the knobs. I closed all the curtains and turned on all the lights. I placed a flashlight next to my bed (in case the electricity went out, I told myself) and my husband's hunting knife under my pillow.

Still, I couldn't sleep. Finally, I phoned the doctor after many sleepless nights. The sleeping pills he prescribed made me feel groggy all day. Yet I needed to sleep. Added to my sleep malady came loneliness and insecurity over being the only resident in this resort during one of the worst snowstorms to hit Oneida County in over fifty years.

Then one January evening, after three months of grieving, everything changed. I was sitting in my living room recliner watching television, eating a TV dinner and thinking about how I didn't have much of a life anymore, when I inhaled a kernel of corn. Coughing and choking, I jumped up from the recliner and proceeded to pound my back into a protruding doorframe, in hopes of forcing the corn from my windpipe. That didn't work. To make matters worse, during the coughing and choking siege, my bladder let loose and I had to run for the bathroom.

While sitting on the commode, I continued to cough and choke for what seemed like forever. Yet even with all the coughing, I still couldn't dislodge the kernel of corn from my windpipe. I started panicking when I got lightheaded.

Was this how I was supposed to die, choking on a kernel of corn? I'd been depressed about not having a life since the death of my husband. But the actual possibility of dying alone had me silently praying.

"Oh, God," I prayed to myself, as tears washed down my cheeks. "I don't really want to die. I do have a life, and I value it. So if you can help me, please do it now."

No sooner had I thought the words than I felt a forceful blow hit me between my shoulder blades, sending the corn flying from my windpipe, out of my mouth, and into the shower stall.

Startled, I half turned and looked behind me as if someone could be there, which was impossible because my back was up against the commode that was up against the wall. Yet I definitely felt a hard blow (almost knocking me off the commode) on my upper back.

Just then I remembered a Bible verse my older sister, Peggy, used to say to me as a child to calm my fears: "For it is written, He shall give His angels charge over thee, to keep thee in all His ways."

As I contemplated this phrase, while feeling truly grateful to be alive, I said aloud, "Thank you, God, for sending one of your angels to keep me safe."

Later, as I was preparing for bed, it occurred to me that I didn't have to be afraid of the dark and being alone anymore. After all, if an angel isn't going to let me die over a kernel of corn, I reasoned, then it is not going to allow anything to happen to me.

Feeling safe and secure for the first time in months, I put the hunting knife back in the box on the closet shelf. From that night on I was able to sleep soundly, without a sleeping pill, and in total darkness. I had conquered my fear of the dark and being alone, all because God had sent an angel to have charge over me.

~Sylvia Bright-Green

Driving on Ice

Trust in the Lord with all your heart
and lean not on your own understanding.
~Proverbs 3:5

I was twenty years old in 1973, living in Kansas City and working two jobs to support myself while attending college. A year earlier I'd been forced to quit Stephens College in Columbia, Missouri due to lack of funds. When an invite came to return to my former college town for a party, I jumped at the chance to reconnect in Columbia.

It was November and I got on the road after Friday's work shift around 8 or 8:30 p.m. for the two-hour drive. The plan was to spend Friday night in Columbia at a local hotel, look around town the next day, and attend the party Saturday night.

My 1963 Corvair convertible was not air tight, so turning on the heater really helped with the outside cold. Ironically, I'd have to roll down the windows to let fresh air in because the smell of gas fumes permeated the car once the heater was on.

It had snowed earlier that day, but roads were clear and driving was nothing out of the ordinary. I had the radio cranked up loud, singing along, enjoying a beautiful moonlit night. About an hour into the drive, I hit an unseen patch of ice that seemed to take complete control of the car.

My high school driver's ed training had taught me to gently pump the brakes when in a skid (anti-lock brakes were nonexistent), but to no avail. The car spun. Then it swerved head first into a ditch dividing the four-lane highway. Simultaneously, the engine died and I was sitting in a car resting headfirst down a forty-degree angle, in utter silence. I was terrified. I was in the middle of nowhere and there were no other cars. I tried a few times to restart the car, but it was dead.

It was freezing cold and all I could see was an empty highway lined with trees, moonlight reflecting on the surrounding snow. To say I was scared was an understatement. I didn't have enough warm clothing to withstand spending the night out there. Cell phones didn't exist at that time. The night could get better or much worse, depending on who (if anyone) stopped to help this lone female stuck in a ditch. To add to my dilemma, I realized no one would even know I was missing for several days.

I sat in the car watching the highway for what seemed like an eternity, hoping a police car would drive by. Nothing. After a while, one or two cars drove past going in the opposite direction. No one stopped. The wind picked up as it made a whistling noise through the slightly tattered convertible top.

I decided to get out and see if there was any place close enough to walk for help. As I opened the car door and carefully stood up on the frozen ground, I looked in every direction to see nothing but snow, trees and a darkened, empty highway.

I didn't have snow tires and would not be able to grab enough traction to get out of that steep ditch, even if my car started. I got back in the car, berating myself for being so stupid. Why did I drive so late in the day? Why did I risk an old car in this weather? Why didn't I tell someone where I was going so that if I didn't show up they'd know to look for me?

I took a deep breath and began to pray. "God," I said. "I'm in trouble. Please, please help me to be safe and get out of this." I cannot remember the rest of my prayer, as I'm sure it turned into babbling at some point. The night grew later, the wind grew stronger. I was getting really cold.

After praying, I sat in the car doing nothing, thinking nothing… just sitting, staring at the wheel and the snow-covered ditch beyond the hood.

What happened next is hard to describe. But it impacted me enough that I still recall the incident vividly, even though it happened nearly forty years ago. Fear of ridicule prevented me from ever sharing this story with more than one or two people.

It seemed like a presence joined me in the car. Was I losing my mind? There even seemed to be a depression from the weight of someone in the passenger seat next to me!

If someone was there to help me, I needed proof. I could not get past the feeling that I was not alone. Okay God, I thought. If you or an angel or something is here to help me, then I'll test it.

I once again turned the ignition key. The car started right up. I couldn't believe it. But now I feared the tires would just continue to spin, as the snow had become frozen ice. "Okay Lord," I thought. "If I'm not going crazy and you are somehow helping me, I'm going to put the Corvair into reverse and see if I can get out of this ditch." Slowly, the car came right up and out of the ditch, almost as if there was no ice at all.

I backed out onto the highway, put the gear into drive and slowly made my way back onto the road. The radio had shut off when the engine initially died. I drove in silence and could not shake the feeling that there was still someone sitting with me in the car, occupying the passenger's seat.

Needing proof that I wasn't going crazy, I decided upon one more "test." I lifted my hands off the steering wheel. Something took over and was steering the car! I know my car. It needed a pair of hands to maneuver properly, unlike newer power steering in today's models. Someone, or something, was steering my car!

Afraid to "test" any further I placed my hands back on the steering wheel and thanked God out loud for this blessing. I did not see any other cars the rest of the way into town. The "presence" remained until I reached my destination. I did not physically see an angel, but there's no doubt in my mind that I was assisted by an unseen presence that night forty years ago.

~Morgan Hill

26

My Snow Angel

It is not known precisely where angels dwell—
whether in the air, the void, or the planets. It has not been God's pleasure
that we should be informed of their abode.
~Voltaire

A warm, sunny day in early November, especially in the Sierras, was a nice surprise. One look at the cloudless blue sky was all it took to convince me to drive twenty miles into the valley to do early Christmas shopping. My husband was content to stay home and rake up the last of the fallen leaves. I called out to him before I got in the car, "Call me if you think of something you want me to bring home." He smiled and waved as I drove away.

Temperatures in the valley are between eight and ten degrees higher than in the foothills where we live, so I enjoyed the warmth and sunshine as I walked from store to store. It wasn't until around sunset when I realized I had been shopping for most of the day. I was surprised I hadn't had a call from my husband as he usually thought of something he wanted from town while I was gone.

I rummaged through my purse for my cell phone only to discover it wasn't there. Not all that surprising as it wasn't the first time that had happened. "It's probably on the car seat or on the floor," I said to myself as I hurried to the parking lot. I put the bags in the trunk and got in the car, but the cell phone was nowhere in sight. After a frustrating search I found it under the seat and sighed with relief. Not only to find the cell phone but also to discover the source of the clunking sound every time I had turned a corner on the drive to the valley.

My husband will have a good laugh about that, I thought, as I dialed our home phone number. I didn't get the chance to tell him. I heard the panic in my husband's voice when he answered the phone. "I've been trying to call you. It started snowing up here half an hour ago," he shouted into the phone.

"But the storm wasn't due in until after the weekend," I said.

"I know, I know, but there was a sudden drop in temperature and it switched from fall to winter just like that," he said.

Another surprise from Mother Nature. That's how things happen in the Sierras, which is why I keep a box of emergency supplies in the trunk and carry chains from fall through the end of spring.

"Well, I guess I'll have to stop and put the chains on when I get up there so I can make it home," I sighed. My husband coughed nervously and cleared his throat. "Uh, I forgot to put the chains back in the trunk when I vacuumed the car out yesterday. I saw them in the garage when I finished raking," he said. I resisted the urge to scream. I checked my watch. The two local auto parts stores were closed by now.

"How much snow is on the ground now?" I asked.

"Only an inch or two. I think you can make it home okay if you leave now and drive slowly and follow the tire tracks in the road when you get to the snow."

I hung up and slammed the phone into my purse. I berated myself for not checking the trunk after he cleaned out the car. It was a constant battle with him to put things back where he found them. Usually it was his stuff, but this time I was the victim of his careless-ness. I had to let a scream out to release my anger rather than carry it home with me.

Big tufts of white swirled in front of the car headlights when I reached the 1200-foot level. I kept the car in low gear and crept slowly toward the 2600-foot elevation where we lived. I started talk-ing to myself and to God. "Help me get home," became my prayer mantra as I repeated it every few minutes.

My biggest challenge would be to get over the reservoir bridge, then up the hill on the other side. The only way to make it would be to keep the car moving steadily and hope the cars and trucks had displaced enough snow so my tires could get traction. I continued my mantra. The snow was falling harder when I reached the reservoir bridge. I blinked back tears.

A truck was driving across the bridge ahead of me. My hopes soared. Those big tires would make a good path through the snow and help my car tires get enough traction to make it up the hill. The truck slowed as I got closer, then stopped. I slowed the car but had to stop a few feet from the truck. I watched helplessly as the driver got out, swept snow off the truck hood and windshield then got back in and drove off.

My car had lost precious momentum. The path from the truck tires helped until I reached the end of the bridge and started up the hill. The car started to swerve. I turned the wheel to correct each swerve. The tires started spinning and the car started to slide back down the hill toward the sloped side of the reservoir. I was on a direct path into the water.

"God, please, I need help right now," I yelled. The car stopped. I pressed my head against the steering wheel and said, "Thank You." Someone was rapping on the window. I rolled it down to see a young man with dark curly hair and sparkling blue eyes. He smiled. "You'll never make it up this hill without chains. I'll push your car to the side. You can walk up the hill," he said.

The car seemed to float effortlessly to the side of the road. The young man came to the open window and nodded. "Remember to take those Christmas gifts out of the trunk when you leave," he said. How did he know there were Christmas gifts in the trunk?

I grabbed my purse and jumped out of the car so I could thank him for his help. I looked around. No one was there. There were no cars or trucks on the road. I looked for footprints but there were none, only a pristine layer of snow growing deeper by the minute. I reached for my cell phone to call my husband but then remembered that reception at this level was poor even in good weather.

I slipped on rubber boots and a hooded sweatshirt I kept under the spare tire, grabbed the shopping bags and started walking toward the gas station at the top of the hill. When I saw the dim light over the door I knew it was closed. My plan to call my husband was lost in the swirling snow around me. I had to keep walking until I got to a house where I could use a phone.

Just as I turned off the main road, a white truck pulled up next to me and the driver got out and came toward me. "Would you like a ride home?" he asked. I nodded and he opened the door. He smiled when I started giving him directions and said, " I know where you live." I looked at him more closely to see if I recognized him and noticed some dark curly hair sticking out of his knit hat. "Are you the young man who pushed my car off the road on the hill?" I asked. He smiled and nodded.

The truck seemed to glide over the road and I was surprised when it pulled into the driveway to our house in a matter of minutes. It takes about ten minutes to cover that distance in nice weather. I thanked him after he helped me out of the truck and turned to wave, but the truck was gone.

My husband was startled to see me come in the front door instead of coming from the garage. I told him about my trip home from the valley. When I finished, he scrunched up his face and looked at me. "I didn't hear a truck pull into the driveway," he said. After a short discussion he challenged me to show him the tire tracks. We walked out to the driveway.

There were no tire tracks, only a deep, smooth white blanket of snow—except where my footprints started and led to the stairs to the house.

Since that experience the term "Snow Angel" has a special meaning for me.

~L.A. Kennedy

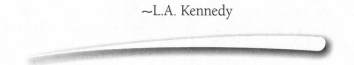

27

Angel on My Shoulder

If you abide in me, and My words abide in you,
you will ask what you desire, and it shall be done for you.
~John 15:7

W hen I was little, I was taught that everyone has a guardian angel assigned to him or her from the moment of birth. I even believed that if I turned around quickly enough, I would catch sight of mine. Of course, that never happened.

I retained my faith over the years, but eventually stopped believing in the existence of an invisible winged being protectively hovering over me to grant my every wish. The cliché "angel on my shoulder" became just that, an outdated expression that belonged in hymns and childish dreams.

I grew up, married and had a child. Although blessed in many ways, life was a constant struggle financially, hitting an all-time low three years ago. My husband lost his job of thirty-five years. We had managed to buy our first home only a year before, and although the mortgage was low, it quickly depleted the small settlement he received as compensation for all his years of hard work.

Jobs were non-existent in our rural area. We maxed out our credit cards within months just trying to survive. Our outlook was bleak, forcing us to face the harsh reality of our situation; we would have to put the house up for sale and rent a small apartment.

We had no equity in our home, so there would be nothing left from the sale to pay off our other bills. Declaring bankruptcy was inevitable, and we began to plan accordingly.

"We need to get the house market-ready," my husband stated sadly. "We'll clean the chimney, empty the septic tank and repaint. We'll also have to file our income taxes so we can declare that debt along with the rest," he added, rubbing his tired, red-rimmed eyes.

I nodded quietly and got up to get the paperwork. We'd filled out income tax forms several months earlier but never filed. Due to the lump sum settlement, we knew we owed thousands of dollars. Now there would be interest and late filing fees as well. I handed him the thick forms with all our other bills and called the chimney sweep to come the next day.

"Don't forget, we still have his coat that he left here last year," my husband reminded me, and I retrieved that too, tossing it on the back of the chair. As it landed, a crumpled piece of paper fell out of the pocket. I bent to pick it up and saw it was an old twenty-dollar bill.

"Wow—that's ancient!" my husband remarked.

"It's still money," I pointed out bitterly, my hands shaking from the temptation to keep it. It was a small amount, but to me, it was a windfall.

I looked at my husband and saw the same thought in his sad eyes. Surely, the owner would never remember it was there, and if he did, well, what proof did he have?

We were silent for a long time. Always of one mind, we reached the same conclusion. I tucked the money back into the jacket. We resumed our discussion of what needed doing, glancing longingly at the coat every so often, but the money remained there.

The next day, my husband went to see a tax accountant to recheck our forms. I waited for the chimney sweep. His fee sat neatly on the table in embarrassingly small bills and change.

He arrived, did his job, collected his money and thanked me profusely for keeping his coat for so long.

"I'm sorry. I meant to come by several times to get it, but just never got around to it." I waved him off with a forced smile.

After he left, I went to make coffee. It would be weak, since I was scraping the bottom of the can to collect the last grains. I reached for the milk I'd been so sparing with, hoping it would last until we received a small check we were expecting. I'd been too stingy! The milk made a glopping sound as soured lumps fell into my coffee.

It was the final straw! In a rage, I threw my cup across the kitchen into the dining room where it shattered against a mirror. Diluted coffee streamed in rivulets down the wall and pooled with the glass shards on the floor.

"Why?" I screamed at a God who I felt had abandoned me. "We're good people. We're honest, work hard, and this is our reward?" I railed. "I know you're busy. I know we're not important, but can you at least send one of those angels you want me to believe in to help us out a little? I'm not asking for a fortune! I just want to keep what little we have!" I screamed, tears saturating my face.

I breathed shakily, trying to compose myself. Grabbing a dustpan and a rag, I bent down to pick up the broken glass. As I did so, I felt a gentle, comforting touch on my shoulder. Startled, I whirled around to see a reflection in a small piece of mirror—a beautiful woman's face surrounded by a bright light. She had the bluest eyes I'd ever seen, and she smiled reassuringly, as if to say, "Everything is going to be all right." A moment later, the image was gone, replaced again by glass shards dotted with coffee splatter. I sat back, filled with a warm sense of peace.

I was still sitting on my heels in a daze when the phone rang. I got to my feet clumsily, reaching for the receiver.

"Hello?" I murmured.

"Honey, are you sitting down? You need to sit down!" It was my husband, his voice raw with emotion.

"What's wrong?"

"Nothing's wrong." He laughed. "Everything's right! I made a mistake on the taxes. We're getting money back—lots of money!"

He went on to explain his error. His jabber made no sense. All I wanted to know was how much our refund would be. When he told me the amount, I gasped.

It was more than enough to pay off all our debts, and still leave us with money to buy food and wood for the winter. I was stunned.

I was replacing the phone when it rang again. It was the chimney sweep. He replied to my cheerful hello with an exuberant one of his own.

"I just called to thank you for your honesty," he began. "I found something in my jacket pocket that I thought I'd lost forever—a twenty-dollar bill my mother gave me forty years ago for my Confirmation. I never spent it because it was the last thing she gave me before she died a week later."

"Well, I'm glad you found it," I told him, guiltily remembering those few ugly moments when I was tempted to steal it for my own needs.

"May angels always watch over you, ma'am," he told me softly, and I smiled, my eyes filling with tears.

"They do," I whispered as I hung up the phone.

~Marya Morin

28

Ashley's Angel

Evening, morning and noon I will pray and cry aloud
and He shall hear my voice.
~Psalm 55:17

When my daughter turned nineteen, she announced to us she was moving from our small mountain town in central California to Pasadena. I wasn't crazy about my youngest daughter moving to the big city, but I remembered The Beach Boys song, "The Little Old Lady from Pasadena." So if my daughter seemed determined to relocate to southern California, that city seemed like a safer choice than most.

After a couple of years of junior college, she and her roommate, Laura, decided to transfer to the university. That meant moving away from the little old ladies in Pasadena. As starving college students they had to settle for a place that was less than advantageous—to say the least.

"We're not living in the ghetto. We're just living in the 'ghett,'" Ashley joked, trying to reassure us. She was right. It wasn't completely frightening, but there were just enough shady characters and siren sounds to keep a mother on her knees every night asking God to send angels to watch over the petite blonde beauty living in Los Angeles.

After parking her car one night, Ashley cautiously began walking to her door when she passed a group of guys who took notice of the fact she was alone. She and Laura had made a habit of calling

each other as soon as they got out of the car and staying on the phone until they were safely inside, but tonight Laura wasn't home either. Pretending to be on the phone, Ashley heard footsteps following her. With her heart in her throat, she breathed a prayer for safety.

Within minutes, she heard a voice behind her. "Sweetie, you're being followed and I am just going to walk with you until you get to your door."

"Normally if some guy calls me 'sweetie,' he's the one I want to avoid," Ashley informed. "But the minute this man opened his mouth, I felt safe.

"He didn't actually walk with me," she informed me. "He stayed a few steps behind. I reached my apartment, put my key in the door, and turned to thank him, but he was gone. He hadn't had time to travel that far, but still he was nowhere in sight."

While Ashley didn't get to express her gratitude to her benefactor that night, I haven't stopped thanking God for answering this fretting mother's prayers.

~Linda Newton

29

The Power of Prayer

Pray without ceasing...
~1 Thessalonians 5:17

"Those stairs. They worry me. I pray every day for your family on those stairs." My husband's "crazy Aunt Anna" was always praying for something. For her, prayer was like breathing. She never stopped until the day she died. She prayed for requests from local churches and lists from televangelists. She prayed for parking spaces, doctors' visits and grocery orders. She prayed herself up and then down the few steps in her small apartment.

Aunt Anna was our family's rock of faith. A widow with no children, she cared for her nieces and nephews, grand-nieces and grand-nephews, as if they were her own. If my children had a pending test, audition, or big game, they'd ask Aunt Anna to pray for them, believing that she had the red phone direct line to heaven. Of course, they knew that they could pray too, but to them Aunt Anna's prayers seemed more powerful.

In her younger years, she visited people in need of prayer. My husband was often sick as a child, and Aunt Anna came to his bedside and prayed for him. Years later, as she became more and more housebound, she increased her prayer time. Her kitchen table served as Prayer Headquarters, strewn with handwritten prayers, journals, Bibles, devotional books, and prayer requests—lots and lots of prayer requests.

And for some reason, Aunt Anna always reminded us that she prayed for safety on our basement staircase.

What was it about those stairs that scared her? With her one withered hand and two arthritic knees, Aunt Anna had three good reasons to fear them. But we didn't. We climbed up and down those stairs each time we left and returned home. The handrail on the left side did seem a bit awkward when descending. Could that be it? Or was it the hard cement beneath the unpadded indoor/outdoor carpeting? Whatever it was, we didn't give the stairs a second thought.

Maybe we should have.

My four-year-old daughter's constant companion was her adorable talking doll Katie. Lauren carried Katie everywhere she went, which was no small feat as the doll was half Lauren's height. Lauren was a petite, quiet little girl with a mass of brown curls. Katie was a huge blond doll that spoke.

One ordinary day, we headed toward the stairs to the garage. My toddler son AJ rested heavily on my hip. Lauren carried Katie as she opened the basement door and started down the stairs.

What happened next took only a microsecond, yet it seemed to happen in slow motion. With the Katie doll in her left arm, Lauren stepped off the landing and made it to the second step before catapulting into the air. Her sneaker's thick rubber sole stuck on the carpet pile, propelling her headfirst down the hard flight of stairs. She rolled head over heels. Behind her, I was powerless to stop the unfolding nightmare as I envisioned my broken and bleeding little girl crumpled on the cement floor.

With teary eyes and pounding heart, I couldn't believe what I saw next. To this day, as many times as my mind replays this event, it seems like a film that's missing footage — as if several frames were lost on the cutting room floor. One second I saw Lauren flying. The next, I saw her twisted body at my feet lying diagonally on the stairs as if an angel had caught her in mid-air and gently laid her there. The rubber bottoms of her shoes faced up at me, her head a few steps down. The giant doll remained curled inside her left arm as her right hand somehow seized the railing on her left side.

Despite Lauren's wide-eyed terror, she didn't cry or even whimper. She just waited peacefully for me to gather her into my arms. As she nestled into my lap, her right hand—the one that held the banister—was balled in a fist. Prying her fingers open exposed a huge wad of contraband gummy worm candies nesting inside. Unbelievable! It was impossible for her tiny fist to have grasped the railing without dropping the candies.

I knew I had witnessed an angelic intervention.

Jesus said that children have "their angels in heaven" (Matthew 18:10) and the psalmist wrote, "He will order His angels to protect you wherever you go. They will hold you up with their hands so you won't even hurt your foot on a stone." (Psalm 91:11-12)

God answered Aunt Anna's prayers that day. Surely He sent an invisible angel to hold up Lauren with his hands and stop her from tumbling further down the stairs.

That day changed our attitude towards prayer, towards the real presence of angels, and towards Aunt Anna. She was so faithful, so sure that God heard her prayers. She prayed over big things and little things, certain that her heavenly Father cared for all things.

As a young mom, I cared about every big and every little thing concerning my children. Taking our cue from Aunt Anna, my family and I now share all our concerns in prayer, not just the "major" ones. After all, the Bible says to "Give all your worries and cares to God, for He cares about you." (1 Peter 5:7)

He certainly did send us an angel in our time of need.

~Susan Allen Panzica

30

Chicken Soup for the Soul

Hope in the ICU

The prayer that begins with trustfulness and passes on into waiting will always end in thankfulness, triumph, and praise.
~Alexander Maclaren

I t was a joyous time for Mother to be in the delivery room as my younger sister gave birth to her first child. Mother said it was an awesome, unforgettable experience to see her granddaughter born. Sara was a small baby but quickly gained weight, reaching the five-pound minimum to be released from the hospital. My sister and her husband took her home.

Shortly after being home, Sara became ill and was re-admitted to the hospital. Mother was still visiting. Unknown to us at the time, Mother prayed for God to take her rather than Sara. Sara began thriving again, keeping down her food and gaining weight. She was again sent home to the care of her parents and grandmother. Mother enjoyed caring for Sara.

A week or so after Sara was released from the hospital, Mother had a heart attack and was rushed by ambulance to the hospital. My other sister and I immediately drove to the hospital. It was a four-hour drive from the town where we lived.

The cardiologist informed us Mother most likely wouldn't survive. "Even if she does," he said, "she will have no memory and be in a vegetative state." He explained, "In the forty-minute ambulance ride to the hospital, her heart stopped three times. Though the paramedics were able to revive her, with each episode the brain was damaged due to lack of oxygen." The cardiologist advised us to call family members.

This is not what we wanted to hear. At age fifty-five, she was too young to leave us. It felt like only yesterday Daddy died (actually thirteen and a half years), and now Mother. "Please God, don't take her," I begged.

While my younger sister had to be home to care for her new baby, my other sister and I stayed in the waiting room outside the ICU. When the nurses allowed it, we would go to Mother's side, hold her hand and talk to her. She was unresponsive, but we kept talking.

One night around midnight, while my sister and I sat in the ICU waiting room, a minister came through the doors from the ICU. We had not seen him go into ICU.

He came directly to us, as if he knew us, and said, "Your Mother is going to be fine." He sat down and prayed with us. As he did, I felt my fear and hopelessness wash away. Within me there was a renewed optimism and sense of wellbeing.

The minister appeared to be in his early sixties with gray-black hair. He looked directly into my eyes as he handed me a business card and said, "Call if you need me." As he looked into my eyes, I felt calm. I was thankful for the minister's visit.

The length of time Mother lay in the hospital bed unresponsive is unclear in my memory. It seemed like an eternity! My sister and I made repeated trips back and forth from Norfolk, Virginia where we lived, to the North Carolina hospital. Each time there was no change; we were disappointed, but I didn't give up hope.

Finally, she spoke. Without opening her eyes, she called out her sister's names. She also called out the names of her children.

The doctor said her ability to speak was a positive, unexplainable sign. She did regain consciousness despite the doctor's initial bleak prediction. The only permanent damage to her brain was loss of short-term memory. I had one last thing to do before we took her back to Norfolk—thank the minister for his prayers.

I called the number on the business card. There was no such number in service. I looked in the phone book only to discover no listing for the church. Upon describing the minister to the ICU nurses and the hospital information desk attendant, I was told no one knew him or had ever seen the minister. My sister and I couldn't have both dreamt him, and I did have the business card in hand.

For me, there is no doubt that during the time we were exhausted and had no hope, God sent an angel to pull us back up. He sent an angel disguised as an earthly minister to carry the message of an upcoming miracle: "Your mother is going to be fine."

~Sara L. Schafer

Chapter
4

Angels Among Us

Angels in Disguise

An Unlikely Protector

It is not because angels are holier than men or devils that makes them angels,
but because they do not expect holiness from one another,
but from God alone.
~William Blake

In early 2001, our daughter Elizabeth was determined to take a bus trip from Iowa to Ohio to meet the young man she'd been writing to for several years. Her father and I weren't very happy with her decision and were especially worried about the many stops in larger cities, but she dismissed our concerns. She was eighteen, had saved up enough money to make the trip, and nothing we said could dissuade her.

When we dropped her off at the bus stop, we hugged her tightly and warned her to be very careful. As the bus pulled away, I found myself saying a prayer for her safe arrival.

That very night, we watched a police drama where a young girl's body was found behind a dumpster at a bus station. "An innocent Iowa girl, raped and murdered," one police offer lamented to the other, after they discovered her identity. My blood ran cold. I looked up to see a matching fear in David's eyes. We were thinking the same thing: We shouldn't have let her go.

Neither one of us got much sleep that long night, tossing and turning and reaching out for each other's hands. Over and over, we prayed for our daughter, repeating the same prayer I'd uttered under my breath at the bus stop: Please Lord, take care of our daughter on this journey. Watch over her.

I breathed a huge sigh of relief when Elizabeth finally called the next afternoon to say she'd arrived at her destination. I told her about the television program the night before, expecting her to tell me I was silly for worrying. Instead there was silence at the other end.

Then my daughter began telling me about the five-hour layover she had at 3:00 a.m., at a bus station that consisted of little more than a single locked building in the middle of nowhere. Just as she approached the door of the structure, a hulk of a man with long stringy hair and bulging tattooed biceps appeared from a nearby alley.

My terrified daughter twisted the doorknob back and forth frantically, to no avail. It was locked tight and there were no lights on inside.

Shoulders slumped in resignation, she did the only thing she could think to do; she sat down on her suitcase and began praying in earnest. She kept her eyes to the ground, trying to avoid eye contact with the fearsome stranger as he approached her.

When she finally dared to look up, the man was standing right in front of her. When he greeted her, she gulped back her fear enough to whisper a shaky hello. As he attempted to strike up a casual conversation, she bravely responded with one-word answers. He stood uncomfortably close to her as he talked. He asked her where she was headed and told her about the girlfriend he was headed to Florida to visit. She gradually relaxed as she realized that despite his rough exterior and language, he meant her no harm.

During the two hours that they stood alone outside, my daughter noticed at least three different vehicles filled with groups of young men drive by, one car circling at least twice. The men looked at my daughter, and then glanced at the big man standing next to her. None of them stopped.

By 5:15 a woman with a ring full of keys arrived, and as she opened the door to the station, Elizabeth heard the man mumble something, disappearing back into the alley. The attendant allowed her to enter the building, despite the fact that it wouldn't officially open for another fifteen minutes.

Once Elizabeth was locked inside, the man returned and tried to open the door. My daughter called out to him that the station wouldn't open until 5:30, and he nodded and walked away. She never saw him again.

Elizabeth waited inside the station for almost three hours, but never saw the man come into the building or get on a bus.

"Mom, if he hadn't been there and one of those cars full of guys stopped, they could have done anything to me. I would have been totally alone in the middle of the night. I could have been that girl in the show you watched."

I gasped in shock, but then Elizabeth added, "Mom, where did he go? The station wasn't crowded. If he really had planned to get on a bus, why did he disappear once I was safe inside?"

I felt a warm sense of peace fill me. I knew then, without a doubt, that God had answered my prayers by sending that burly bodyguard to watch over my daughter. "He was God's angel," I told Elizabeth, but she wasn't so sure.

"He didn't look like an angel, or talk like an angel," she responded uncertainly.

"If he had looked less intimidating, would his presence have hindered any of those cars from stopping?"

Beth went quiet as we both considered what might have happened if that formidable-looking man hadn't been standing so protectively close to her.

Were it not for that fortuitous encounter at the closed bus station, Elizabeth might not have made it as far as Ohio to meet the young man who would eventually become her husband and the father of her three children.

I know for a fact that angels exist, though we might not always recognize them when they visit us. Sometimes God's angel can be a big, burly man with tattooed arms.

~Mary Potter Kenyon

An Angel of Calm

The magnitude of life is overwhelming.
Angels are here to help us take it peace by peace.
~Levende Waters

Going to school during my older brother's intense six-year battle with drug abuse was an ordeal in itself—hiding my distress daily from friends, pretending to be carefree. It should have been over after he died. But the stress of his murder highly suspected to be at the hands of a dealer eight months earlier had left me even more anxiety-ridden. Especially the day that my best friend begged me to accept a ride home from her after school. I could see tension in her hands as she fumbled for her keys. What a pair we were. If ever two young girls needed a miracle, it was us.

Mandy had driven her family's blue boat of a car to school on her own as she occasionally did. "I can't take long," she said, in her usual nerve-wracked manner, "but you're really on the way…." Then, almost like a whispered afterthought, "My mother said it was okay."

I tried to mask my shudder. What would happen if Mandy got home a few minutes late?

Mandy was such a different person inside the walls of school. Laughing, talkative, caring. But no sooner would the final bell ring than she'd begin a slow, distracted freeze—a tightening of her body as she'd grip her books to her chest and race, stumbling, out to a car waiting at the curb. It didn't matter if we were in the middle of a conversation coming out of class. She'd get that fearful look and rush out.

Often, I watched Mandy jump into the car, hanging her head low. The driver appeared to be chewing her out for taking too long, flashing angry eyes and waving her hands in Mandy's face.

Connecting the dots I realized poor Mandy was being abused, at least verbally.

Not wanting to hurt her feelings, I slid in the passenger seat even though I was nervous about accepting a ride from such a new driver—and a jittery one at that. But what could happen in just two miles?

Mandy backed out of the school parking lot and pulled out at the light. It seemed like we were moving at a snail's pace, but I was glad she was cautious. Carefully, she swung left from the busy boulevard onto the side street leading to my neighborhood. At that moment, from nowhere, a car was coming straight at us!

"Mandy!" I cried at the splintering sound of two cars colliding head-on, rocking us backward. We'd barely been going—what, fifteen miles an hour? Still, we sat there, stunned.

Mandy gripped the wheel, her face and knuckles white as snow. "Wh-what d-do I d-do?" she whispered. I stared back.

I had no idea. I didn't even drive. What do you do when someone hits your car? Did we have to call the police? (This was pre-cell phone days, and we'd have had to bang on a stranger's door to call anyone.)

The other driver slammed out of his car, irritation darkening his face. I could run home, I thought wildly... get Mom... but Dad had our only car at work. Poor Mandy began to shake. It wasn't her fault. But how could we prove it?

Just then, an urgent knocking on Mandy's window made us jump. She lowered the window, where a man not involved in the accident had suddenly appeared. Dressed like a businessman, his expression was calm. Confidently, he patted Mandy's hand still on the wheel. "It's okay," he comforted her. "Don't worry. I've talked to the other driver and he knows it's his fault. Neither of you has much damage."

Mandy looked up at him wordlessly, focusing as if on a lifeline. Tall and strong looking, his words and manner made me strangely calm. The sudden peace inside the car seemed almost otherworldly.

"Here's what you need to do," he said, explaining step by step how to obtain the other driver's insurance, information she should get and give, what to look for in her glove compartment. Flashing her one more assuring smile, he repeated, "Don't worry."

The two of us opened the doors and stepped out. Quietly, Mandy began talking with the other driver. Things seemed to be going smoothly enough and Mandy had stopped shaking. It had only been a moment when I turned to thank the man who had advised us, but — glancing up and down the street — I could find no one around. Anywhere. No other cars were on the street and there was no activity at any of the houses.

Come to think of it, I hadn't seen or heard any cars besides Mandy's and the other driver. Never heard any doors shut anywhere, or even footsteps. And — I wondered then — when had he had time to talk to the other driver before us?

Soon we were on our way and pulling into my driveway. Mom greeted us at the door, where the story spilled out. "Stay for tea, honey," Mom urged her. "You could use a minute before you get going."

Certain she'd refuse, I was amazed to find Mandy follow us in and take a seat in the wing chair. Cradling steaming cups in our hands, we were silent.

"Mandy," I said thoughtfully. "Did you notice… that man just… disappeared?"

She nodded, slowly.

"Girls," Mom said, "I think God sent you an angel today."

Tears pooled in Mandy's eyes and I could feel that same choking back I always felt when I watched my favorite movie, *It's A Wonderful Life*. Especially in the moment when little Zuzu tells Jimmy Stewart about every time a bell rings. "That's right, honey!" he'd exclaim exuberantly. "That's right!"

That afternoon, Mom called Mandy's mother and smoothed the way for her to stay and talk over cookies for a bit. It was the first of many days when she would somehow manage to steal away to spend an hour or so with us after school. I never knew all of what she confided to Mom, but soon Mandy moved in with a beloved grandma who had been praying for her all along. Since that day of the accident, we both had fresh hope in new beginnings.

Sometimes, I'd walk down that street coming home from school, looking in open garages or doorways, just to make sure. But I never saw him again. Something in me knew. He had been no ordinary man.

The memory of his reassuring, calm presence, framed in the window behind Mandy's white-knuckled grip, reminds me that God cares personally about our sorrows and fears. So deeply that He still sends his angels as He did in the Bible. And they still have the same message. Do not worry. God is with you.

~Pam Depoyan

Angels Don't Need Your Address

The golden moments in the stream of life rush past us and we see nothing but sand; the angels come to visit us, and we only know them when they are gone.
~George Eliot

It was a typical last weekend of summer mania at the beach, and of course I wanted to be part of the madness. My husband thought that a quiet barbeque at home would suffice. But given his gentle and accommodating ways, there we were lying supine on our rainbow-striped towels like sardines in a tin. If we inched forward, backward, left or right, we would be quite intimate with our beach neighbors.

I was thrilled to hear the ocean roar, feel the mist on my face, taste the saltiness in the air. My husband said he could have easily duplicated this experience back home by playing one of those new wave CDs in the background (the ones that sound like a combination of an eerie violin and waterfalls) while he sprayed me with a mister and fed me potato chips.

I put him under the umbrella and headed for one of my famous beach adventures. Seashell collecting followed by a hunt for sea glass, a walk along the jetty and the ultimate reward—wading, dipping, diving and eventually riding back in on my own private wave.

We headed home, sun-drenched and parched and in dire need of showers. And that's when I noticed that my owl necklace, a thirtieth birthday gift given to me by my dad just one week before he passed away, was not where it should have been and always was: hanging right below the I Love You necklace given to me by my husband on our wedding night.

My two most favorite men on the planet and my two most treasured gifts, and now one was missing. I was frantic as I searched every room in the house. I asked my husband if he recalled seeing the necklace on me while we were at the beach. He couldn't be sure and neither could I.

All I could be certain of was that I was heartbroken.

I grabbed the car keys and headed back to the beach. My husband thought I was crazy and rightly so. Nine miles of beach, thirty thousand beachgoers later—did I really think I could locate one teeny necklace?

I knew I had to try. At least there was a Lost and Found. Maybe, just maybe, someone came across my necklace and turned it in. Then cynically I thought, maybe, just maybe with the price of gold someone did not.

What if it came off in the ocean?

I was unwilling to even consider that as a possibility.

I rushed onto the beach and didn't know where to begin. The lifeguards were long gone but a worker sweeping the boardwalk had access to the Lost and Found. One deck of playing cards, three beach chairs, and more than six coolers were stacked along the wall but no necklace anywhere.

I noticed an elderly man slowly walking the sand with a metal detector in his hand. I raced up to him and, nearly breathless, asked if he had come across a necklace.

He opened his yellowed weather-beaten hand and showed me his bounty thus far—nickels and quarters but mostly pennies.

The old man said I could write down my name and address and if he happened to come upon my necklace he would gladly return it to me. I wanted to hug him so I did.

I also wanted him to have sufficient postage to mail it back to me so I gave him a crumpled up $5 bill that he re-crumpled and put in his vest pocket.

I raced back to my car to find something to write with (and on) and found a dull-tipped eyebrow pencil and a napkin.

I scribbled my name and address and ran back as fast as I could.

The old man was gone.

I searched for a while and then went home.

My generous husband offered to replace the little blue owl with a new one.

I turned down his loving gesture, as there could be no replacement. My dad, despite being hospitalized for the better part of seven months, had found a way to buy me that necklace and not miss my thirtieth birthday. I had learned about it at his funeral.

There had been a fundraising event in the lobby of the hospital a few days earlier where merchants were selling their wares. Having gotten wind of this, my dad had asked one of the orderlies if he could wheel him downstairs.

On display in a small white box on a corner table he spotted the owl necklace and knew he had found the very best gift of all. My dad always told me how wise I was, even as a little girl, wise beyond my years he would say. Wise like a wise old owl.

Without money to pay for the owl, my dad had to barter with the vendor. He offered to build something in his occupational therapy class like a magazine rack or a wooden boat in exchange for my birthday gift.

The vendor gave my dad the owl with an IOU and Dad's favorite nurse brought it home to gift-wrap as though it had come from Tiffany.

I would later learn that this kind vendor had just lost his father to cancer and was so moved by my dad's gumption and dignity that he never had any intention of accepting any money.

Three days after combing the beach for the fourth and final time a package appeared inside our screen door.

I don't know who delivered it or who sent it, as there was no return address nor any postage of any kind.

Inside was a crumpled up $5 bill and my owl necklace.

First I cried.

Then I kissed that beautiful owl.

Then I put my necklace back on where it belonged.

And only then did I realize how silly I had been.

I never needed to worry about writing down where I lived. Angels don't need your address.

~Lisa Leshaw

Daniel and the Pelican

If we were all like angels, the world would be a heavenly place.
~Author Unknown

As I drove home from work one afternoon, the cars ahead of me were swerving to miss something not often seen in the middle of a six-lane highway: a great big pelican. After an eighteen-wheeler nearly ran him over, it was clear the pelican wasn't planning to move any time soon. And if he didn't, the remainder of his life could be clocked with an egg timer.

I parked my car and slowly approached him. The bird wasn't the least bit afraid of me, and the drivers who honked their horns and yelled at us as they sped by didn't impress him either.

Stomping my feet, I waved my arms and shouted to get him into the lake next to the road, all the while trying to direct traffic.

"C'mon beat it, Big Guy, before you get hurt!"

After a brief pause, he cooperatively waddled to the curb and slid down to the water's edge.

Problem solved. Or so I thought.

The minute I walked away he was back on the road, resulting in another round of honking, squealing tires and smoking brakes.

So I tried again.

"Shoo, for crying out loud!"

The bird blinked, first one eye then the other, and with a little sigh placated me by returning to the lake.

Of course when I started for my car it was instant replay.

After two more unsuccessful attempts, I was at my wits' end. Cell phones were practically non-existent back then, and the nearest pay phone was about a mile away. I wasn't about to abandon the hapless creature and run for help. He probably wouldn't be alive when I returned.

So there we stood, on the curb, like a couple of folks waiting at a bus stop. While he nonchalantly preened his feathers, I prayed for a miracle.

Suddenly a shiny red pickup truck pulled up, and a man hopped out.

"Would you like a hand?"

I'm seldom at a loss for words, but one look at the very tall newcomer rendered me tongue-tied and unable to do anything but nod.

He was the most striking man I'd ever seen—smoky black hair, muscular with tanned skin, and a tender smile flanked by dimples deep enough to drill for oil. His eyes were hypnotic, crystal clear and Caribbean blue. He was almost too beautiful to be real.

The embroidered name on his denim work shirt said "Daniel."

"I'm on my way out to the Seabird Sanctuary, and I'd be glad to take him with me. I have a big cage in the back of my truck," the man offered.

Oh my goodness.

"Do you volunteer at the Sanctuary?" I croaked, struggling to regain my powers of speech.

"Yes, every now and then."

In my wildest dreams, I couldn't have imagined a more perfect solution to my dilemma. The bird was going to be saved by a knowledgeable expert with movie star looks, who happened to have a pelican-sized cage with him and was on his way to the Seabird Sanctuary.

As I watched Daniel prepare for his passenger, I couldn't shake the feeling that I knew him from somewhere.

"Have we ever met before?" I asked.

"No I don't think so," was his reply, smiling again with warmth that would melt glaciers.

I held my breath as the man crept toward the pelican. Their eyes met, and the bird meekly allowed Daniel to drape a towel over his face and place him in the cage. There was no struggle, no flapping wings and not one peep of protest—just calm.

"Yes!" I shrieked with excitement when the door was latched. What had seemed a no-win situation was no longer hopeless. The pelican was finally safe.

Before they drove away, I thanked my fellow rescuer for his help.

"It was my pleasure, Michelle."

And he was gone.

Wait a minute. How did he know my name? We didn't introduce ourselves. I only knew his name because of his shirt.

Later when I called the Sanctuary to check on the pelican, I asked if I might speak with Daniel.

No one had ever heard of him.

I was beginning to think my mind was playing tricks on me.

As we discussed my baffling experience over dinner, our little girl Julie was convinced that she knew Daniel's true identity.

"Mommy, I'll bet he's your angel. That's why you know him," she insisted.

"But Daniel didn't have wings, honey." I smiled, passing the green beans to my husband.

"A lot of angels don't have wings, Mommy."

"How do you know this?"

"I see them sometimes. They're just people like you, me and Daddy."

I put down my fork and gave her my full attention.

"Julie, why do you think the people you see are angels?" I asked.

"Because God is in their faces."

After dishes were washed and bedtime prayers were said, it was time to sort through the confusion whirling through my head.

I read somewhere that young children are able to see what adults can't because their innocence hasn't yet been tainted by the skepticism of a grownup world. It must be true. My baby daughter seemed to have the inside track on something her incredulous mother could barely comprehend.

Moreover what she said made sense.

I prayed for a miracle and Daniel suddenly appeared. He not only knew how to capture a pelican, but had a big cage in his truck and was on his way to a place where the bird would be safe.

And the glow radiating from Daniel's beautiful eyes was pure and loving, like the adoration of a father for his child. As Julie said, God was in his face.

If Daniel was my angel it would explain his familiarity. My spirit might know him even if I didn't recognize him in the flesh. And he'd know my name without being told.

Then I recalled struggling to hold back traffic while trying to get the pelican off the road. Perhaps the bird wasn't the only one in imminent danger. I was so preoccupied that it didn't occur to me that I was in danger of losing my own life while trying to save his.

It was a precious and humbling revelation—to be so cherished by God that He would send one of the Heavenly hosts to protect me. I'd heard that angels watch over us, but I was handed tangible evidence of their existence.

What an amazing gift.

~Michelle Close Mills

Stranded

Not all of us can do great things. But we can do small things with great love.
~Mother Teresa

My mind started wandering. I had been driving on I-79 North in our newly acquired used Jeep Cherokee with my pregnant wife through the mountains of West Virginia for nearly two hours. No radio. No cell phone service. No stop lights. No rest areas. No vehicles on the road other than ours. The only noise we heard was the slow drone of the wiper blades moving back and forth, reminding me of the metronome my fifth grade piano instructor used to keep me on tempo. The slushy mix of snow, rain, and sleet started picking up, making it harder and harder to focus on the seemingly endless road before us.

It was the night before Christmas Eve and we were making the long trek home to rural Pennsylvania. I was attending graduate school in Kentucky and our winter break had finally arrived. My wife and I had to work earlier in the day so we got off to a later start than we would have liked—forcing us to drive in utter darkness the entire trip home. We didn't really mind the drive though, knowing that in eight hours we would be enjoying eggnog in front of a warm fireplace with our family.

BOOM!!!

"Did you hear that?" I asked my wife.

"Yes. What happened?"

"I must have hit something," I said.

I pulled the vehicle off to the side of the road to check out the damage. I grabbed the flashlight from under my seat.

"We got a flat!" I yelled. "I'm going to put on the doughnut."

One by one I grabbed our Christmas presents, placing them on the sloppy ground. I finally made it the bottom of the pile, grabbing the jack, our only source of hope on this wintry night.

"Great, just our luck, it's broken! The car dealer sold us a vehicle with a broken jack! Now what?"

One by one I placed the saturated Christmas gifts back into the vehicle, replaying in my head how I could have made such a mistake. I returned to my seat and started wondering what our next move might be. We took a moment to assess the situation and offer up a quick prayer.

We laid out our options:

Option 1 — It looked like there was a house way off in the distance. I could ring their doorbell.

Option 2 — The next exit was fifteen miles. I could walk to the exit and my wife could stay in the car until I returned.

Option 3 — We could wait it out in the warmth of our car until the gas ran out — hoping that another vehicle would stop and perform a modern-day Good Samaritan deed on our behalf (even though we hadn't seen another car on the road for nearly two hours).

Neither one of us liked options one or two, considering the fact that we were in the middle of nowhere in West Virginia — so we decided on option three.

I reclined in my seat, not expecting to see another vehicle for several hours, if at all. I shut off the wiper blades so I could have a normal conversation with my wife. But before I uttered the first sentence, I heard what sounded like sirens. I looked in the rearview mirror and shouted as if I had just won the lottery: "A police car!"

The policeman pulled alongside our vehicle, asking us how he could be of service, telling us that his name was Officer Anderson. I told him about the flat tire and that we didn't have a working jack or cell phone service. Without hesitation, Officer Anderson hopped out of his vehicle, grabbed the jack from his car, plopped down on the soggy grass, and started changing the tire. He then told us to stay inside where it was warm while he found us a mechanic. He eventually found us one, but it was forty-five miles away. He told us that he would follow behind us until we made it to our destination. So for the next hour and half, Officer Anderson followed behind our vehicle, even though it was way out of his jurisdiction.

When we finally arrived at our exit, Officer Anderson told us to follow him to the mechanic and that he would give us a ride to a hotel. Before he left, I felt compelled to ask him for his police station address so I could send him a proper thank you, and to ask him a question that I had been mulling over since the moment he stopped to help us several hours before:

"So why did you stop?"

After a long pause, he looked me directly in the eyes and said:

"I stopped to help you and your family because someone stopped and helped me and my family when we were in need many years ago."

Officer Anderson's words have been reverberating in my heart and mind ever since that night. His words (and actions) have provided me with much hope in my life when we have been in difficult situations and needed help—and there have been many. His words have also been the driving force behind my mission in this life—to reach out and help those who are in need, to those who are hurting, to those who need compassion, to those who need someone to help carry their burdens.

The truth of the matter is that we all need an Officer Anderson from time to time. Life gets challenging—a flat tire, a broken relationship, an unforeseen illness, a sudden job loss, or an unexpected bill to pay. But like Officer Anderson mentioned, he stopped and helped us because someone stopped to help him first.

The day after Christmas I decided to contact the police station to properly thank Officer Anderson for his service. The police chief answered and I started recounting the amazing act of kindness we had received from one of his officers. The police chief responded, "I'm very glad you received the help you needed the other night but there isn't an Officer Anderson at our station."

To this day I'm not sure if there really is an Officer Anderson who roams the mountains of West Virginia on I-79 north or if he is simply an angel, but I do know that this amazing act of kindness has drastically changed the course of my life.

~Tom Kaden

The Nick of Time

Be an angel to someone else whenever you can,
as a way of thanking God for the help your angel has given you.
~Eileen Elias Freeman,
The Angels' Little Instruction Book

While many people believe that they are surrounded by angels and tell stories about angels having helped them out of tight spots, I must admit that I always fell on the more skeptical side whenever I heard about an angel encounter. Coincidence, I usually thought, when someone told me about how "their" angel lent them a hand. Good timing. Nothing more than being in the right place at the right time. Until, that is, I met an angel of my own.

It was 1990 and I was looking for a job. Not just hoping to find one, but pretty desperate to get something that would help pay the mortgage of the new house my husband and I had just bought. After answering an ad in the paper and landing an interview, I set off one bright winter morning, more than a little nervous, but dressed in my interviewing best to wow my potential boss.

My interview was in the downtown section of the city we had just moved to, and I was fairly certain that I knew how to get there. But to be safe, I gave myself an extra half hour.

Finding the building was a piece of cake, but what I hadn't counted on was having no place to park downtown in the middle of the morning on a busy Monday. The building was in the middle of a block filled with office buildings, restaurants and a few older houses, and every parking place I saw was already taken.

I circled the block several times, a feeling of panic rising in my chest every time I turned a corner. Although I'd allowed ample time to get to the interview, I hadn't factored in fruitlessly driving around downtown in search of parking.

As I slowly made my way down the street for what seemed like the hundredth time, I noticed a woman with flaming red hair standing at the end of a driveway, one hand on her hip and the other holding a broom she was using to sweep snow off her sidewalk. She waved at me and I slowed down.

"Are you lost?" she asked when I rolled down my window. "I've seen you go by half a dozen times at least."

"No, I'm not lost. I'm trying to find a spot to park. I have a job interview in five minutes in that building across the street."

The woman smiled sympathetically. "Park in my driveway," she offered. "I'm not going anywhere."

"Are you sure?" I asked.

"Of course I'm sure! And hurry! You don't want to be late, do you?" The woman gestured toward a spot she'd just swept clear of snow and I gratefully pulled my car into her driveway. After thanking her again, I ran across the street and made it to my interview with a minute to spare. Afterwards I returned to get my car.

The red-haired woman was still outside sweeping. "How'd it go?" she asked.

"I think it went all right," I told her. "Thank you again for your help."

She smiled at me. "Isn't that what folks are supposed to do, be kind to each other? I hope you get the job."

That night I told my husband about the woman who'd offered me a parking spot in the nick of time. "I'd like to bring her something to thank her," I said. "Maybe a plant or some cookies. I'll take her something tomorrow."

The next morning, Tuesday, I drove back downtown, with a small African violet plant on the car seat next to me. For some reason there were plenty of parking spots that day and I was able to park directly in front of the generous stranger's house. But as I rang the front doorbell, there was no answer.

"No one lives there!" someone called out to me after a few minutes. A neighbor appeared on the steps of the house next door.

"Yesterday a woman who lived here let me park in her driveway," I replied.

The neighbor shook her head. "I don't think so. Helen went into a nursing home last month and she passed away on Sunday."

"Did Helen have red hair and blue eyes?"

"No. Helen had blue eyes but her hair was white. She was quite elderly. It must have been someone else." The neighbor started back into her house before stopping. "That's funny though. I think Helen did have red hair, a long time ago. She always said her hair used to be the same color as Lucille Ball's." The neighbor eyed the plant I was holding. "Nice violet," she said.

A shiver ran down my spine as I remembered what Helen had said about being kind to each other. Walking over to the neighbor's house, I handed her the violet. "Enjoy," I told her. "I'd like you to have this."

Her eyes widened. "What for?"

Shrugging, I replied, "As a thank you to Helen."

Later that week I was offered the job, and for several years I drove past Helen's house twice a day. And every time I did, I thought about the angel I'd met and her kindness to me, kindness I still try to pass on to others whenever I can.

My encounter with Helen showed me that meeting an angel isn't about coincidences or good timing or being in the right place at the right time. It's about being kind to each other whenever we possibly can.

~Nell Musolf

Roadside Assistance

*The LORD will command His loving kindness in the daytime, and in the
night His song shall be with me — A prayer to the God of my life.*
~Psalm 42:8

I t was a rainy Sunday summer afternoon and my friend and
I had been driving for an hour. We drove quiet backcountry
roads that took us past cow pastures and horse farms and not
much else. We drove secluded dirt roads — not a home in view
for miles. As we rounded another bend we passed, for the second
time, the same roadside eatery we had passed twenty minutes earlier — the one with the "Closed" sign hanging in the door.

With our gas tank needle pointing towards "Empty" we resisted
the temptation to pick up a serious-looking hitchhiker for the express
purpose of having him assist us in finding our way. His countenance
disturbed us, but just what it was about him that troubled us neither
of us could pinpoint.

When we pulled into a gas station in the rural countryside of
Lancaster County, Pennsylvania, we finally admitted to each other
that we were, indeed, lost.

Before the age of technology — before GPS navigation and cell
phones — there were road maps. Fortunately, we had a Pennsylvania
map. We had just pulled it out of the glove compartment when a white
car pulled into the gas station on the opposite side of the pumps.

Headed home after a five-day camping trip at a Christian music
festival, my friend and I were anxious to get back to civilization that

included hot showers and warm beds. My friend dutifully studied the map while I slid out of the driver's seat and made my way towards the office of the gas station.

I smiled and nodded at the people in the car next to ours—an elderly couple. The man driving the car had white hair and wore a white shirt. His wife also had white hair and had a white cardigan thrown across her shoulders. She held a happy-go-lucky white Poodle in her lap. The woman smiled back at me and nodded.

The elderly gentleman rolled down his window and called out, "You won't find anyone in there—the station's closed on Sunday."

"Oh, okay, thanks," I replied, disappointed. How foolish of me to think that I would find an open gas station in the middle of Amish country on a Sunday afternoon.

"I see you've got Jersey plates. Headed home? You missed your turn about three miles back. You should have turned right just after the stone mill."

"Oh—there were no signs. And… well… as a matter of fact, yes, we're headed back to New Jersey. We've been driving in circles for an hour."

"Well, good thing you didn't pick up that hitchhiker back there. He's a troubled man," the elderly gentleman replied.

I looked over at my friend, whose mouth hung open in disbelief. With the map opened fully on her lap, she said in a low voice, "How did he know? There was no one following us on those roads and he pulled into this station from the opposite direction."

His next comment interrupted our discussion. "If you want to follow us, we'll get you back to the Interstate and then about two miles east there's a gas station where you can get some fuel."

I leaned into the driver's side window of the car. "How did you know we needed gas? And how did you know we were lost?"

"Well, let's just call it divine intervention," he quipped as he smiled. His wife chuckled and the Poodle stood at attention with his little tail straight up in the air. "I'll pull out of the station and you can follow us to the Interstate."

"We can't thank you enough. You are so kind. Can I give you some money for the extra gas and for your trouble?" I asked.

"Oh no—that won't be necessary. We're only a few miles away and we're heading in that direction."

"Well thank you again." I smiled at them and slipped back into the car.

As we meandered through the countryside my friend and I speculated—could it be that these were angels sent to help us find our way and protect us? Could it all be just a coincidence—an elderly couple from the area, out for a Sunday afternoon drive, who came across two lost Jersey girls? Irrespective of who and why, we were thankful for their assistance.

As we made our way closer to the Interstate we saw the gentleman pull to the side of the road, roll down his window, and point at the exit we needed to take just ahead. We waved goodbye as we passed them and I used my turn signal to indicate I understood his directive. As we ascended the entry ramp to the highway my friend looked back to wave again. She gasped—the car was gone. "Look in your mirror," she instructed. Amazed and speechless, we headed home.

Later that night, lying in my cozy bed after a hot meal and a cool shower, I picked up my Bible and randomly opened to the book of Hebrews, Chapter 13. I began reading.

"Let brotherly love continue. Be not forgetful to entertain strangers: for thereby some have entertained angels unawares."

At that moment the events of the day became clear. Our escorts from earlier in the day were not strangers living in a lonely town in Lancaster County, Pennsylvania. I quickly called my friend to share with her the confirmation of our earlier suspicion—angels.

Today, in those moments when I become impatient with others, I remember that verse from Hebrews and recollect our experience. Would anyone ever believe us? Probably not, we surmised back then. We had encountered angels unaware who treated us with kindness and compassion. How could I ever do anything less?

~Elisa Yager

38

The Jolly Bus Driver

Laughter is the shortest distance between two people.
~Victor Borge

I was sixteen years old and had enough money to buy a bus ticket out of town. Destination—my sister's house in Kellogg, a small mountain community in northern Washington state.

The bus ride would take me north through Walla Walla, Washington then on to Spokane. A snowstorm was underway but I wasn't worried. I had a few dollars in my pocket and the open road ahead of me.

The Greyhound lumbered out of the terminal. I felt safe and warm snuggled up against the window. A rest from running away, I was living in the moment with no worry about what came next. I soon drifted off to sleep and didn't wake for some time. When I did wake up, the bus was stopped. Wiping the sleep from my eyes I looked around to see that I was the only one on the bus.

Shaking off the stiffness in my legs, I stood and walked down the aisle. Peering out the door I could see the small terminal. Through the darkness, I could barely read the snow-crusted sign above the door. Welcome to Walla Walla. Tired and hungry, I went back to my seat and snuggled down against the cold. The driver came back on the bus. I heard his rough voice bellow at me.

"Hey, you down there!"

"Oh crap," I whispered, shrinking down further in the seat.

"You seem to be the only passenger going on, young lady. You better go in and warm up. I doubt if we are going any further tonight."

I didn't move; I just slumped more in the seat.

"Suit yourself," he snapped.

I was in no mood to make a new plan and found myself choking back the lump that had formed in my throat. "Don't cry," I told myself. "Nobody is going to see me cry." It was then he stepped on the bus. He was dressed in a bus driver uniform with a funny old-fashioned cap. He looked like Santa Claus—a big man with a white beard and suspenders that wrapped around his round belly.

"Might as well come sit up front, young lady. Looks like you are the only one going on to Spokane," he said. Slowly I made my way to the front of the bus. "Might as well take that front row seat," he laughed.

Cautiously I sat down in the front row seat across from him. The biggest flakes I had ever seen blanketed the window.

Off we went into that blizzard, just me and the jolly bus driver. It was odd for me to take such a chance. I remember thinking that this could turn out bad. As I sat staring into the darkness, we began to talk and laugh. At one point, I drank cocoa from his thermos and laughed so hard that it shot out my nose and ran down my coat. I don't know when I fell asleep; I just remember the humming of the wheels rocking me to sleep.

It seemed like I had just shut my eyes when I woke to warm sunlight beaming through the windshield. Standing, I stretched and yawned and twisted my long hair up under my cap. Slinging my backpack over my shoulder I looked around for my jolly driver. The bus doors were open and I stepped into the cool morning air. He was gone. It was still cold outside. I crossed my arms and tried to shake off the chill. Slowly I made my way into the bus terminal. I was in Spokane. We must have driven all night. I sat down and looked through my last bit of change to call my sister to come pick me up. While I wandered around the terminal looking for a phone, I decided to go to the counter and ask about the bus driver. He had been so nice to me and I wanted to thank him.

"Hello," I said to the clerk.

"Yes, destination?" she asked.

"Oh," I stuttered. "I'm not going anywhere I just came in last night from Walla Walla."

The woman gave me a confused, hard stare.

"Anyway," I continued. "I was wondering if I could speak to the driver."

The woman rolled her eyes from me to her paperwork. Looking up she said, "No, no you couldn't have come in on that route, it must have been another bus. Let me see your ticket and I will see."

Puzzled, I began to search my backpack and I checked all my pockets. I couldn't find it.

"Shoot! I must have lost it," I said, shaking my head. "Really, that bus right over there." I pointed. Then I described the driver and our ride through the blizzard from Walla Walla.

The woman gave me a long hard look and said, "No you were not on that bus last night. You couldn't have been because the pass was closed. We didn't have any buses running that route last night." She stood and continued, "What are you up to anyway? Are you on drugs or something?" Confused, I started backing away from her. "Stay right there," she added. "I'm going to call someone."

I caught sight of the door, turned and ran. I ran and ran until I thought it was safe, stopping outside of a small convenience store. Sitting down on the slush-covered curb, I rested, with the bus ride running through my mind. I knew it was real. Otherwise, how did I get there? I could almost hear the driver's laugh as I looked down at the cocoa stain on my coat. I laughed and went to find a phone to call my sister.

She was happy and worried to hear from me, and said she would pick me up in a couple of hours.

As I waited I thought again about the jolly bus driver. Who was he really? I truly believe to this day that an angel drove that bus.

~Susan R. Boles

39

The Angel in the Plaid Shirt

God not only sends special angels into our lives, but sometimes He even sends them back again if we forget to take notes the first time!
~Eileen Elias Freeman,
The Angels' Little Instruction Book

Was he an angel? More than twenty-five years later I remember him as plain as I remember what I had for breakfast this morning. Considering my poor memory these days, that's saying a lot.

My daughter was in school for the day. My husband Buck had just stormed out of the house after another disagreement, the nature of which I cannot recall. There were so many arguments those days. Much of our dissension revolved around his deteriorating health and trying to maintain our monument business while he continued to work full-time as a 911 dispatcher.

Two jobs were too physically demanding for him, and he wanted to quit working at the sheriff's office because the monument business was more lucrative. I protested because I felt the monument business, with all the lifting and hard manual labor, would soon be more than he could handle. Besides, if he weren't employed by the County Commission, he'd no longer have insurance. We needed the health insurance coverage desperately.

Buck had suffered a near heart attack; his cholesterol and

triglyceride levels were astronomical, and he was diabetic. What I didn't know then was that in years to come he would need to have several amputations, would lose much of his eyesight, and go on dialysis.

On that warm spring day all those years ago, I cringed when the doorbell rang. We ran our monument business out of our house and I presumed this would be a customer. I brushed my hand across my cheek to wipe away a stray tear.

An older man, slightly bent and wearing a red plaid shirt and overalls, stood on the porch. I opened the door and invited him into the living room. I offered him a seat but he remained standing. He spoke in a calm deep voice that seemed to personify peace, but it was his eyes that totally mesmerized me. They were the bluest, deepest, calmest eyes I had ever seen. I could not look away.

He inquired about buying a monument and held up a brochure he had about our business. I offered to show him stones we had in the lot available for sale, but he declined. I am certain that through-out our conversation he noticed my red eyes and the sniffles I tried to hold back. Kindness and warmth radiated from this man and the comfort was almost more than I could bear at that dark moment in my life.

As he turned to go, his crystal eyes never left my face. Before he closed the door behind him, he said, "It will all work out."

I cried more vigorously. Being in the presence of someone who made me feel consoled started my weeping once again. But this time it was different. The sobs were cleansing and renewing. I felt like all my worries had been washed away.

I never did tell my husband about my encounter with this man. Instead, I tried to remain quiet about what I thought he should do. A day or two later he said, "I've been thinking about what you said. I believe the best thing would be to sell the monument business and continue at the Sheriff's Office. That health insurance is more impor-tant than the extra money we would make with the tombstones."

A few months later, we sold the business. Through the years, Buck endured many hospital stays and spent the last years of his life in a nursing home. So, indeed, the insurance had been of utmost importance. Yet what I remember most from that time was the slightly stooped man dressed in farmer's attire who walked into my living room and led me beside the still waters.

An angel? He must have been. He soothed my troubled soul.

~Shirley Nordeck Short

Chapter
5

Angels Among Us

Faith in Action

The Boy on the Bike

A prayer in its simplest definition is merely a wish turned Godward.
~Phillips Brooks

I never gave much thought to anything of a heavenly or spiritual nature until my daughter Sarah started getting sick just a few months after her birth. Even so, I prayed for her desperately as the months went by and her illness progressed. I longed for God to hear my prayers and intervene. While I wasn't sure of my own religious beliefs at that point, I didn't want Sarah to suffer more because of my lack of faith or failure to pray.

Even my most urgent prayers were not enough. Just four days after her second birthday, in June of 1998, Sarah passed away from complications of a mitochondrial disease. Everything changed for me that day. I wanted to die. I wanted to go to sleep and never wake up. Then the pain would stop. But no matter how eagerly I awaited a visit from death, it wasn't my time to go.

I was still wavering in my faith at that point, and so was my husband Chris. But I knew I needed to find out if my daughter was indeed in Heaven. Then I might have some hope of joining her there someday. If God were merely a myth, an enduring fabrication of an ancient society, then I would no longer have a reason to live. I physically ached through every inch of my body, my emotions were raw, and my grief paralyzed me.

Chris and I had been married nearly eleven years when Sarah passed away. Except for attending an occasional wedding, we hadn't set foot in a church since the day we were married in one. A few weeks after Sarah died, we made our first trip to a nearby church in search of answers to some very basic questions. Was there really a God? If so, was Sarah in Heaven? Was she okay? Our answers came quickly and in a way so heartening and extraordinary that we couldn't have dreamed or imagined it.

One Sunday after church, just a few weeks after Sarah's death, Chris and I were having a heated and teary-eyed discussion on the existence of God and Heaven. We had become quite emotional at the thought of never seeing our daughter again. In the midst of his pain, my husband raised his arms toward the sky and cried out to God saying, "Show me a sign that Sarah is with you—that she's really okay."

Within seconds, we heard a voice. We looked out the bay window in our living room. The light, warm breeze through the open window was mingled with the sound of someone singing. A closer look revealed the source of the music.

A young boy who appeared to be somewhere between eight and ten years of age was riding his bicycle in circles around our cul-de-sac singing "Amazing Grace." His voice was high and sweet like a choirboy. He continued to sing out the words as he made a few laps around our road. He then rode out of our cul-de-sac and reemerged a brief moment later singing another hymn. Although I didn't recognize the song he was singing, I heard enough of his words to know that he was singing about his love for the Lord. He made one final lap and then disappeared.

The neighborhood we lived in at that time had a lot of young children. We knew the children around us, most by name and others by appearance. We knew which children lived in which houses. This boy was clearly not from our neighborhood. We had never seen him before that day, and we never saw him again.

Chris and I stood there, stunned, in awe, and momentarily speechless, looking at each other. We both knew that this little boy was an angel sent from God to comfort us. Chris asked for a sign, and God gave us one. At that very moment, I was certain that my precious daughter was safe in the arms of the Lord.

My life has not been the same since that day. Though many years have passed since Sarah's death, I still miss her. She is a constant presence in my heart and mind. I know I will never see her graduate, go to college, get married, or have children of her own. Yet I also know that our separation is merely a moment in the whole of our lives. Every day I am grateful that God gave us our daughter and an angel to show us the truth. Both of them were here for brief moments, but their impact endures.

~Sheryl Grey

The Floating Angel

Coincidence is God's way of remaining anonymous.
~Albert Einstein

I sat quietly watching my fifty-year-old husband, Bruce, as the team of UCLA physicians told him he had less than a year to live. He looked stoic, strong, handsome, and physically seemed ten years younger than he was. This could not be true. There had to be a mistake. He was always so full of life. To him it was an adventure and a joy. And he made it that way for me and our two sons. He could not be dying.

Bruce asked the physicians several questions. It was Stage IV cancer. They would treat it aggressively. They were, however, in agreement on the prognosis. Six months, perhaps a year at the most. They were sure.

We stood alone in the dreary, gray afternoon at the door of the medical center. A man and woman held tight in one another's arms. The man softly crying for just a moment or two, the woman whispering in his ear, "I'm so sorry. I'm so sorry." An odd pair, noticing no one coming or going through the doors, lost in their own story.

Bruce took a deep breath and said, "Let's go get something to eat." We walked slowly to a small nearby restaurant, where he talked positively and optimistically. Then we drove home.

Bruce did not die that first year, nor the second. For eight long years he battled with courage and a smile as he went through numerous experimental treatments, multiple surgeries, chemotherapy, and radiation.

Each day past that first year was a gift and he lived it as such. No wasted time, no complaints. Loving life and loving others as he always had.

When the pain was less, treatments fewer, or he was enjoying a brief remission, we traveled around Italy, snorkeled off Key West, visited with family and friends, attended college graduations for our sons, celebrated a wedding, and held three of our grandchildren in our arms. And each of us pretended for the other that he would recover.

Then one of the routine tests found new tumors in his spine. Though we remained positive with and for each other, it was becoming obvious his time was brief.

One morning shortly after we got those test results we were preparing coffee in the kitchen of the condo we had recently purchased and remodeled. Bruce spoke quietly: "Kandy, last night an angel kissed me."

"Oh, you had a dream," I responded, moving about the room.

"No."

"Then it must have been that time, you know, just before you fall asleep," I offered.

"No," he repeated. "It was as real as me standing here talking to you." My husband was an extremely rational person. I knew what he was telling me was what he believed and he was not on any pain medication at the time.

I sat down across from him at the table. I wanted to hear more. "What was it like?"

"She was beautiful. Her hair was long and it flowed all around her. She was very light, glowing. And she floated over me."

I was so caught up in the details that I foolishly asked if she had wings.

"No," he answered seriously.

He went on. "She touched my face with both her hands and

leaned down and kissed me. Then she faded away...." He moved his hands to illustrate.

He described his experience as calmly and believably as if he were giving the opening lineup to a baseball game.

I paused for a moment to process what he had just said.

"Bruce," I began, "you are very blessed. You've had what's called a visitation."

I did not know anything other than I believed what he described had really happened to him.

If that were the end of this story it would of course be comforting, especially considering what my husband was about to go through. However, that was not the end of the story. It was the beginning.

As I mentioned, we had remodeled a condo and I had purchased a lovely Italian table for the entry hall. I wanted just the right accessory for it. One afternoon, several weeks after our conversation in the kitchen, I went to an upscale furniture store that was having a sale. As soon as I walked in, I saw a tall terra cotta angel mounted on a metal stand.

I immediately recognized it as one I had seen previously in that store and had always liked. However, at the time I had no place for it in our apartment. Now, it was absolutely perfect for the hall in our condo. I was delighted. I remembered that it had not been extremely expensive. I decided I would purchase it regardless of the price. I noticed that it did have a large red sale tag attached.

I quickly walked over to examine it further.

She had a delicate face, long flowing hair, wings, and gently held a shell in her hands. Knowing I was buying it anyway, but out of pure curiosity, I turned over the red sale tag to read the new price. There, handwritten beneath the amount, it said "The Floating Angel."

I could not believe it. It could not be coincidental.

I brought her home and placed her exactly where I had planned. She sat there for the next year as Bruce grew worse and his disease ate away at his body, but not his spirit. Although his death was long and filled with uncontrollable pain, his faith never faltered.

After he died, I questioned God a great deal. All of the "whys" and "what ifs" haunted me. How could Bruce be gone?

I stayed with my oldest son and his family for several months. Each morning before I went to work I would walk several miles, and pray and cry, and cry and pray. Nothing seemed to comfort me. I could not find peace. The grief was inescapable.

Then one of those lonely early mornings I begged God to send me a sign that Bruce was all right. An inaudible voice broke through my wall of grief and said, "You had your sign when Bruce was here. It was his angel."

I have had moments of disbelief and doubt along this path since. However, at times I remember that morning Bruce described in beautiful detail how an angel had kissed him. I like to believe that perhaps she prepared him with her visit.

And sometimes I pass the statue I bought that day, lightly pat her head and say "Hello, Bruce's angel." She always reminds me of the real angel without wings who my husband believed briefly floated over him one night.

Was it simply a terra cotta statue, simply with long flowing hair, simply named "The Floating Angel," simply in a store I visited to buy a decorative accessory, simply a few weeks after my husband's experience, simply there directly in front of me? Simply coincidence? Simply miraculous.

~Kandy Petillo

I Wanted to See a Miracle

It's not that we pray and God answers; our prayer is already God answering.
~Richard Rohr

One pleasant afternoon in May, I loaded my two-year-old, Beth, and four-month-old, Christine, into our van to go to a special event. Charles and Francis Hunter, who had a reputation as miracle-working evangelists, were speaking at nearby Stranahan Great Hall. And I wanted to see a miracle.

When we arrived, the parking lot was crowded, but I finally found a spot at the far end. Inside the hall, I grabbed a seat on an outside aisle and stretched a quilt on the floor so my girls could nap.

Although it was a weekday afternoon, nearly every seat was full. The Hunters' worship music and message were powerful and I sat in awe—so glad I came. I overheard people share how their physical problems were healed after the Hunters prayed for them. It was amazing to see so many people being touched by the Lord.

During the offering, I noticed a strange thing. One of the ushers kept scanning the back of the room.

When the meeting was over, I waited a few minutes until the crowds thinned out. I thought I would let Beth sleep a little longer before gathering my Bible, notebook, and quilt and squeezing them into the diaper bag. Christine was already awake, but content.

After a few minutes, it seemed like a good time to exit. With one arm I held the cumbersome diaper bag and Beth's hand. With the other arm I carried Christine in her carrier, and headed for the hallway exit. Feeling overloaded, I looked at my girls' beautiful faces, yet felt glad I had brought them along. They had been so good during the meeting.

As we walked toward the stairway, I realized my car keys were buried in the bottom of the diaper bag. I carefully placed the baby carrier with Christine on the flat railing at the top of the stairs so I could get into my bag. I thought it would be easier to get the keys out sooner rather than waiting until I got to my car.

Keeping one hand on the carrier while digging for my keys, I thought to myself: Don't put her on that ledge. You know it is not safe. But I ignored the little warning, rationalizing that I would have the keys out in just a second. After all, I had one hand on her.

Suddenly, before I could blink, the carrier slipped through my fingers and flipped upside down, hitting the cold, stone floor! I was stunned. I couldn't believe what was happening. Christine and the carrier fell about four feet and she landed on her face. Shock rippled through me as people around me gasped in horror.

"Oh, Jesus, help!" I panicked as I grabbed my screaming baby, while terrible thoughts flooded my mind. How badly was she hurt? Would she live through this? How could I have been so careless?

Standing nearby was a young brunette with long, pretty hair who had witnessed the whole thing. Her countenance stayed oddly peaceful and unchanging. While others gasped, she was calm and collected.

The woman walked slowly toward me as I knelt sobbing and hugging my precious baby. Through my hot tears, I watched her approach us. She reached out her hand to comfort me. Her brown eyes were tender and comforting and her hands were warm against mine.

With a little wave, she motioned to the strange, watchful usher, who suddenly appeared in the little crowd around me. Together they helped me gather my things and escorted us to our van in the nearly empty parking lot. It took a few minutes to walk to the far end of the parking lot, where I had parked. I was relieved that Christine had stopped screaming.

A tiny purple bruise was forming on her left cheek, but she didn't show any other signs of injury. As a nurse, I studied her pupils carefully to see if they were changing in size, which would indicate a concussion. Thankfully they stayed the same.

When we reached our van, I buckled Christine's seat belt. As I reached out to put Beth in her seat, I turned to thank the kind lady and usher, but they had vanished! I looked in every direction. Where did they go? They had been there just seconds before. I couldn't believe they had disappeared. There were no cars parked nearby. As I scanned the large parking lot, I could not see them anywhere.

Suddenly, a perfect peace filled me. Somehow I knew my precious baby would be all right. Right then and there, I thanked God for His mercy and for preserving Christine's life. It then dawned on me — God had allowed me to experience a miracle.

Twenty-two years later, the memories came back once again as we celebrated Christine's wedding reception at Stranahan Great Hall. Yes, unwittingly, Christine had chosen to have her reception in the same place where the accident occurred so many years before.

Joy filled my heart seeing Christine, the beautiful bride, dancing with her new, handsome husband. And there was Beth, her lovely matron-of-honor, enjoying the festivities with our whole family. What a wonderful wedding reception and evening it was! I felt so thankful.

Tears welled in my eyes as I remembered how good God was to me on that day long ago. He had sent angels when we needed them most. Although I didn't see the brown-eyed lady or the watchful usher in our crowd that night, I will bet they were there.

~Judy Gyde

Faith in the Fog

And whatever things you ask in prayer believing, you will receive.
~Matthew 21:22

My job delivering newspapers seven days a week was tiresome and I relished the idea of a mini-vacation. A relative of mine who lived in Nashville, Tennessee invited me to her house for the Thanksgiving holiday, and wanted me to arrive the week before so that we could spend some extra time together. The day I planned to leave I took the usual four-hour nap that I took every evening before delivering my papers. But instead of going to the paper station when I got up, I headed to the freeway. It was around 2 a.m. I decided I would drive as far as I could, and when I got tired I would stop somewhere in Georgia for the night.

The ten hours from Boca Raton to Atlanta were fairly uneventful, but heavier traffic slowed me down on my way to Chattanooga. After about fourteen hours of driving I knew it would be prudent to stop for the night. But I had reached Chattanooga, and I had only three more hours to go. Since I wasn't tired, I continued.

What I didn't know about was the fog on I-24, in the area of Monteagle, where the highway crosses the Cumberland Plateau. There hadn't been any fog at the lower elevations.

I had gone a few miles before the fog set in thick, and it was getting worse by the minute. Before long, I could barely see in front of me. It felt like I was coasting down a hill but unable to reach the bottom, where I hoped it would level off. I had shifted into second gear to keep my speed down, and my old Plymouth was fighting to maintain a safe speed around curves and what seemed to be a never-ending slope. My hands had begun to perspire as I gripped the wheel and worked the brakes.

I wanted desperately to find a place to pull over and rest, but all I could see out the window was guardrail after guardrail. I prayed aloud. "Oh, dear God, please let this nightmare end!" Almost immediately, and out of nowhere, there were taillights in front of me. Hallelujah, I wasn't alone! Luckily, the car was going the same speed as I was and I could easily keep up with his taillights leading the way. I breathed a sigh of relief and thanked the Lord for allowing me to catch up with what appeared to be the only other car on the road. Curve after treacherous curve we drove, down, down, mile after mile and then finally we came to a level stretch. It was still very foggy but the car in front of me continued to be my beacon and my savior. I decided that as soon as we got off this mountain, I was going to roll my window down and thank that person from the bottom of my heart. Maybe I could toot my horn to get his attention as I passed in front of him. Whatever it took, I would do it.

As we neared the bottom of the pass and with the fog lifting, I could see the mountain in my rearview mirror. And to think I wanted to pull over to the side of the road when there were no sides to pull over on! I shuddered to think I might have gone over a guardrail if it hadn't been for the car in front of me. But now I began to wonder where my fearless leader had gone. The car had been there a second before and there were no exits, just the road in front of us that would take me to Nashville. I sped up a bit and although I could see cars in the oncoming lanes, I was the only car in my lane. No one was behind me and no one was in front of me for as far as I could see.

It took me a few minutes to take it all in. When I finally did, I pulled over to the side of the road to gather my wits. My eyes filled with tears when I realized what had just happened. If I never believed in guardian angels before that day, I certainly did from then on! A car had suddenly appeared in front of me when I needed it the most, and when danger had passed, it disappeared as quickly as it had arrived. I strongly believe that God sent someone to the mountain that night to calm my nerves and take away my fear so that I could keep my car under control around those curves. I have never once doubted it! Praise the Lord for safely guiding me through that dangerous foggy mountain pass!

~Trish Castro

Getting the Point

The angel of the LORD encamps around those who fear him,
and he delivers them.
~Psalm 34:7

I t was one of those glorious spring days when everything feels right with the world. I was profoundly happy, with a wonderful husband, a one-year-old son, and an organist job I loved at the church where I'd grown up. It was a Thursday evening, and choir practice had just ended. Feeling exhilarated, I ushered everyone out of the church, then locked myself safely inside, eager to squeeze in some additional organ practice before heading home to my family.

Climbing up on the bench, I pulled out my postlude for Sunday (a rousing Bach piece), cranked up the volume and began playing. The dramatic piece was a perfect match for my exuberant mood until—suddenly—I felt a firm, warm finger dig into my spine. Instantly, an electrically charged aura engulfed me, giving me an eerie sense that my waist-long hair was standing on end.

Astonished, terrified, I stopped dead, fingers hovering above the keyboard, my breath shallow, ears listening for any movement from behind. Agonizing seconds passed while I gathered my courage to turn and face whoever stood behind me. Heart pounding, I drew a shaky breath, spun around, and saw... no one!

Or had someone slipped behind a nearby pew?

Abruptly, the air around me returned to normal, and I calmed down a bit. Dropping from the bench, annoyed by this surreal interruption, I strode through the church, inspecting pews, back rooms, windows, doors. Everything was locked up tight. Nothing was amiss yet clearly I'd sensed something—or was it just my overactive imagination?

Skeptical now, and eager to resume practicing, I returned to the organ and fired up my Bach. But instantly—not two measures later—that firm, insistent finger was at my back again, the air charged with an irrefutable sense of urgency.

This time, I didn't question. As my music died, I whispered with uncanny conviction: "Okay, God, I get it. I'm outta here."

Uneasy yet strangely un-fearful, I turned off the organ, grabbed my things, and exited the church I'd known and loved since infancy. Outside, I took a slow, hard look around me. The spring evening was still lovely and warm. The birds sang sweetly. A gentle breeze rustled the leaves. Yet I was certain that something life-changing had just occurred, and in that moment I couldn't help wondering… would I ever know, exactly, what it was?

Early the next morning, I was yanked from sleep by the blast of a telephone.

"Wendy," cried Father Barrett, our minister, "did you notice anything unusual at church last night?"

My eyes popped open. Wide awake now, the story of my previous night's adventure tumbled out.

There was a pause.

"Well," Father Barrett sighed at last. "I'm glad you left when you did because the church was broken into and robbed of all its silver and gold. This morning, when questioned by police, a neighbor recalled seeing a dark utility van parked after hours in the library parking lot next to the church. They must have been waiting for you to leave."

My skin prickled. My head reeled as the inexplicable events of the previous night started to make sense.

"Someone was watching over you, Wendy," Father Barrett offered kindly.

At that moment, I knew he was right. My guardian angel had persisted in bugging me until I trusted, on blind faith, that it was time for me to go. But in the days and years to come, I was haunted by the possibility that had I only stayed longer, my beloved church might have been spared the travesty of a break-in and burglary. Maybe the bad guys would have given up and gone away! In no small way, I felt responsible, burdened by the sense that I'd deserted my church in her hour of need.

I was twenty-eight years old when this happened; I'm fifty-nine now. I went on to have two more beautiful sons and, today, I'm a grandmother to three children as well. But I'm a pretty slow learner when it comes to major life lessons because only recently did it dawn on me that I did not let my church down, after all. To the heartless thieves, I was just an expendable commodity compared to the monetary value of those precious metals. I see now that I was in very real danger, and I'm glad that I followed my instincts. I wasn't expected to be a super hero who "saved the day" that beautiful spring night. Far from it, I was meant to do exactly what I did:

STOP.

GET OUT.

GO HOME.

BE SAFE.

Far wiser than I, my guardian angel made sure I lived to see another day, to be there for my family and to savor the many blessings of this life.

~Wendy Hobday Haugh

No Accident

You may ask me for anything in my name, and I will do it.
~John 14:14

Nothing was going right that morning. My husband was due to be released from the hospital after cancer surgery and I was frantic to get everything done before I picked him up. The electric bill was overdue. I had to get to their office and get it paid before noon or they would turn off the electricity. I had totally forgotten about it in the couple of weeks of turmoil we had been through. I had just gotten the air conditioning fixed that morning, so I was running late after waiting for the repairman.

Trying to calm myself and get to the electric company before the deadline, I got my purse and checkbook and headed out to pay the bill. I kept telling myself to calm down. "God is in His heaven and He is going to see us through this."

As I drove downtown, I decided to take the scenic route beside the old cemetery. For some reason it always comforted me to pass by there. It was a special cemetery in our town that went back to the Civil War days. Cole Younger of the notorious James-Younger Gang was buried there as well as many of the town's founding fathers. As I drove past the cemetery, I mused about what a nice and decent Christian man Cole had become after his release from jail. He became a mentor for troubled youth and everyone called him "Uncle Cole." He was also one of the founding fathers of the early Youth for Christ in our area. That is why our town held Cole Younger Days every year. He had done a lot of good for our little town, and we strove to keep those memories alive.

As I drove past the cemetery I said a little prayer for all of our deceased ancestors who were buried there. Just as I reached the corner of the cemetery a car came barreling through the stop sign. All I saw was a flash of brown before it was going to hit my driver's side door. I remember thinking "Oh! God save me." The next thing I knew my little four-cylinder car took off like a rocket. It was almost surreal how fast it sped up. Then I came to a stop in the yard on the opposite corner of the road. I looked up and saw the other car also stopped in the yard. Inside were a woman and a little girl.

We got out and looked over our cars, and amazingly there were no scrapes or damage to either car or ourselves. As we stood there musing how lucky we were, the little girl said, "Mommy did you see the angels pushing our cars?" We started giggling that, yes there were angels around us, just to humor her. Then we noticed a large beer truck that had pulled to the curb. The driver came over to see if we were all right. His face was completely white as he exclaimed, "I never believed in angels but I sure do now. I was right behind you and saw that there was no way for you to avoid the collision. Suddenly there were angels all around your cars. I saw the cars actually pass through one another and yet there isn't a scratch on any of you or your cars."

Amazing. A child and a stranger had seen what neither of us had figured out. We knew we were very lucky but had no idea how blessed we had been. God is in His Heaven and His angels are watching over us.

~Christine Trollinger

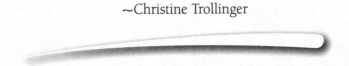

Delivered by Angels

Prayer is not overcoming God's reluctance;
it is laying hold of His highest willingness.
~Richard C. Trench

I bolted upright in bed feeling pressure and a stabbing pain, and then breathed a sigh of relief. I was expecting my third child and had been hospitalized on Mother's Day with intense labor. By evening, it was declared "false labor," and I was discharged. Now, forty-eight hours later at 2 a.m., I had a fluid discharge. My delivery day had finally arrived. My overtly huge baby bump hung from my petite body, so heavily that to get out of bed I had to roll onto my side, sit up and dangle my feet over the side, plant them firmly on the floor and then support my stomach as I stood up.

As I reached for the phone, I realized I was bleeding profusely and could be having an at-home-delivery with no assistance. My husband worked nights and my two young children were asleep. I wrapped myself in the sheets until help arrived. The minister's wife took my children to her home and I was rushed to the hospital.

As I was being admitted, I detected concern in the voices of the staff, suggesting that this was not a routine delivery. I had a rare blood type and needed a transfusion. A supply was ordered from the blood bank and was on its way. Further tests revealed that the baby was in distress and I was rushed to X-ray.

My doctor gently delivered the sad news. The cord was wrapped multiple times around the baby's neck and enlarged tumors or growths were blocking the birth canal. "Your baby is dead and your life is in jeopardy." A surgeon was on his way. "Meanwhile," the doctor said gently, "if you have anything to make right, this is the time."

I replied, "No. It's okay. I do that every day." As I was wheeled into surgery, I noticed on the big clock that it was 8:00 a.m. Anesthesia was administered and I drifted into oblivion. My body was lying on the operating table, while a spiritual replica floated above. The operating wall opened into a massive dark tunnel. A glass-smooth sea appeared at the end of the tunnel. Beyond the sea at the top of a high hill, I saw a city shrouded in white lights. As my spirit-body was being drawn by angels into the tunnel, I said, "I can't go now. My two young children need me."

When I opened my eyes, I was in a hospital bed in a private room. A nurse came in and quickly announced to the staff, "She's awake." Then she turned to me and said, "We're bringing your baby." Remembering the doctor's words, I thought she had the wrong room and whispered, "I don't have a baby." But I did! I had been asleep for two days. The nurse explained that during surgery, when the monitor began the steady sound of death, my surgeon fell to his knees, held up his glove-covered hands and prayed. He must have seen the angels, too, because he rose quickly and continued operating, saving both of us.

The tumors were surgically removed. They were all benign. After a few days of recovery and observation, my healthy baby girl and I were going home.

~Vi Parsons

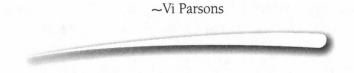

The Shoppers

Prayer is the soul's sincere desire, uttered or unexpressed.
~James Montgomery

I t has taken me a year to process what happened and sit down to tell this story, which begins on a midnight shopping run. My father was dying, and I left him with my son while I went to the grocery store to pick up some things I thought he would enjoy. As I walked into the store, I hoped to see someone I knew so I could talk about my father's quick decline.

I pushed the cart up and down the aisles, trying not to become emotional. Then, as I picked up an item and turned to place it in my basket, I saw two women coming toward me. They didn't have a basket or any groceries. One was very tall and the other very short. But their height difference was not what captivated me. It was their faces and eyes, which were so kind and loving.

The women came straight to me, and one of them took the item in my hand and placed it in the cart. They just stood there smiling at me, as if they were waiting for me to speak. I began to tell them my father's story. They smiled and told me how great God's love was for my father; that, indeed, God would heal him, even if it was not while on this earth. They told me that God has a beautiful place where my father would soon be. They told me not to be afraid, and then they prayed for me, right there in the grocery store. I had a wonderful feeling of peace as they turned to leave. I watched them walk down the aisle.

I believe that Our Loving, Heavenly Father sent these two angels to give His message. I am so thankful to Him for caring about His children so much that He would turn a midnight shopping trip into a peace that passes understanding.

~Ruth Ann Roy

Backseat Driver

Make yourself familiar with the angels, and behold them frequently in spirit;
for, without being seen, they are present with you.
~St. Francis of Sales

Six years ago my life seemed to be at a standstill. My faith was waning as I started questioning the painful events that had taken place throughout my life, even wondering whether God and the spirit world were real. I doubted myself, too. Was I a good mother? What was my purpose in this life?

I remember driving down the expressway with my four-year-old son, Dylan, headed toward Chicago with nothing but worries on my mind. As I drove, I asked myself questions. How was I going to pay my rent on time? Who was going to watch Dylan while I worked the next Saturday? And I reminded myself that my car needed an oil change.

Traffic came to a screeching halt. The freeway always jammed up just before the famous Chicago bottleneck, where basically four lanes merge into one. As my car stopped, I heard a voice in my left ear shout, "TURN RIGHT, NOW!"

Without hesitation my hands gripped the steering wheel, my foot hit the gas pedal, and I quickly steered my car onto a truck-stop ramp conveniently located directly to my right.

Seconds later I heard a loud squealing noise. I looked toward the spot where we had been and saw a large Cadillac smashing into the green car that had been in front of us before I swerved from that lane.

The entire back end of the green car looked like an accordion. I couldn't breathe. That could have been us!

The thought of almost losing my son or something terrible happening to him made me feel sick to my stomach.

I checked my rearview mirror, praying that Dylan was okay, as if we were victims of the accident. To my surprise, he was happily playing with his Spider-Man action figure making swooshing noises as if Spider-Man was swinging from building to building.

Still alarmed, my focus quickly turned to the road. My defensive driving mode kicked in. My hands gripped both sides of the steering wheel and I continued to watch my surroundings. What just happened? Whose voice did I hear? Were the other drivers okay? And how was I able to respond so quickly?

The voice had been that of a man's. It sounded human. And it was loud. It was as if someone sitting in the back seat on the driver's side had leaned over, put his mouth to my left ear and shouted those three words. "Turn right, now!"

I hadn't even given myself time to think or wonder if I was hearing things. I reacted instantly as if guided by someone else.

The only explanation was that an angel had intervened that day for two reasons. First, my son and I were supposed to be unharmed and on a safe path. And second, to confirm that God and angels do exist and that everything was going to be okay for my son and me. I truly believe this was God's way of getting my attention and helping me reconnect with Him.

Immediately after the accident, I quickly became a believer again. I no longer questioned my reason for living. Since then, life has become less complicated and I try not to sweat the small stuff. Although I may never know exactly whose voice spoke to me that day, I'm convinced it was my own guardian angel.

~Kristen Nicole Velasquez

49

Chicken Soup for the Soul

Faith in Cape May

Angels assist us in connecting with a powerful yet gentle force,
which encourages us to live life to its fullest.
~Denise Linn

"Ready to go to breakfast?" My husband, Walter, came into the room.

"I'm ready." We were vacationing in our favorite place—Cape May, New Jersey—and staying in our favorite bed and breakfast inn.

I hesitated before going into the breakfast room. I'm not misanthropic, just shy, because I have a spinal cord injury and walk with a walker; it is a subject that can be difficult to talk about with strangers.

In I went, anyway. We sat down, and shortly afterward two women sat at our table. We introduced ourselves, explaining that we lived in northern New Jersey, almost three hours away.

The women introduced themselves: Mary and Michele. Mary told us, "Michele and I are from Pennsylvania. We've been friends for many years. We do getaway weekends every once in a while."

Michele told a story about her son as a little boy, and I told a story about our son, Jeff, when he was young too.

Michele and Mary were good people and I liked them instantly. They put me at ease with their casual conversation, and I relaxed.

Michele excused herself briefly. She needed to go back to the room to call her family.

Mary detailed their trip, saying that Michelle is a very spiritual, religious person who was bringing her on this vacation because of some personal difficulties. "The way things are in the world, sometimes I wish I could get a sign from God that He is still watching us," Mary said sadly.

I smiled at her as I thought that maybe my story could help. Somehow, I knew that it wouldn't bother me to retell my story this time.

I told her about my two spinal cord surgeries, my nearly six months in rehab, of how I worried about Jeff, who was four years old at the time, and how I wanted to do the right thing for him. So, one day I phoned the county mental health facility for some advice.

Instead of being transferred around, as I fully expected, I found myself talking to a woman who answered the phone at the main number. When I told her that I needed help to keep Jeff grounded through all of this, she offered her help.

We introduced ourselves. I told her my name, not quite believing I could find help this easily.

"My name is Norma."

"That's easy to remember — that's my mother's name." I was more incredulous with each passing moment.

I told her the trials that my family and I had endured during the past year, about the fact that my medical condition had improved, but was not close to where I thought it should be. This was depressing me. I didn't want my fears to be transferred to Jeffrey.

"I'm glad you called," Norma said. "You have been through a lot. I understand what you are saying about your spinal surgery — I am an RN."

Over the next several months, there were more calls to Norma. They were filled with friendship, understanding and good advice for me. As I progressed, with Norma's help, the telephone calls became less frequent. But Norma was always close, even if only in my thoughts.

There was one incident, I emphasized to Mary, that stands out in my mind to this day.

One day, I confessed to Norma that I couldn't understand how God had allowed this to happen to my family and me, but especially to Jeffrey. I told her how guilty I felt for having those feelings.

I will never forget Norma's comforting words to me: "Don't worry, Donna. God gets blamed for a lot of things. He is used to being blamed for things that happen on earth. He understands your frustration—and your anger, too."

I was so relieved to hear that! It was just what I needed to know: that God understood me, that He wasn't angry at me. Norma's personal counsel helped me in so many ways. She was my friend and she sounded as though she knew just how God felt about me.

Shortly thereafter, I wanted Norma to know the full impact she had not only on me, but on Walter and Jeffrey as well. Her influence was nothing short of miraculous—just as miraculous as our initial telephone contact had been.

I dialed the number that had connected me to the one person who had helped me without ever telling me her last name, someone who never charged me for her counsel or for taking the time to listen to me. This time, however, Norma didn't answer.

I continued my narrative to Mary:

When the receptionist answered, "County Mental Health... how can I help you?" I asked to speak to Norma. What I heard next absolutely stunned me. "I'm sorry, but there is no Norma here. Is there a last name?"

"No, she never gave me her last name. But I've talked to her at this number many times."

My astonishment turned to incredulity as the conversation progressed. "I'm sorry, there is no one by the name of Norma here, and there hasn't been, at least since I've been working here."

I thanked the receptionist, and hung up the phone more convinced than ever that Norma was truly an angel.

As I finished my story, Mary smiled, even as her eyes welled up with tears. She grabbed my hand, and said, "What a story! Thank you for sharing it with me! Is it all right with you if I share it with Michele, too? I know she'll appreciate it as much as I do."

The next morning, hung on the outside of our door was a bag with a note of thanks from Mary and Michele and several gifts. including the delicate figure of a Victorian angel. What a lovely tribute to Norma, my angel, who helped me once again while also helping my newfound friends.

~Donna Lowich

Praise Him

Remember the wonders he has done, his miracles,
and the judgments he pronounced...
~1 Chronicles 16:12

I had been burned in a fire and told that I would need skin
grafts on certain parts of my body. I had also been told that my
hand had been so severely injured that it was unlikely I would
be able to move my fingers and play the guitar again. This
really discouraged me, as I had a praise concert to do in three days
and I would be forced to cancel. More importantly, it seemed that I
would never regain full use of my hand.

That night after coming home from the hospital, I lay in my bed,
discouraged and exhausted. I was too tired to offer some big prayer
of faith. I simply wanted to go to sleep and get ready for my next
hospital visit. I was told that in the morning they were going to peel
away the damaged skin and then take skin from other parts of my
body to repair the damaged areas.

After falling asleep for a couple of hours I awoke to a feeling of
warmth all over my body. As I opened my eyes, I saw an enormous
angel staring at me with a grin that stretched from ear to ear. He was
so large that he had to bend all the way forward to miss the ceiling.
Although he stood at the end of my bed, this caused his face to be
only a couple of feet from mine.

I had never seen such brilliant, joyous eyes or a smile so warm
and kind. Somehow, in that moment, I knew everything was going

to be all right. The angel never promised a healing or some great deliverance from my pain. He simply said, "Praise Him."

As he stood there, I got out of bed, knelt down and said, "God, I don't understand why all this happened, but I know that you love me and are in control of my life. Whatever you want to do is fine with me; I turn it all over to you." As I was doing this, the angel lifted his face to the sky, raised his voice in praise and then disappeared. The odd thing was that as he rose up, my ceiling disappeared and I could see the star-filled sky. That was the last thing I remember from that night.

When I awoke the next day, I stumbled into the bathroom. As I looked into the mirror I noticed that the burns on my face had disappeared. I tried to move my fingers through the bandages, and to my amazement I could. This was incredible, as my fingers had melted together from the fire and had no feeling. As I removed the gauze and looked at my fingers, they were perfectly normal. My wife and I could not wait to go to the hospital that day and have them check me out. As the doctor inspected all the areas he had seen the day before he just stared in amazement and said, "This is truly a miracle."

To this day, when I am experiencing challenging situations and have the urge to complain and get discouraged, my mind goes back to the simple instructions of that angel: praise him!

~Ken Freebairn

Chapter
6

Angels Among Us

Angelic Visitors

Entertaining an Angel Unaware

Angels can fly directly into the heart of the matter.
~Author Unknown

"Will this blizzard ever end?" I asked myself as the gigantic snowflakes cascaded down, making visibility difficult even at midday. The weather was not helping my grief and depression, which seemed to be deepening with my confinement in the house. My family lived in a two-story condominium unit on Loring Air Force Base in Limestone, Maine.

My father had died earlier that winter. It had been the Monday before Thanksgiving, around 5:00 p.m. I listened as laughter and excited squeals drifted into the kitchen as I prepared our dinner. My husband, Jim, was playing with our children, Patrick and Kristi, in the living room. The phone rang. It was my brother-in-law, Harry. He insisted on speaking with Jim.

Jim, pale and shaken, told me, "Your father fell dead at the state fish hatchery while mending a fishing net this afternoon at work. He was laughing and talking with a co-worker when his heart failed him. The funeral will be on Friday in order to give us time to get there."

I didn't have time to process the news and grieve. We had to eat, pack and leave as quickly as possible. However, I kept asking God, "Why did we have to leave Little Rock AFB, Arkansas, twenty miles from my hometown, in August and move here, two miles from the Canadian border? Why couldn't we have stayed there? Why were we denied these last few months of his life? Why was he taken during this Thanksgiving week?"

Since all the planes had been grounded due to the blizzard, we had to pack the car and drive more than 600 miles to Jim's parents' home in New York City, then rest for a few hours before continuing the trip. It was hazardous traveling in the blizzard combined with the darkness of night. We still had more than 1,200 miles to travel before arriving in my hometown. We only stopped to eat and rest for a few hours, allowing Jim to sleep. My heart was broken, but I wouldn't allow myself to cry when the children were awake. We didn't want them more upset than they already were. The trip was very hard on them.

On Thanksgiving Day when we stopped to eat, I struggled in my grief and resentment of my dad's death as I saw families celebrating the holiday. I still couldn't accept or understand why God would take my dad. I had received a letter from my mother several days prior to his death telling me how well they were and that Daddy was planning to retire in February. They wanted to come and visit us in late spring. I was angry with God, and I resisted the fact that His presence, love, and comfort surrounded me. I kept asking Him, "Why did You allow this to happen?"

Here we were, weeks later, in the middle of another blizzard, and I was still dealing with my grief and depression. The Christmas holidays hadn't helped me. I couldn't sleep at night and when I did, I would wake up crying. I felt the walls pressing in on me. I went through my daily routine robotically.

The children and I were upstairs. They were napping and I was trying to rest when the doorbell rang. I went downstairs in disbelief that someone would be visiting in this weather. The temperature was forty degrees below zero. I opened the door and a pleasant, friendly lady asked if she could come in. As she entered, she introduced herself and thanked me for inviting her into my home.

"You can come in, but I'm really not feeling up to having company. I lost my dad a couple of months ago."

"I am so sorry. I do understand what you are experiencing because I also had great difficulty in accepting my father's death," she said with immense compassion.

Those words opened the door for me to ask her, "How long did it take before you started sleeping all night? I wake up crying and then I can't go back to sleep. I am very tired. Also, I am so angry because God took him just three and a half months after we were transferred from the base close to my hometown."

She spoke in a quiet, comforting tone. "Be patient and give yourself time to heal. Don't stop yourself from crying. Let the tears fall until you no longer have any. Crying is a release of your feelings; don't be afraid to tell God that you are angry because your father died. He wants you to tell him everything you feel. Then, He can begin the healing process in your heart. When you hang onto anger, it will turn to bitterness and turn you away from God. In time, you will find your waking in the night crying will decrease and eventually will stop. Always thank God for His comfort, understanding, forgiveness, and love. Also, always ask for His strength to sustain you as you begin each day."

She stayed until we had discussed every feeling and question I had. When she got up to leave, she gave me a little hug and said, "You are going to be fine." And then she left.

After a couple of days, I wanted to call and thank her for her visit and let her know how much she had helped me. I couldn't find her name in the phone book. I asked all of my neighbors if she had stopped at their homes. No one had seen or talked with her.

When I couldn't find a trace of her, I recalled what my mother taught my siblings and me. She always welcomed and offered food and water to strangers. She told us that we should never turn anyone away because we are told in Hebrews 13:2 (NAS): "Do not neglect to show hospitality to strangers, for by this some have entertained angels without knowing it."

Had I entertained an angel unaware? I can't say for certain, but I do know and believe that God sent her to minister to me in my grief, depression, and anger.

~Minnie Norton Browne

Spiritual Therapy

An angel from heaven appeared to him and strengthened him.
~Luke 22:43

Patience. That was one of my strengths, according to my fellow teachers, friends and family. However, as I struggled through caregiving for my widowed mother-in-law, I wondered if I'd had everyone fooled... including myself.

Mother had fallen in her kitchen on her eighty-second birthday right before her older son, Danny, was to take her the fifty miles to our home for a special dinner. Charles had made lasagna, a family favorite. Even though in pain, she'd insisted on Danny taking her for the celebration. The next day Danny took her to the doctor before returning to his home in Mississippi.

On Thursday morning almost a week later, we received a call from Uncle Thomas. He and Aunt Louise had stopped to check on Mother. They knew the doctor had diagnosed her with a broken pelvic bone and prescribed pain medicine for her.

"Charles, your mother is on the floor at the foot of her bed all tangled up in the sheet and the quilt. She's talking strangely and can't get up. Looks like she may have been there all night," Uncle Thomas explained.

We abandoned our plans for the day and rushed to her home in Summerville, Georgia. Another visit to the doctor revealed no additional broken bones but we learned he'd been talking to her about moving to a nursing home. He'd detected early signs of dementia, which she'd successfully hidden from us. The trauma of the fall and the pain medicine combined to increase these signs. Continuing to live alone was too dangerous, so I stayed with her.

Mother's home health care team included a petite brunette physical therapist who could have been in her mid-thirties to early forties. She certainly displayed patience as she gently worked with Mother on the strengthening exercises needed due to her broken pelvic bone.

The physical therapist handed me a stretchy yellow band. She told me, "You can use this stretch band to do the exercises with Mrs. Pettyjohn."

"Look Mother! We can do exercises together now," I exclaimed. I wrapped the ends of the band around my hands, placed my foot in the middle and held it tightly while stretching my leg straight out then back to the floor, feeling the gentle resistance. Mother's less than enthusiastic look clued me in to her impending stubborn refusals to exercise.

With her typical soft-spoken voice, the physical therapist said to Mother, "We've done enough for today. Would you like me to help you lie down for a nap?"

Though she usually resisted taking naps, Mother agreed. Soon the physical therapist joined me in the kitchen.

"Would you like something to drink?" I asked.

"No thank you." She smiled and, from behind glasses, her kind dark brown eyes connected with me.

She pulled out a chair from the table and sat down. I followed her lead.

After listening to my concerns and frustrations, she said, "Why don't we pray?" Afterwards, she stood up to leave.

"Thank you so much! That really helped." I hugged her. As she drove off, I enjoyed a renewed sense of calming peace.

The therapist returned a few days later for the next session. After completing the exercises with Mother and helping her get comfortable, she turned her attention to me.

"I brought a couple of books you might enjoy reading. They belong to my daughter but she doesn't mind if you borrow them.

They are some of her favorites so I'll need to get them back when you're finished with them." She smiled and handed me two historical fiction books by Judith Pella—*Frontier Lady* and *Stoner's Crossing*.

"Thank you," I said, glancing at the covers and flipping through the first book. "They look interesting."

The therapist's continued visits helped Mother improve her mobility. She always took a little time to converse and pray with me.

"Today is our last day for physical therapy," she told Mother. "Continue with the exercises to keep building your strength."

"I haven't even finished with the first book yet," I told the therapist as she prepared to leave.

"That's okay. Keep them until you're through reading them," she said.

"I'll still be here with Mother unless we find a better solution. I could mail them back to you when I've finished. What's your address?"

"No, you don't have to do that. You live in Dalton, Georgia, right?" I nodded yes. "I'm over there sometimes and could just come by to get them."

"Well, if that's what you'd rather do," I hesitantly responded.

"Yes," she gently but firmly replied.

A month or two later, Mrs. Pettyjohn had another serious fall that required hospitalization at Redmond Park Hospital in Rome, Georgia and rehabilitation at Wood Dale Health Care Center in Dalton, Georgia.

Suzanne, the nurse on her home health care team, had worked with the doctor to establish a health care plan for Mother after her fall on her birthday five months earlier. She administered medications and made sure any necessary resources were available for Mother's health care. Suzanne also coordinated visits from specialists and documented everything related to Mother's treatment. Now she was helping us with some of the arrangements and needed information for the transition to the hospital then rehabilitation.

I wanted to be sure that I could return the books to the therapist; therefore, I asked Suzanne how to contact her.

Suzanne paused from her writing and looked up. Puzzled, she said, "I don't remember that physical therapist."

Why didn't Suzanne remember the physical therapist? Why was the therapist so evasive when I tried to learn how to contact her? Why did she insist on being the one to contact me? How can I explain her helpfulness to Mrs. Pettyjohn with the physical therapy and to me with the emotional and spiritual therapy?

Now sixteen years later, the books are still sitting on a shelf in my home. I finished reading them many years ago but have never heard from or seen the physical therapist again.

"Don't neglect to show hospitality, for by doing this some have welcomed angels as guests without knowing it." Hebrews 13:2 (Holman Christian Standard Bible)

~Pamela Millwood Pettyjohn

Roadside Angels

Angels have no philosophy but love.
~*Terri Guillemets*

L aughter resonated in the car as we drove away from Funland. We—my dad, his cousin Richard, my older sister, and I—had spent the day enjoying the rides and tasty treats at the small amusement park in Dad's hometown. It was a much-needed respite from the recent strain caused by my parents' impending divorce. That's what our "dad and daughters" vacation to Maine was supposed to be—a chance to get away, forget the pain for a while, and simply have fun.

"The bumper cars were the best," my sister said with a grin. "Especially when you got stuck in the corner and everyone kept running into your car."

"Yeah, but I got you back on the water boats," I countered, tugging on her still-wet shorts.

In the front of the car, Dad and Richard laughed at our playful banter, pleased to see us having a good time. Richard's hearty chuckle quickly changed to a violent coughing fit when his orange soda caught in his throat. Dad shifted his gaze from the road to glance sideways at his cousin and… WHAM! In that instant, our family's little world was sent into a tailspin and an extraordinary encounter was set into motion.

Our tiny silver Renault Le Car drifted across the centerline and straight into the path of a three-quarter-ton truck barreling down the road. Tires squealed, metal crunched, and glass shattered as the two vehicles collided head-on. The seatbelt cut in and stung my skin as the car spiraled out of control in the middle of the road. I squeezed my eyes shut to erase the dizzy blur around me and one thought repeated in my seven-year-old mind, "Jesus, help us. Please, Jesus, help us."

Almost as abruptly as it started, the car came to a standstill on the side of the road beside an open field. The eerie silence in the vehicle was painful and terrifying. "Daddy?" My whisper echoed in the stillness. "Daddy?"

My dad, still dazed from the impact, stirred in the driver's seat. "Girls... girls. Are you okay?" When he turned to look at us, my stomach lurched and my reply stuck in my throat. Shards of glass were mingled with blood that dripped down my daddy's face.

Despite his own obvious injuries, Dad got out and helped my sister and me crawl from the back seat. Other than my sister's bloody knee where a previous scab had been scraped off when she hit the seat in front of her, we both climbed out of the totaled car safe. He then tried repeatedly to rouse Richard. No response. The impact of his head hitting the windshield had left Richard hurt and unconscious.

The field near where our car landed was on a less traveled road on the outskirts of a small town. That was before everyone had a cell phone, so it appeared that help would not be imminent. The best hope for an injured father, two small children, and an unconscious family member was the off chance that someone traveling down the road would stop to offer assistance.

Dad led us away from the road and our demolished car, and into the open field. Imagine our surprise when we walked into the field and two women were waiting there. Although we did not know them, they smiled and greeted us like they had been expecting us all along. One of the women motioned toward the wreckage and reassured my dad. "Don't be afraid and don't worry about your girls. Just take care of what you need to do. We will keep your children safe."

I watched him hike down the road to a distant house in search of a telephone and marveled that my protective father had left us with strangers. Why would he just leave us, especially when we were afraid? It was so unlike him.

Then the strong and comforting hand of the woman beside me closed around my shaky one, and my anxiety faded away. In its place came a deep calm. For the first time in over a year of turbulence, I did not feel afraid. Even in the midst of a crisis.

Before long, police cars and ambulances arrived with sirens blaring and lights flashing. My sister and I sat safely in the field and watched emergency workers hustle around the scene of the accident, as the two women stood quietly alongside. Always the inquisitive child, I took the opportunity to study the two strangers who watched over us.

What was it about them that made me feel so peaceful and safe when I trusted so few adults? Neither of them was extraordinary in appearance. Both appeared to be middle-aged, of average size and with shoulder-length silver hair. The clothes they wore were simple. They weren't particularly attractive women, yet there was an underlying beauty that was undeniable when they smiled at me. They spoke very few words, other than to whisper reassurances that everything would be okay. I had never met either of the women, yet I felt more comfortable remaining in the field with them than if I had been in the presence of my own family members. I didn't even know their names.

Our helpful strangers stood close by later while the paramedics examined my sister and me and when they decided to take her to the hospital for further examination along with my dad and Richard. My grandfather arrived to take me with him.

Before leaving, I grabbed the hand of the woman closest to me, whispered a thank you, and turned to go. She kept hold of my hand, called me by name and said, "Don't be afraid. You will be okay. Everything will be okay."

I spun back around to wave a goodbye to the two kind women, but they were gone. In an area with a flat, open terrain and no close buildings or vehicles, they had simply vanished in an instant. Even as I climbed into Grandpa's truck, that same inexplicable peace remained and warmed me to the core. Everything would be all right.

There are many things in life that remain a mystery to me. However, one truth is extremely clear. God sent two of His angels to help my family that day. Through those "roadside angels," His love, comfort, and presence were revealed to two wounded men and two scared little girls who desperately needed it. I was only a small child on the fateful day, but the memory and the promise from God will stick with me forever. He sends His angels to go before us, to be alongside us, and to follow after us. No matter who you are or where you go, you are never alone.

~Jo Brielyn

Blue Bug Angel

In Heaven an angel is nobody in particular.
~George Bernard Shaw

I was the daughter that Aunt Bea never had. A childhood kidnapping and rape had left her barren. When my mother was diagnosed with cancer shortly after I was born, Aunt Bea cared for her. I was fourteen when Mama died. Various relatives invited me into their homes, but how could I leave Aunt Bea, who had cared for me since babyhood? Why would I want to live with people I barely knew? Aunt Bea needed me as much as I needed her.

When I grew up, I moved to Los Angeles. Aunt Bea remained in San Antonio running her own neighborhood grocery business. I worried nightly about my elderly aunt, on her own, on the wrong side of town, ringing up sales that barely supported her.

One night, later than I would have expected her to telephone, Aunt Bea called sounding breathless and anxious. I pictured my seventy-five-year-old aunt, 1,300 miles away, alone, vulnerable, pushing broken English to the limit when no one was around who understood her native Spanish.

Her voice trembled as she said, "Some boys came into the store. They stole sodas and beer from the cooler and ran out the door. I screamed at them to stop. I had to chase them."

"Where are you now?" I blurted out, near tears.

I pictured the meager cash register. I envisioned a cold hospital room—bandages!

"I'm in the living room. The police just left. The store's locked up."

"Are you hurt, Aunt Bea?"

"Just my knees," she replied with a moan. "My legs gave out when I chased the boys. I fell to the ground and watched them disappear in the distance. I screamed at them and then looked up to the sky and prayed."

Thank God there had been no confrontation.

"Then I saw the girl," Aunt Bea said.

"There was a girl, too?" I gasped.

"She wasn't with the boys," Aunt Bea explained. "At first, I thought it was you. I didn't see her until I ran outside. Suddenly, she was lifting me up from the ground and asking me if I was all right."

Probably a customer, I thought. She must have seen the boys running from the store. That was bound to look suspicious.

"She never bought anything," Aunt Bea went on. "She just lifted me up, helped me inside and telephoned for help. When I finished talking to the police, she was gone."

It had probably been someone who hadn't wanted to get involved, I surmised. And she had probably thought that Aunt Bea was in no condition to conduct business after her ordeal. Of course, my aunt was always in condition to conduct business.

"What did she look like?" I asked, thinking I might remember her from the neighborhood.

"She was tall and slim," Aunt Bea began. "Her skin was very fair. She looked like an Americana. She had long light brown hair like yours. It fell straight across her back. I guess the little blue bug car that I saw parked alongside the store was hers. There was no one else around and no other cars stopped."

Thirteen hundred miles away in my California apartment, I sat in wonderment as I listened to Aunt Bea describe the girl who had helped her. I was tall and slim. I wore my golden brown hair long. Despite my Mexican roots, my skin was as fair as an Irish girl's. Anyone describing that girl might have described me. There was more.

When I had first moved to Los Angeles, I had fallen in love with the colorful profusion of Volkswagen Beetles. The little cars roamed the LA freeways like giant insects. Within a few months, I had traded in my cumbersome Pontiac for a cute sky blue bug. In San Antonio's hot, humid climate the radiator-free, air-cooled VW Beetles were as rare as snowstorms.

Thirteen hundred miles separated me from my beloved Aunt Bea. Yet someone who looked like me and who even drove the same kind of car as I did had appeared at my aunt's grocery store. This angel had helped Aunt Bea through the aftermath of a terrifying crime and ordeal. The angel had summoned help and then disappeared when the police arrived.

My beloved Aunt Bea passed away thirty years ago, but I still share this story with others. Inevitably, listeners smile and say, "That was an angel." I call it my Blue Bug Angel story.

~Susana Nevarez-Marquez

55

Heavenly Help

Prayer is the mortar that holds our house together.
~Mother Teresa

We knew it was coming since the day he was born. Our little boy was born with a terminal genetic disorder. We tried to cram a lifetime of happiness into his short years, and secretly in my heart, I prayed that his passing would be gentle on him as well as the rest of us.

That fateful morning something told me to make his favorite breakfast. But we were too exhausted from a sleepless night, and I fed him some leftovers instead, an act I regret to this day. He fell asleep for a midmorning nap on some thick quilts in the den. Usually I'd leave him undisturbed, but still another voice urged me to put him on his miniature bed. I'm glad that, in spite of my fatigue, I managed to do at least that.

He died from a strong seizure during his nap.

The grief weighed down my mind and body so heavily that for days after I didn't want to get out of bed. But my two other children, whose hearts also were torn from their chests, watched me, frightened. They needed to be fed; they needed clean clothes. They needed a mother who could show them how to carry on despite the pain.

Almost against my will, my body did climb out of bed, went through the motions of fixing spaghetti with meat sauce, stuffing dirty jeans and T-shirts into the washer, washing dishes and listening to bedtime prayers. I marveled at how my arms seemed to move as though something or someone was carrying me along, moving my body for me. I watched my hands moving about. It wasn't by my own effort. I felt like a marionette.

"Something or someone is lifting me out of bed and moving this body for me," I told my husband. In his own grief, he just nodded.

One night, after the kids were tucked into bed, I sat on the sofa, weeping bitterly. How can a heart hurt so much and still keep beating? And yet, it kept beating through the excruciating physical and emotional pain. I didn't want to live anymore. Not without my precious little boy.

"Dear God," I pleaded. "Please let me go with him." I dissolved into sobs, my head pounding, my insides hollow except for the searing pain. My prayers were answered in a different way. In God's mercy, my nights soon were filled with dreams of joyous reunions with my little boy. I gradually regained my strength and my unseen help slowly withdrew, leaving behind a barely perceptible sense of grace and peace.

One day, my neighbor stopped to chat and see how I was doing. The day Alex died, she said they saw the paramedics, the police, and finally the funeral parlor's van pull up and then away from our home. My extended family's cars flooded the driveway and street and she hadn't wanted to intrude. But the next day, she found her own little boy, only four years old, leaning out the bathroom windowsill, chatting amiably and waving.

Knowing that the window faced the often-neglected side yards of our houses, she grew alarmed at who could be out there talking with her boy.

"Who are you talking to?" she asked her wide-eyed little boy. He scrambled down from the windowsill.

"The angels."

His mother gave him a quizzical look. "What angels?"

"The angels with the little boy at Lori's house."

Feeling weak, she looked out the window and scanned the view. "Where are they?"

He pointed to the roof of my house next door and then scampered out the door to get his lunch, leaving his mother stunned. For reasons unknown, she could neither see the angels nor the little boy with whom her son chatted.

Still standing in the street next to my car, she explained her reason for not telling me sooner. "I didn't want you to think that my son was crazy for talking to angels and Alex when no one else saw them."

Crazy? It made perfect sense. There was no way I could have survived that past week without divine help. I felt it. It made perfect sense that an innocent, pure-hearted child would be able to see these angelic beings when the rest of us, hardened by a cynical world, could not. My heart felt grateful to know that angels came to escort my little boy to heaven while helping me deal with his parting.

I tell my story to people, including those who don't readily believe in angels and an afterlife. Their reactions vary. But even hardened doubt softens into wonder. Those who wonder find themselves one step closer to believing. And believers smile at this sweet confirmation that angels truly are among us.

~Lori Phillips

56

Back in Business

We are like children, who stand in need of masters to enlighten us
and direct us; and God has provided for this, by appointing his angels
to be our teachers and guides.

~St. Thomas Aquinas

In August 2005, after moving 1800 miles to a rural area without friends or family, I suffered a head-on crash with a speeding drunk driver. Luckily, neither I nor my then-husband died, but I had a dislocated shoulder, two crushed knees and a fractured back. I went from being a healthy wife and mother, enthusiastic about farming our newly acquired nine acres, to a person who could do nothing without help.

I was in extreme pain, depressed, and angry—angry with the other driver, even though he died, angry with God for letting it happen, and even angry with my family, which was waiting for me to turn back into myself. I alternated between my bed and a recliner, where I looked out my second-story window at nature passing by. My husband left me and I felt guilty whenever I asked my thirteen-year-old daughter to help.

One neighbor brought a used wheelchair. I never tried it. Self-pity is powerful. It sat by my bedside every day. Finally, sweating, panting, crying, and screaming in pain, I found a way to hoist myself and my motionless legs from the bed into the chair. What freedom! Despite my new freedom, most of what I wanted to do required legs, or was outside. I was still useless. Rural gravel roads and walkways don't lend themselves to wheelchairs. Another neighbor offered a walker, saying "You're out of bed, so try something new." My only thought was, yeah, right.

After a tornado, our roof began to leak. I had to get bids. Explaining the problems without showing the contractors what was wrong didn't work. They left with too many unanswered questions. Needing the roof repaired, I called the two best contractors back. It took over an hour to drag myself outside with the walker while trying not to scream in pain. Even with good bids, neither of them could start for weeks. I told myself I was done trying to walk—ever.

The next day two gentlemen showed up unannounced. They had been referred by another contractor who had refused to bid since he was working out of town. Saying they were "gentlemen" is generous. The older man looked as if he'd been a hard drinker at one time and hadn't gotten his hair or beard cut or combed in years. His younger protégé was someone who had just been released from prison who needed work. Both wore shabby clothes and mud-caked boots.

Nevertheless, I was desperate. Plus, the older man mentioned that while everyone else in the area was very busy, he could start immediately. So I dragged myself out of the house again. The elder man spoke easily, and the younger one was gentle and respectful, getting me a chair to sit down. They both did all they could to put me at ease, and each had a ready smile. After measuring everything and confirming how I wanted the repairs done, they gave me a business card and promised to give me a quote shortly.

Before leaving, the older man asked me what had happened. When I explained, he said he knew just how I felt. "Some ten years ago, I fell off a three-story building, hit a concrete wall and broke my back in two places. I was in the hospital for seven years, and told I would never walk again." I was stunned and said so! He limped slightly, but had walked all over and climbed my two-story barn. He said, "No, don't be amazed. Doctors mean well, but they never take into account what God wants to do. I told myself I'd probably be in pain my entire life, but that I wasn't meant to sit and waste away, so I had to focus on moving whatever I could, without thinking about how much it hurt."

I sat there, lost in thought. He waited a while and then said, "You can do it too. Maybe you won't be what you were before. But if you give up trying, you'll never find out."

In the days after I kept thinking that if he could do what he had done, maybe I could do more too. I found myself doing a little more each day. I'd be lying if I said it was easy or that I felt no pain. I surprised both myself and my daughter with how much less I grumbled, and how much more I accomplished. Each day brought new small victories and celebrations.

When I didn't receive the visitors' bid, I tried calling. Their number wasn't in service. Puzzled, I called the person who had referred them, and asked for a call back when he returned. It took five days for him to do so. Imagine my shock when he called and said he'd never sent anyone my way! I gave him the names, the phone number and a description. "No, I don't know anyone by that name. I've never heard of them. If I were going to refer someone to you, it wouldn't have been someone that looked the way you described them."

I felt sure that someone in my extremely small, "everyone knows everyone" town would have seen these men. At the very least, my disabled neighbor, who lives along the main highway where it intersects my dead end country road, and who sits outside all day should have seen them come or go. No one knew anything or had seen anyone fitting either of the men's descriptions. No one had even heard of them. The more I asked, the crazier everyone thought I was.

Despite the mystery, I had a new spirit. I got stronger. Not whole, but a little bit more able each day. My toes and legs began to move. Not perfectly, but movement nonetheless. For the first time in a long time I dreamed of a new future.

These men didn't have wings or halos. But they came to encourage me when I'd completely given up. After their visit my life improved in ways that I never imagined. I feel truly blessed, as written in Hebrews 13:2, to have entertained angels unawares.

~Kamia Taylor

Father, Son, and Brother

Yet if there is an angel at their side, a messenger, one out of a thousand,
sent to tell them how to be upright.
~Job 33:23

My son Mike and I had a rather tumultuous relationship ever since the day my ex-wife called and said, "Come get him. I can't do a thing with him."

I was thrilled to get my son back and looked forward to using my own parenting methods on him. Mike had gotten into trouble with the law on several occasions. On the day I picked him up, I told him I would not tolerate such things. If he got into trouble with the law while he lived with me, I would let the law handle it. Of course, being fourteen years old and knowing all there was to know about the world, he didn't believe me. After living with me for two months, he found himself incarcerated in a juvenile facility in our county.

This started a long string of events where he would promise to stay out of trouble and then go right back to his old ways. We had some great times together and some times of terrible grief. When he was thirty years old, he was working for a man who cut logs for a living. One night Mike took off in the man's pickup truck that had two chainsaws in the back along with some other logging equipment. None of us had any idea where he went. Word was put out to law enforcement agencies, but Mike and the truck could not be located.

My lifestyle had changed for the better, and I was traveling in a motor home and selling jewelry at various events to make a living. While I was selling at an event in Quartzsite, Arizona, I got word through a long grapevine that Mike had been killed in an accident in California. I found out he had married a woman who had two children, and they had another child of their own. The youngest baby had stayed with her grandparents while her daddy, mom, and two brothers went to the store. All four of them lost a battle with a train at an unmarked crossing on their way home. I had a granddaughter I had never met or even knew existed. And she was an orphan.

I was about seven hundred miles away from where my son was going to be buried, so I took off the next morning to attend the funeral. I got into the small town on the morning of the second day of my trip, arriving just forty-five minutes before the funeral was to start. A man met me at the door of the church and explained that he was an assistant pastor for the church and folks called him Brother Bob. He said my son's wife's family had requested that he help me through the whole process since I had never met any of these people and certainly didn't know them. I hadn't even know until three days before that my son had gotten married and was a father.

The coffins were in a side room off the main sanctuary of the church. They were left there so the family could spend some time alone with their loved ones before the main service. Brother Bob was a rather short, stout man, but he did manage to hold up my three-hundred-pound body when I almost collapsed at the first sight of Mike in a coffin.

He knew a great deal about Mike's past. The one thing I remember him telling me was not to beat myself up over everything that had happened in our relationship. There were many other factors that led to this moment, and all of them were not my fault. He quoted several passages from the Bible that were comforting, and he prayed with me. He got me seated in the sanctuary before the service started and then left to attend to some other duties.

After the service in the church, we all went to the cemetery for a graveside ceremony. After that, we returned to the church for a huge meal that had been prepared by volunteers. After I finished eating, I sought Pastor Paul Simmons and thanked him for the services he had performed. I asked him where I might find Brother Bob so I could thank him for his help. He got a quizzical look on his face. "Who?" he said.

"Your assistant pastor, Brother Bob."

"I'm sorry, but we only have one assistant pastor here, Brother Luke. He's a young, tall man with sandy red hair."

I went to each member of the family and asked if they had seen this man who called himself Brother Bob. I said he was short, stout and wearing a black suit, white shirt, and a black, string western-style tie. He was also balding. None could remember seeing him and none of them said they asked anyone to be there to specifically help me. I told all of them I was talking with him in the side room off the sanctuary before the service. Still no one remembered seeing him. I guess I was the only one, but he was as real to me as this keyboard I'm typing on.

On my way back to Quartzsite, I had a lot of time to think. I came to one conclusion. All of my son's in-laws had been friendly and helpful, but Brother Bob was sent especially to help me through this whole horrible process. I guess angels come in all shapes and sizes. They don't have to have wings or golden halos. They can be short, stout, and balding, but they can still be angels.

~Gary R. Hoffman

Night Angel

Then no harm will befall you, no disaster will come near your tent. For he will command his angels concerning you to guard you in all your ways.
~Psalm 91:10-11

The first time I spied the elderly woman rocking in the wicker chair in the corner of my bedroom, I was ten. I was old enough to realize a stranger had appeared in the middle of the night, but not old enough to appreciate the reason behind her visit. Sitting up in bed, I peered into the full-length mirror to my left and caught the woman's reflection—her gentleness persuaded me to remain silent despite my urge to scream. For unexplained reasons, I trusted this stranger and settled into bed.

Palpable warmth spread across the room as she rocked with her hands folded in her lap and a grandmother-like kindness about her. Instinctively, I knew she meant no harm. The real harm lay in the next room—an abusive mother who made frequent trips to my bedside to unleash her rage. On this night, my mother busied herself with late-night television. While my visitor rocked, I drifted to sleep amidst sounds from the TV down the hallway.

The next night, I pulled the covers over my head at the first creak of the bedroom door. Light from the hallway sliced through the darkness, and I stiffened, preparing for my mother's wrath. Feigning sleep, I prayed she'd lose interest, become distracted by something outside the room, or experience a rush of guilt and leave. Unfortunately, she remained focused but, eventually, she tired of the beating and left. While I choked back my tears, I stared at the empty rocking chair.

Throughout the next five years, the comforting figure perched herself in the corner of my bedroom. When I heard my mother approaching, I glanced toward the chair and caught the woman nodding, giving me the strength and confidence to endure. This serene soul wasn't there to fight my battles, only to ensure that I wasn't alone in my struggles. There were tests along the way and moments of doubt. Times when she failed to come. Times when my mother came. Times when I wished myself dead. Somehow, at fifteen, I knew it was part of a much bigger plan.

The following year, my mother left without saying so much as goodbye. Sadly, so did my guardian angel. More than likely, she needed to console another frightened child. Yet, after thirty years, my angel hasn't been forgotten. Each night, while kneeling at my children's bedside, I offer a prayer of thanksgiving: Thank you my night angel, sent by The Almighty Father, for giving me the fortitude to endure the wounds of childhood. Most of all, thank you for the safety of my children—that I chose not to repeat the acts of violence I experienced but to follow your example of guarding the vulnerable. Amen.

~Cathi LaMarche

The Cowboy

Children often have imaginary playmates.
I suspect that half of them are really their guardian angels.
~Eileen Elias Freeman,
The Angels' Little Instruction Book

I was seven when I saw the cowboy. My brother was three, and in the throes of a cowboy obsession. He wore his white cowboy hat and holster with two cap guns everywhere he went. He also was in the throes of a strange unrelenting illness that caused him to rock back and forth, gasping for breath, and become delirious with fevers. They called it asthmatic bronchitis at first. Later they realized it was a series of feverous infections and asthma brought on by allergies. I just knew that my mother rarely got to sleep through the night. My parents were very concerned.

Bedtime meant nasal sprays and vaporizers and if he wanted to wear his holster to bed, he did. But I hardly noticed all of that on this particular night, because I was having my best friend Kelly sleep over. We played games, ate snacks, tried to scare ourselves with ghost stories and then settled in to sleep in the living room, just down the hall from my brother's bedroom. Kelly was on the couch and I was on the loveseat. My mother had turned off the lights and had gone upstairs to bed, and Kelly and I were quietly talking when something caught Kelly's attention. She sat up, looking down the hall and whispered for me to come over to the couch.

I went over and saw what she saw. There was a translucent

cowboy, just like those in the old westerns my dad watched on TV sometimes, just like the molded plastic figures my brother played with in his Fort Apache play set! It walked down the hall and into my brother's bedroom. Kelly and I just stared. We were transfixed. It was a very calming presence and in spite of our prior ghost stories, we were not afraid. Just then, we heard my brother calling out, "Mum! There's a cowboy in my room!" His voice was not fearful, but excited. My mother came down the stairs immediately and after a while got him back to sleep. Kelly and I also settled into peaceful sleep.

The next morning at breakfast my mother scolded me for "messing around" in my brother's room during the night. Kelly and I were confused. My mother was very upset, going on to say that we had no business moving things around, that it was very important that he have his vaporizer and fan blowing on him all the time. We were clueless as to what she was talking about. She said it must have taken both of us to move the big box fan that she had in his doorway, and that she couldn't figure out why we would do that. Finally, my brother stopped her tirade by explaining, "The cowboy must have moved it!" Yes, that made sense. Kelly and I agreed it must have been the cowboy. We solved that mystery, or so we thought.

My mother became enraged. She thought we were ridiculing my brother in his "delirium" and disrespecting her at the same time. Now I was worried. Not only my integrity, but my future sleepovers were at stake. Kelly and I both explained to her exactly what we had seen that night, and my brother told it from his perspective.

I still wonder if it was the fact that I have never lied to her before, or that we were all so calm about this, or that my brother slept through the rest of that night that stopped her anger. Maybe it was divine intervention. Suddenly, my mother's anger disappeared and she was listening intently. She believed us. We wanted to know what this cowboy was, and why he had come. After a few days of thinking about it, my mother was the one who offered the explanation. She said it was my brother's guardian angel, there to protect and not to scare. All of that air blowing on him must have been harmful, so the angel moved the fan. It made sense. Kelly and I loved to tell that story. We had seen an angel. Our classmates were fascinated.

After that, my mother had other brushes with my brother's guardian angel. She never saw the angel, but she saw the effects of its presence. There was the miraculous prevention of a car accident that would have hurt or even killed my brother in the back seat. My mother was stopped in traffic and gripped the wheel tightly to brace herself for the car that was approaching too quickly in the rearview mirror. She watched as the car's brakes screamed and the car seemed to lift up to avoid hitting them. She saw the amazing branch that hung down from seemingly nowhere for him to grab to save himself from drowning in a fast-rising creek. I never saw the cowboy again, but I knew he was there. Though I never saw my own guardian angel, I knew without question that she was with me always. After all, that would only be fair.

Years after that, I had forgotten about the cowboy. I was consumed with fear for my brother's life as he had become a Marine and was fighting in the Persian Gulf War. My parents watched CNN without interruption, listening for the casualty count each day. All of our nerves were on edge, not knowing if he was dead or alive.

During that time, I took a phone call from a woman that my mother had known briefly years before. She acknowledged how strange this was, but needed to pass along a message she received in a dream. My mother was not home, so I received this urgent and unusual message. She told me that she had a dream that my brother's angel was with him and was protecting him and that we should not worry because he would live through this war. I was stunned. The cowboy was still there! How could I forget? Through tears of joy, I shared with her the cowboy story. She was good to call; this was a very welcome message for us. I told my parents, and this knowledge eased our worries. He did come home from the war, no doubt with the cowboy by his side.

My own children know this story well. We are very considerate of our guardian angels, and very grateful to them. I am also very grateful for having had that glimpse of an angel. The experience has formed my faith, my personality, and made indelible impressions on the lives of my friends and family. In so many ways, I have been blessed by my brother's cowboy.

~Kristine Peebles

60

The Assignment

Our perfect companions never have fewer than four feet.
~Colette

We all know someone who loves angels. You know, the kind of person who has every nook and cranny of her home filled to capacity with those endearing porcelain, china or dollar store nickknacks?

I have always pictured an angel as a soft, feminine form with cascading luminescent tendrils of hair, porcelain skin and eyes the colour of the Caribbean Sea. That was until... I actually met one.

Not the feminine form I'd imagined, but feline. Not cascading tendrils or porcelain skin, but soft, silky, taupe fur. Beautiful turquoise, soulful eyes, albeit somewhat crossed. Yes, my angel was a Siamese cat!

My daughter Jessica was nine years old at the time. She had fallen off the monkey bars in the playground. A compression fracture wrapped in a cast was her souvenir after spending eight hours in the emergency room. Nice gift to get the week before summer vacation! At our one-week checkup with the orthopedic surgeon, X-rays were taken, an exam made, and we received disappointing news.

Although things looked okay on the outside, the bones weren't in perfect alignment. The surgeon recommended a return visit to the operating room the next day to remove the cast and re-set the bone. My daughter was terrified, especially when she learned that her dad and I weren't allowed to be with her during the procedure.

The ride home was very quiet. You could see the worry in her watery eyes and in her body language. There was no consoling her. After encouraging her to have some lunch I suggested she go outside to get some fresh air.

At her age, most kids were pining for the latest video game or electronic gadget, but she was pleading for a cat. Being an only child was lonely and I had always felt guilty about not providing her with any siblings. I was trying to come up with an activity to distract her, when all of a sudden I said, "Look!"

A beautiful Siamese cat was walking atop the fence in our yard. Strutting her form like an Olympic gymnast, she was showing off her beautiful lines and languid curves.

Where did this exquisite cat come from? We'd lived in this neighborhood for fifteen years and had never seen this cat before. I couldn't believe it. The one thing that would truly make my daughter happy had just appeared out of thin air! The cat dismounted with gymnastic perfection and crossed the yard to softly rest at my daughter's feet.

She let out a meow as if to say, "All is well; I'm here for you." That Siamese angel was hugged, rubbed, petted and loved all afternoon. She followed my daughter everywhere and was a faithful companion and confidante. I kept peeking outside in utter disbelief.

Dinnertime rolled around and I regretfully called my daughter inside. Her trusty companion kept vigil outside the patio door for a few minutes, making sure she was in good hands. Then as quickly and quietly as she had come into our little world, she vanished, her assignment here on earth completed.

We never saw that cat again, but we have a photo that we truly treasure. I was so moved by the encounter that I wrote this story and originally titled it "Angels Among Us." I was thrilled to be able to submit it to this book with the same title.

~Catherine Rossi

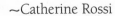

Angels Among Us

Healing Touches

Nothing Less than Miraculous

When angels visit us, we do not hear the rustle of wings,
nor feel the feathery touch of the breast of a dove;
but we know their presence by the love they create in our hearts.
~Author Unknown

I was still in the intensive care unit, but the crisis was over. The ventilator had been removed and I was breathing on my own. My kidneys began to function on their own again too, releasing me from the portable dialysis machine that occupied a corner of my hospital room. My one remaining limb was still tethered to the IV pole—endless fluids dripped into my veins.

No longer in a drug-induced coma, and weaning off the heavy narcotics, the fog began to clear from my mind. I now understood that I had been an unwitting soldier on a microscopic battlefield. The bacterial infection that invaded my body tried valiantly to render itself victorious. Strep A necrotizing fasciitis, commonly known as the flesh-eating bacteria, hit hard and fast, and by design left carnage in its wake. But I survived the war.

Even in my celebration of victory, I was devastated by the collateral damage sustained from this battle. My right hand... gone. The lower halves of both legs... gone. The left half of my chest... gone.

The gravity of my situation hit me. As I lay flat on my back, unable to move, I began to wonder how I was going to manage my two small children, a husband, a home, my job.... I began a mantra of "how am I going to make it?" I was in a continuous loop of fear and despair.

But amidst my panic, I felt something shift. My fear subsided a little, and my thundering heart began to slow. I had an inkling of something refreshing, almost pure, like the way the air smells right before the rain comes on a summer's day. Then I felt it entirely.

An incredible presence in the small confines of my hospital room enveloped me. I sensed a giant hand that encompassed my battered, useless hand lying next to my head on the pillow. The words "I am with you" were spoken in my ear. My desperate mantra uttered only moments earlier was replaced with profound peacefulness—a settled calm within my soul. As I opened my eyes, I saw an amazingly beautiful light shimmering right by me.

"What just happened?" My nurse, Sarah, raced into my room. "Cindy, are you okay? What just happened?" she asked again with a sense of urgency that verged on panic.

"Oh Sarah," I said, as tears poured from my eyes. "I just saw my... angel." I was hesitant to name it, but the word slid from my mouth nonetheless. There certainly wasn't any other explanation, and it seemed that now wasn't the time to analyze, to dissect what had just occurred.

"I knew something happened. We saw it, Cindy; we saw it on the monitors." Sarah was now crying too, her blue eyes wide, and a tremulous smile was spreading across her mouth. At that moment, she looked like an angel herself.

I had many monitors hooked up to me, all of which kept track of my vital signs. They recorded the much-needed data to a central station in the ICU. A tech monitor was watching my readouts when he noticed some startling changes.

He beckoned Sarah to come look at what he was witnessing. As they looked at the readings from my monitors, they saw an increase in my precariously low blood pressure, a slowing of my racing heart, and an increase in my blood oxygen level. For weeks, my medical team had made every effort to stabilize my vitals, and now, within an instant and without explanation, they became normal.

What I witnessed directly, Sarah and the tech witnessed indirectly, but we all witnessed the same thing—something unexplainable, something glorious.

Over the next few months, my healing was deemed "nothing less than miraculous" by the team of doctors who were monitoring my care. My stay at the hospital ended in May, which far surpassed my doctors' expectations that my discharge from the hospital would most likely be in September. I was in a physical rehab facility by the middle of May and home with my family by July.

I believe that my healing was "miraculous," that I survived for a reason. As my recovery continued, it became clear to me that I had a debt to pay for not just once, but twice, being given the miracle of life. My mantra changed the night my angel appeared. My new mantra began, "How do I repay... how do I give back?"

My journey over these past fifteen years has provided me a lifetime of lessons. I have learned that I am not alone in the vast sea of life, a small cork bobbing along trying to keep my head above the water. I have come to acknowledge that we are all corks bobbing along in the same sea. But instead of going it alone, each one of us helps to hold the other up. We stabilize each other, lending support to keep each other steady. I have learned that through helping others I feed my soul and my healing continues.

I believe that all of us, whether or not we feel we have a debt to pay for our own miraculous lives, are here simply to help each other live better lives; and when we open our hearts, our hearing gets better and better.

I wasn't sure what to believe about angels before the night my ethereal visitor came to me in the ICU. Now I not only believe... I know.

~Cindy Charlton

Shortcut to Peace

You'll meet more angels on a winding path than on a straight one.
~Terri Guillemets

The day I decided to commit suicide was the day I met my guardian angel. It was July 4, 1975, and my mother had sent me to buy her some cigarettes at the grocery store on the edge of my small Louisiana town. I was a thirteen-year-old girl with low self-esteem who bore the psychological scars of too many beatings from a mother who fought her own demons.

To say my childhood was unpleasant would be an understatement. And by the time I became a teenager, I was tired of fighting with my mother, tired of feeling like I was worthless as a human being and simply tired of living.

The walk to the store was uneventful, but on the return trip I decided to try a shortcut I thought would take me back to my house. It was a dirt path running beside a levee with a canal full of water for the rice fields that surrounded my hometown.

The farther I walked, the more depressed I became as I thought about how much I hated my life. I wasn't allowed to make any friends and years of isolation, beatings and being treated like I was worthless had taken their toll. Before long, tears were running down my face as I came to the conclusion the only escape from the hell I lived at home was to kill myself. But how?

Suddenly I had an idea. I would simply walk into the canal and drown myself. The world wouldn't miss me and I wouldn't have to endure any more abuse from my mother. The thought of dying didn't even scare me. I just thought of it as going to sleep and never having to wake up again to the incredible sadness of my life.

As if my body had a mind of its own, I felt myself walk to the water's edge. The surface was smooth as glass and all the noises of nature around me were suddenly quiet. Too quiet. Like the whole world was waiting to see if I would go through with my plan. And that's when it happened.

Just as I was about to slip into the water, I felt this incredible push from two invisible hands shoving me away from the canal's edge. The force was so strong that I flew halfway across the road and landed in the dirt. It took me a moment to catch my breath and collect my thoughts. As if I was waking from a dream, I looked around me. I had been alone on that dirt road before and there was still no one in sight. Who pushed me? Who kept me from carrying out my plan?

A peace came over me in that moment and the memory of that day remains with me still. My life at home was still hell until I left at age seventeen, but I didn't feel quite so alone after that day. I moved out on my own after graduating high school and had a few more opportunities to feel the presence of my guardian angel as I struggled to find a place for myself. Each time I was desperate for some sign that God had not forgotten me, that there was a purpose to my life, my angel would come to me and remind me that I am never quite alone. Now I reach out to others through my martial arts and my writing with the hope that my words will somehow bring them peace in their hour of need. It's the only way I know to repay my guardian angel for giving me a second chance at life.

~Donna L. Martin

You'll Be All Right

In all their distress he too was distressed, and the angel of his presence
saved them. In his love and mercy he redeemed them;
he lifted them up and carried them all the days of old.
~Isaiah 63:9

Pulling into the driveway, I could see that the hotel bore little resemblance to the depiction on the chain's website. The soft pink stucco I expected to see was a far cry from the actual Pepto-Bismol tone. The pool was accessible only by walking past large, pungent dumpsters to the far side of the parking lot. The east edge of the building was connected to a busy liquor store, and nearby food options were limited to one restaurant and a donut shop. But the room had been prepaid and there were no refunds if I cancelled.

I parked and went into the small lobby. I could see that it doubled as the breakfast area and made a mental note to forgo that meal. However, as the manager, Mr. Patel, and his assistant, Nila, greeted me with smiles and welcoming conversation, I reminded myself that it was only for one night.

I had returned to the area for business and pleasure. A poet and singer, I had scheduled a music rehearsal followed by dinner with friends from high school. After church the next day, I would drive to a planning meeting for a women's retreat before heading home. It would be a tight schedule, with little time for anything not already planned. The rehearsal over, dinner was a welcome time of relaxation, with conversation lasting for hours before I forced myself to return to the hotel.

Short on sleep, I was hard pressed to emerge from the covers on Sunday morning. If I skipped church, I could sleep for another two hours and still make my meeting. That thought lulled me back to pleasant dreams, only to be jarred into reality by the incessant buzz, buzz, buzz of my alarm. It was almost as if the heavenly Father was speaking to my heart, telling me, "Rise up, Daughter. I have other things in store for you today." I hurried to get ready, knowing that if there was any traffic at all, I would be late.

As I stepped from the wide curb into the parking lot, I felt my right ankle give way and then move to an unnatural angle. When the outside of my foot hit the hard asphalt surface, I heard a loud pop! Looking around, I evaluated my situation. I was sitting at a ninety-degree angle with a twelve-foot wide wall that ran between the front door of the lobby and the night window.

I craned my neck in both directions. No one inside the office could see me. Too early for housekeeping, the door to the laundry room behind and to my left was closed, and the other guests appeared to still be tucked away in their rooms.

I knew that any traffic that passed through the parking lot was going one of three places: the hotel, the liquor store, or the restaurant. I also knew that no matter the destination, the drivers of the cars always seemed to be in a hurry and traveled at speeds well above the posted 5 mph. That would give them little time to avoid a person sitting in their path.

There were no cars in front of the liquor store, but a breakfast crowd had the eatery's parking lot packed. Since there was a substantial hedge between the businesses, I was invisible to the diners as well. I had visions of being flattened, much like the pancakes being served.

I brushed the loose asphalt from my now red, pitted palms and tried to lift myself from the ground. No matter how I maneuvered, I could not rise up more than a few inches, and any pressure on my foot was excruciating. I was stuck.

I tried hollering, "Mr. Patel! Nila! Can anyone hear me?" There was only silence. Then, out of my peripheral vision, I saw her. I had never even noticed the phone booth at the far side of the liquor store, but now standing next to it was a very large woman.

"Are you okay, honey?" Her voice was not sweet like the endearment she used, but instead, deep and gruff. I could only stare as she approached, her features becoming clearer. She was dressed in men's blue jeans, a black crewneck T-shirt and a denim vest. There were two chains of graduated lengths hanging between two belt loops on her pants, and her black Doc Martens made a heavy, ominous sound as they came toward me. A blue and white bandana covered most of her short dreadlocks and gave her face a severe quality. I had always prided myself on being comfortable around strangers, but I had to admit, I was leery of this woman.

She asked again, "Are you okay, honey? Do you need help?"

"I fell and I can't get up." As I heard the words come out of my mouth, I flashed on a familiar medical alert commercial and a slight chuckle lessened my tension. In the next moment, she had reached my side. I could now see the tattoos that covered her skin. She spoke again.

"Do you think you can get up?"

"I've tried, but my foot hurts too much," I answered.

She held out her hand, and after a slight hesitation, I reached up to take hold of it. I was surprised at how strong yet gentle her grasp was and, even more so, how effortlessly she lifted me from the ground. I attempted to steady myself, but any pressure on my foot brought unbearable pain.

"Can you walk?"

"I'm not sure."

She continued to hold my hand while I bent down to get a closer look at the now swollen and bruised appendage. Rising up, I brushed the remnants of dirt and gravel from my slacks.

"You'll be all right."

I realized then that she was no longer holding my hand, and I looked up, expecting to see her standing in front of me. But she was gone. Not just from my side, but gone from my sight. She had disappeared. There was no explanation, save one. I had no doubt that I had been visited by a rescuing angel. As the words passed through my mind, a car rounded the corner. I knew that I had been spared from serious injury, and maybe even death.

Somehow, I limped to my car. I continued onto church, to my meeting and then made the more than two-hour drive home. Each time the pain struck, her words echoed in my mind, "You'll be all right."

It was the next afternoon before I could get in to see my doctor. After a preliminary examination, he asked his nurse to take X-rays. Before long, he came back into the room and held up the films so I could see them.

"I don't understand. There is a V-shaped piece of bone completely out of place. You shouldn't be able to put any pressure on that foot. How in the world did you manage to walk in here on your own?"

I smiled, and without a care as to how it might sound, I said, "Let me tell you about my angel."

~Sandy Lynn Moffett

64

The Great Physician's Helper

"For I will restore health to you and heal you of your wounds,"
says the LORD…
~Jeremiah 30:17

At thirty-five I found a lump in my right breast. It was hard, unmoving and without pain. Despite having a clear exam only six months earlier, the invasion seemed bigger than a pea.

The next day I found myself in fight mode. My great-grandmother was 104 when she passed. My grandmother was still healthy at eighty-seven. My mother didn't take a single prescription and never wore out during full days of antiquing. I reasoned the lump was nothing.

I went into fight mode. I called work to tell them I'd be late. I double-checked that my insurance card was in my billfold. I methodically got dressed and then sat staring at the clock until I knew my doctor's office opened. At a minute after eight, I called.

When I told my doctor what I'd discovered, he tried to reassure me. "You don't have a family history of breast cancer and you're too young. It's nothing."

In his office, he examined the area. "Hmmmm. Why don't we send you for an X-ray?" He pulled out my chart and made a note or two. "It's likely something benign. I'll get you set up."

Twenty-four hours later, I had the X-ray. Shortly after the buzz of the machine, the technician announced he'd return in a few minutes. When he came back, he said, "I consulted with your doctor and we agree you need an ultrasound."

"An ultrasound? Like a pregnant woman would have?" I was confused.

"Yes, it's similar. We'll just do an ultrasound of your chest area."

By the time I dressed, the address for my next appointment was in my hand. It had been too quick. Obtaining an appointment doesn't happen fast unless it's urgent, right? In my mind the quick scheduling felt like a confirmation of my fears. Cancer.

The lubricant during the ultrasound felt cold. I shivered and asked the technician if I could see the monitor as she proceeded. I probably shouldn't have.

The dark spot looked like a rotted apricot.

The technician said she would send the results to my doctor. I left the office in a state of numbness. I kept revisiting what everyone was saying. When I closed my car door, I burst into tears. My hands shook until I clasped them in prayer. Several minutes passed before I could safely navigate traffic.

That night, my husband and I lay in one another's arms and talked about what we would do with the diagnosis that we were expecting.

"There's a chance it's not." He refused to speak the word too, and tried to sound hopeful.

"Well, if it is, you need to hurry and buy those concert tickets you've promised me for years."

We could have heard a mouse squeak. He played dumb. Then, we both laughed. It didn't matter what the diagnosis was, he had no desire to see Barry Manilow.

The next day the biopsy was scheduled.

"Count backwards from ten, please." The anesthesiologist stared at a beeping machine over my head.

"Ten… nine… eight…"

At some point I heard a male voice over my left shoulder. "It's malignant. But you will be okay." I tilted my head and saw a tall gentleman. His hair gleamed and matched the white of his clothing. He looked like he'd been dipped in bleach. It wasn't my doctor or the anesthesiologist I'd met before blacking out. An extra doctor? A nurse? It didn't matter.

I smiled and he returned the smile. His countenance of peace made me believe. He reassured me.

The next thing I remember was leaning over a basin as I threw up in the recovery room. Anesthesia always treats me special. Despite my stomach issues, I found myself humming.

We left the clinic and my euphoria didn't dissipate. I actually laughed when I told my husband he needed to buy those Barry Manilow tickets. My chatter made up for his silence.

As we walked into the house, the phone rang. When I recognized my doctor's voice, I put the call on speaker.

"Gail, we need to talk. Is your husband with you?"

"What do we do next?" I didn't want to belabor the discussion.

The silence on the other end of the phone worried me even more. Was it too bad to even treat?

"Well, first I need to tell you the diagnosis."

"Oh, I heard the man tell me during the biopsy," I said.

Longer silence.

"Gail, I never had a chance to tell you because you were sleeping so hard. That anesthesia worked well on you." The doctor chuckled.

"Well, whoever it was, I heard someone over my left shoulder, an older gentleman said it was malignant, but I'd be okay."

"Gail, there was no one over your left shoulder. We were working on your right side. And I didn't say anything after I determined malignant cells."

I thought this was odd. Although he continued to discuss the treatment plan, I focused on my unknown visitor.

As soon as we hung up the phone my husband said, "It's funny. You had this odd smile plastered across your face as you told me it was malignant." My husband reached for my hands. "I figured you were still tipsy from the anesthesia. Now I wonder if your surprise visitor made you giddy."

"I feel such peace about the whole thing. God sent me an angel." We hugged. "He said I'd be okay. And, you know what? I believe him."

As we continued to talk about my experience, we both thanked God for His messenger. Peace enveloped me like a fluffy down comforter and carried me through a year of testing and treatments.

It's been fifteen years and I rarely think about this challenging period, but the gift from the Great Physician's angel remains in my heart.

~Gail Molsbee Morris

65

The Angel in the Bright Green Jacket

Angels descending, bring from above,
Echoes of mercy, whispers of love.
~Fanny J. Crosby

The late summer heat stuck to me as I slowly helped my husband into the cool of the waiting room. Rog, who was several days post-operative from a major operation to correct stenosis of his spine, was precariously holding onto me, almost too weak to stand. I was looking around frantically for someone to help me, but there seemed to be no hospital personnel in the vicinity. Just as I was beginning to attempt to get my husband across the room to a chair, a tiny woman (I'm 5'2" and this women was no more than 4'10") suddenly appeared at my elbow.

"I will stay with him," she said. "You go find a wheelchair."

Something about her rich dark eyes gave me the confidence to hand him over to her. I hurriedly ran outside, where I had seen some wheelchairs parked beside the entrance. Returning to the waiting room, I deftly positioned the chair behind my husband, locking the wheels just as his legs gave out.

"Thank you for your help," I said, looking deep into those amazing eyes.

The woman smiled, then bent over and kissed my husband's

cheek, whispering into his ear. At this point, I had knelt down to position the foot guards. When I stood up, she was gone.

"Where is she?" I asked Rog. He looked puzzled. I quickly scanned the room, then turned and looked out the door, which I knew had not opened, because each time someone came in or out, a blast of hot air came pouring into the waiting room. In addition, I had not heard any footsteps. The woman had on heels, which would have echoed across the floor.

"She couldn't just disappear," I said as I pushed Rog down to the doctor's office. "This is strange."

"Ya," Rog agreed. "Maybe she was an angel."

At this point, we were sitting waiting for the doctor to see Rog. I looked at my dear husband—something had changed. His face looked less stressed and his eyes had lost their fear.

"What makes you think that?" I asked. Rog wasn't one to make comments like this. I could tell he was serious.

"When she whispered in my ear, she said, 'Don't worry. Everything will be fine.' I just felt such peace. I can't put it in words."

Rog's condition got much worse before it got better. The first operation failed. However, through a series of what I can only describe as miracles, we found the leading surgeon for his type of condition, who not only saved Rog's life but also restored our faith in the medical system.

As for the little woman—I asked several people in the waiting room that day if they had seen her. No one had, which was strange to me because not only was she very small, but she also had long, black hair that went well below her waist and the brightest green jacket I had ever seen. Even in a crowd, she would have stood out!

Several weeks after his final operation, Rog looked up at me (something he had not been able to do for a long time). "You know," he said, smiling, "I just remembered—green is the color for healing. See, she really was an angel!"

~Linda M. Rhinehart Neas

Coffee Shop Angel

Likewise I say to you, there is joy in the presence of the angels of God...
~Luke 15:10

The day started out well. My husband was at work and my daughter Sarah, usually prone to grumpiness, was unusually quiet and content. It was about a year and half since she had been born. Adjusting to being a new stay-at-home mom had been difficult, but I had made it through the hump. Yet, I was troubled.

I had suspected something was different about Sarah for a while now. Incessant crying fits lasting for hours were one indication. Resisting body and eye contact was another. Multiple visits to the Children's Hospital in the middle of the night to diagnose the problem only resulted in perplexed, disinterested ER doctors shrugging their shoulders and dismissing my concern with the standard, "She's fine. It must be a behavioral problem."

Then, one Wednesday, we were out for our usual Baby Chat session run by a local medical center. Women would get together and chat while their babies under the age of two played and interacted on the floor.

The nurse running the program at the center pulled me aside and suggested that I have Sarah examined by a specialist in developmental disorders.

"She is exhibiting signs of autism," she told me gently. "I'm not a doctor so I can't say for sure, but maybe you should see someone."

Then she hugged me when the tears started to spill down my face. I was oddly relieved. Someone else had noticed. It wasn't just me. Now I was going to use all my strength to help my family and daughter get through a possible autism diagnosis.

With all these thoughts running through my mind, I decided to put Sarah in the stroller and go for a walk to the neighborhood coffee shop. The birds were singing and the sun was shining—a typical cheesy start one would see in a happy novel or romantic comedy.

Then the crying started. I was used to the crying. I tried everything—a bottle, walking, rocking, singing—it just wouldn't stop. It was especially hard for me because of the people, the ones who whisper and stare. We all know them.

Mostly they had disapproval on their faces. I could almost read their minds as they speculated about what kind of mother I was: "Why is her child so bad? Why doesn't she discipline her?"

Their sanctimonious sneers and cold stares affected me deeply, yet I could understand them. Before I had my own child, I reacted the same way. I vividly remembered one incident in a mall parking lot, where I observed a mom negotiating with her son, begging him to get into the car so they could go home. I recalled how I shook my head and thought, "Just pick him up and put him in the car!"

Now I was on the receiving end of the judgmental stares. Now, I was the flustered mother constantly holding back tears, pleading with my baby, and trying to find every way possible to calm her irrational behavior. Now I, who had never understood those mothers, pleaded for understanding through watery eyes.

Standing helplessly in the entryway of the coffee shop, I didn't know what to do. Standing still made her cry. Moving the stroller made her cry more. Picking her up made her scream. I felt frozen with frustration, indecision and exhaustion. I avoided the stares as more tears welled up in my eyes.

Then, suddenly, I felt a presence at my back. I turned around to see the friendly smile and gentle eyes of a woman. She was dressed in a coffee shop uniform. Her nametag said "Joy."

"Here, you need this more than I do," she said, handing me a coffee card. I looked down at the gift card in my hands. I couldn't possible take this! I started to protest but she dismissed my objections. "Employees get one coffee card a month as a bonus, so don't worry about the cost." I thanked her profusely. She cooed at Sarah, who had miraculously stopped crying.

I looked up again when I felt her hand on my shoulder. She smiled.

"Hang in there," she whispered, before turning to clear tables.

Taking advantage of Sarah's sudden quiet mood, I rushed to the counter and purchased a much-needed coffee and donut. I shared the pastry with my little girl, smiling at her intense examination of the donut pieces I had placed on her stroller tray.

I had thirty minutes of blessed relief. Sarah had nodded off with a bottle, and I felt so relaxed that I could have dozed myself. Reluctantly, I rose from my table, discarded my garbage and looked around for my coffee angel. She was nowhere in sight.

I grabbed the stroller and walked over to the counter inquiring about where I could find Joy. The young woman behind the counter furrowed her brows in confusion.

"We don't have anyone by that name working here."

I protested, but she just shook her head. She had no idea who I was talking about.

I have visited that coffee shop many times over the last few years, and have never seen the woman again. Not long after that day, Sarah was given a diagnosis of autism. When I have a stressful day, or feel lost and overwhelmed, I think of Joy and the strength and support she gave me. I believe in my heart someone is watching over me and my little girl and that we are never alone.

~Christine Pincombe-DeCaen

Chicken Soup for the Soul

Two Pounds of Divine Intervention

Angels deliver Fate to our doorstep—and anywhere else it is needed.
~Jessi Lane Adams

There was a time I believed in coincidence. But that was prior to meeting my four-legged soul mate. Now, I am sure there is something much bigger at work in the universe. There also was a time when it irritated me to have people equate their pets to humans. Again, that was till it happened to me.

I had just been given a death sentence. At forty-five, a random virus had attacked my heart and left it functioning at a mere thirteen percent. Just like that. Active, working, raising kids one day. Being wheeled out of the hospital and lifted into the car to go home and die quietly a week later. What happened during that week is still a mystery to me.

Unable to take care of even the basics of my everyday living, I spent my days looking at cute puppy faces at various pet adoption sites online. Quite a contrast… someone who should be making her final arrangements, instead, filling every moment viewing and fantasizing about owning one of these yipping, yapping little furry balls full of life. Even I, the eternal optimist, knew this was the most ridiculous idea I had ever entertained. But I wasn't hurting anyone. And it filled my days and gave me hope. It became an obsession when I had nothing left.

The days stretched on. My test results remained grave. There was no improvement. And yet, I was still here. Sort of in limbo. Then, one day I received an odd and unsolicited e-mail from a woman who stated she had just the puppy I was looking for. What? What puppy? I hadn't made any requests for puppies (except in my mind). I was only window-shopping! She said she would be at an address near my home that Saturday and to please stop by.

Against his better judgment, my husband drove me to this mysterious location. I huffed and puffed up the driveway and into the yard where puppies of every size, shape and color ran with wild abandon. People were coming and going quickly and leaving with "puppy care packets" and their new additions. I still was a little mystified about how I even got here or why I came.

Soon all the puppies were off to their respective new homes, the yard was empty and quiet, and the woman turned to me.

"Can I help you?" Our brief conversation revealed that she had no idea about any e-mail regarding a puppy. I felt a little silly and more than depressed as I headed back down the driveway. It was about this time that a matronly woman emerged from the house and into the yard, wearing an old-fashioned floral apron. I offered a weak smile as we passed, and from the corner of my eye noticed a shaggy black and white head and little black nose poking out to see what was going on. I was immediately intrigued. As I got closer, the nosey little rag mop nearly jumped into my arms. If I had died right then, I would have died happy.

But my excitement was soon derailed when the woman said, "Don't take an interest in this one. She has severe heart problems and won't be with us much longer." What? Did she say what I think she said? Heart problems? Jackpot! My new "baby" was already in my arms and covering me with kisses.

After lots of grave warnings and signing of waivers, etc., my new puppy and I made our way to the car to break the news to the next naysayer. But jumping from seat to seat and right on my husband's shoulder, I didn't have much to do with convincing him. He was sold. So home we went. To our home that would never be the same.

And, as they say, the rest is history. And still is. That was ten years ago. Jasmine and I haven't spent a day apart since then. The vet never found a trace of any heart issues with her, and my test results began to show gradual improvement from the day I brought her home, and I am still here a decade later.

So, yes, I'm a believer in fate, divine intervention, or what have you.

Coincidence? Not so much.

~JP Jackson

The Night
My Angel Came

And the prayer of faith will save the sick, and the Lord will raise him up.
~James 5:15

I had stood in the doctor's waiting room because if I sat down, I would not be able to get out of the chair. It had taken half an hour for my friend Joann to help me out of the car. Other patients watched me with pity.

Shortly, the nurse came to escort me to see the doctor, who sat at his desk with my file and test results laid before him. His expression was sober, and I knew that I was in for some bad news.

With a sigh, he looked up and greeted me as his nurse helped me into a seat. He got right to the point. The diagnosis was grim. There were herniated discs in my neck and back. Without back surgery, I would be paralyzed and in a wheelchair within six months. My world was shattered.

I was dazed as Joann drove me back to the facility in silence. What should I do? It was not a simple surgery, and according to the doctor, success was not guaranteed; but without it, I would be paralyzed.

I was a single mom with two sons, the assistant administrator in a residential program for mentally challenged children. It was a freak accident on a missionary trip to Jamaica that had left me crippled and in constant excruciating neck and back pain, with sciatica too. After months of treatment, prescribed bed rest, medication, and physical therapy, the physician gave me the ultimatum. It was a shock, but before making a decision, I decided to go home and pray.

The days passed with no change in my condition. I could hardly get around, yet I managed to continue my office responsibilities with a lot of help from the staff. I felt that I probably should have the surgery, but I just couldn't seem to schedule it.

One morning, when it took almost an hour just to get out of bed, I decided that I'd better make the call before paralysis set in. I started to dial the number. My heart began to pound, and my palms were sweaty. That's only natural, I thought, but I hung up. Somehow I just couldn't go through with it.

I'm not sure if it was that night or several nights later that I had retired early, just to try to get relief from the pain. Suddenly, I awoke from a deep sleep. The bedroom was dark, and the door was closed, but a gradual light appeared near the foot of my bed. I looked at the window, but it was dark outside. The corner of the room gradually got brighter and brighter when suddenly the form of an angel appeared, sitting on the foot of the bed. The angel was very tall—its head almost touched the ceiling even while seated. The light became so bright that the whole room lit up from its presence.

I squinted and wondered if I was dreaming. I looked around just to make sure I was not seeing things. The angel did not speak a word, and yet a sense of peace and wellbeing now filled me. The angel's presence gave me a deep assurance that everything was going to be all right. All my questions were unanswered, and yet every former fear was quieted.

I don't know how long this visitation lasted, but the angel just disappeared and the room darkened. Every bit of confusion and panic had left me.

The next day and for some months to follow, I still suffered from pain and limited movement. But I had decided that I would not have the surgery. If paralysis came, I would cope with it. I knew I was not alone. An angel watched over me, and I was at peace about my future.

The day came when I realized the pain was diminishing. I no longer needed a walking cane. It happened gradually, but eventually every bit of pain left, and I was fully restored.

This experience happened over thirty years ago, and there has never been a recurrence of this condition. I'm sure my angel still looks out for me.

~Penny Smith

The Stranger

*Do not forget to entertain strangers, for by so doing some people have
entertained angels without knowing it.*
~Hebrews 13:2

"Do you believe in angels?" I asked Papa one day while we were hanging out together, just the two of us.

"Well," he answered, "sit down and I'll tell you a story." As I scooted next to him on the porch swing, he began telling me about when he was a little boy.

"Times were tough back then," he said. "People didn't have much. My parents worked hard at the mill to provide for me, my brothers and my sisters. Food was scarce, but somehow we always managed to have enough.

"One day my brother, Jim got very sick. He was shivering, but when I touched his skin, it felt like he'd been sitting next to the hot stove all morning. My mama called for the doctor and he came to our house right away.

"'Give your son this medicine twice a day,' he told my mama. 'Make sure he gets plenty of rest, and I'll be back to check on him in the morning.'"

"What happened?" I asked.

"Well, when the doctor came the next day, he said Jim's condition had worsened. And over the next few days, he grew sicker and sicker.

He couldn't eat and eventually grew so weak that he couldn't get out of bed.

"Finally one day after checking him over, the doctor told my mama that Jim had contracted a rare virus and there was nothing else he could do for him. He helped my mama make a bed for Jim in the kitchen near the stove so Jim would be comfortable and warm."

"Oh, no," I gasped. "What did your mama do then?"

"She sent my older brother to the mill to get my daddy, and then she started cooking supper. She made some cornbread and heated up some milk to go with it. While we were waiting for my brother and daddy to get home, there was a knock at the door. Thinking it was my daddy, I ran to answer it. There stood a tall, thin man who I had never seen before. His clothes were dirty and he carried a small knapsack in his arms. My mama came up behind me and asked, 'Can I help you sir?'

"You see, because we lived in a mill village, there were always people passing through. They would jump the rails and ride from place to place looking for work. Word had spread that my parents were generous people so we often had strangers stopping by asking for food.

"'Yes, ma'am,' the stranger answered. 'I was wondering if you might have a little food to spare.'

"'Well,' my mama answered, 'we don't have much, but it's enough to warm your bones. Come on in.' As mama fixed the stranger something to eat, he glanced at Jim on the bed near the stove.

"'Is that your boy?' he asked.

"'Yes,' my mama answered with tears welling up in her eyes. 'He's very sick and the doctor says he's not gonna' make it.'

"'Do you mind if I lay my hands on him and pray?' he asked.

"'Not at all,' Mama answered. The stranger kneeled down next to Jim and placed one of his dirty, callused hands on Jim's forehead, and with the other he held onto Jim's hands. He closed his eyes and mumbled something that I couldn't quite make out. I looked over at my mama and she seemed to be praying along with the stranger. Her head was hanging down, her eyes were closed and tears were streaming down her face. I grabbed her hand and she gave mine a squeeze. After praying for my brother, the stranger ate the warm milk and cornbread mixture, thanked my mama for her generosity and went on his way.

"The next morning, Jim was up running around chasing my older brother and begging my mama to let him go outside. When the doctor arrived to check on Jim, he seemed a bit confused.

"'What did y'all give this child?' the doctor asked my mama. 'I've never seen anything like this. His illness is gone... completely vanished.'

"'Thank you dear Jesus,' my mama exclaimed. Although we searched for the tall stranger who had prayed for Jim, we never found him. My mama said that maybe he was an angel. She told us that sometimes God sends people into our lives to test us. She said that in the Bible, God says, 'For I was hungry, and you fed me. I was thirsty, and you gave me a drink. I was a stranger, and you invited me into your home... and the King will say, "I tell you the truth, when you did it to one of the least of these my brothers and sisters, you were doing it to me!"'"

Papa leaned in close and whispered, "Now, I don't know for sure if the stranger was an angel or not, but I can tell you one thing...."

"What's that?" I asked.

"We should always help people in need. Because you just never know...."

~Christy Westbrook

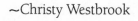

A Touch of Comfort

Prayer enlarges the heart until it is capable of containing God's gift of himself.
~Mother Teresa

I t was the lowest point of my life. After the breakdown of my marriage, my children and I had moved out of the only home they knew. We hadn't had time to finish unpacking the boxes when I got a phone call that would change our lives even more. My best friend's house had burned to the ground that morning; her three sons and three nieces, still asleep in their beds, were lost. They were living in an older mobile home on a beautiful piece of mountain property, where they had planned to build a house. Her sister and brother-in-law were outside working the garden when the fire started; my friend was taking her husband to work. The old home burned down so quickly that they were unable to get in to rescue the children.

Another friend and I made the six-hour trip to be with her. There are no words of comfort that can take away the pain of that loss. I could only give her someone to lean on, someone to talk to, someone to pray for her and offer any kind of assistance I could. We stayed until after the funeral, feeling helpless to ease her pain. The heaviness in my heart was nothing like the burden they carried, but it began to wear me down.

My children were going through their own grief, having been playmates with her children. When they returned to school after summer break, I got a call from my son's teacher. "I'm calling because of a disturbing picture your son drew in class today," she said. "It is a picture of a house with huge orange and red flames coming out of it. Was there an event in his life to explain this?" I told her about the tragedy and she promised to keep me informed if my son showed signs of needing help to cope with it. At the time my children seemed more concerned about me instead of processing their own loss. I was so involved with my friend's loss that I worried I wasn't providing what they needed.

One day my friend called me in a panic. She could no longer "smell" her youngest son. "I could always remember how he smelled in the evening after playing all day. He would climb onto my lap, lay his head on my shoulder, and I would rock him. He always smelled like a mixture of dirt and sweat. After he died I would sit in the rocker and I could still feel his weight against me and remember how he smelled." She cried, huge sobs that tore at my soul. "I can't smell him anymore!" I listened as she cried, connected by the phone line and praying that would be enough. There are no words of comfort for a grieving mother who can't remember the scent of her child.

We stayed on the phone for close to an hour; most of the time no words were spoken, only her sobs and my silent prayers. When we ended the call I was drained. I felt so inadequate to help my friend. I felt like a failure as a friend, a wife and a mother.

I went to my room to rest for a while. The late afternoon had heated my room to an uncomfortable temperature, so I pushed the blanket down to the bottom of the bed to lie down on the cooler sheets. I was overcome with grief and despair and cried uncontrollably until I was overcome with exhaustion. The autumn evening had crept in, cooling the room considerably. I was lying on my left side, feeling cold, but too exhausted to bother reaching down to the bottom of the bed to retrieve the cover.

I began to drift off to sleep, when I felt the covers being pulled over me. Then I felt the weight of someone sit on the bed behind me. Someone began to pat my shoulder as if to give comfort. My daughter, I thought; she must have heard me crying and come in to comfort me. It was not uncommon after the fire for her to crawl into bed with me during the night. I remember thinking that I should roll over and give her a kiss, but I was just too tired and allowed myself to drift off to sleep.

I slept deeply through the night, never changing position, and woke up refreshed. I smiled at the memory of my daughter coming in to comfort me, then remembered something: my children were with their dad. No one was home but me.

I sat up in bed, trying to wrap my mind around this information. Was it an angel? My grandmother or another relative who had passed on? One thing was certain—I was visited in the night by someone who offered me comfort. I felt energized from a night of restorative sleep. On the darkest night of my life, God made sure I wasn't alone. It not only brought me comfort that night, but the memory brings comfort every time I start to feel despair. On the darkest night God will shine a light.

~Beth Arvin

Angels
Among Us

Love from Beyond

Not Forsaken

God could not be everywhere, so he created mothers.
~Jewish Proverb

The baby hadn't moved. I should have been concerned, but I was nauseated, hot, and in desperate need of a nap. As I sat on the couch, nodding while the sounds from the television began to fade, Grandma Maudie's voice called out to me. "Kathy Pollard, I know you're not sleeping sitting up like that. Get your tail to your room and lie down. Give that baby some breathing room."

I slowly opened my eyes so I could fully view my grandmother, sitting at her sewing machine with a cigarette dangling from her mouth. On a good day I would have sat up and argued with her, maybe tell her to mind her own business. But I was thirty-eight weeks into a pregnancy I was more than ready to see come to term, and with all of the vomiting and general discomfort, I didn't have the energy to partake in any kind of dispute. "Okay, Grandma," was all I managed to say. Besides, I knew I would be asleep as soon as my head hit the pillow.

As soon as I lay down, the air in the room seemed to split from ceiling to floor and open up, allowing a breezy wave to break through the gap. I eyed the peculiar phenomenon and then saw my mother. She looked like she was surfing on that wave of air, and she was coming toward me. I should have been excited, curious or even awestruck over seeing her. However, my mother had died three years earlier—shot to death by my stepfather—and I had not forgiven her or God for leaving me behind. I frowned and turned away to show my discontent. I did not care if she would be hurt by the dismissive gesture; she had wounded me first, reneging on a promise to always be there for me.

I felt her presence hovering by the bed and trembled because, after all, she was supposed to be in Heaven doing afterlife things, not standing in my bedroom as if she wanted to have a chat. I remained tight-lipped, hoping she would get the hint and leave. However, she would not move. She would not vanish, or do any other ghostly thing except shimmer and sway. Annoyed by her dogged determination, I turned to look up at her. "Why are you here?"

"Are you okay?" The sound of her voice soothed all of the hurt I had carried in my heart the past three years, and I realized how much I missed my mother. Nevertheless, I was stubborn and I gave her a contemptuous frown. "Why do you care?" I wanted her to sass me and to say something like, "I care because I'm your mother and I asked you a question," but instead her face molded into sympathetic love.

"Are you okay?" she repeated as she stood waiting on that breeze, her body gently flowing up and down with the swaying of the wave.

My mother's patience disturbed me and I wanted her to vanish from my sight. I did not want her to see my shame from my being short with her. "Yeah, I'm okay," I whined.

She looked at my stomach and worry lines formed across her brow. "Are you sure?"

I thought about the baby. He still hadn't moved. But, I hadn't forgiven her for leaving me. I tightened my lips, narrowed my eyes, and clenched my jaw. "Leave me alone," I said.

My mother tilted her head and looked at me with eyes so full of love and compassion, I almost wept. "Okay, Kathy." She shrugged her shoulders, turned and rode away on the wave of air.

I watched my mother float away until she was a tiny speck of light. When that light vanished, I sat up in bed, threw my legs over the side and rubbed my belly. The baby still did not move. I stood, stretched and decided I would eat some leftover chili. Maybe the spiciness would energize the baby.

Grandma looked up at me as I walked by her on the way to the kitchen. "I thought you were sleepy."

I could barely hear her over the whir of her sewing machine and I spoke a bit loudly so she would hear me. "Mama came to visit."

The whirring stopped and Grandma jumped from her chair. "What did she want? What did she say?" She grabbed my arm and pulled me toward the couch. Then she forced me to sit down. "Tell me everything."

I yanked my arm away. "She looked at my stomach and asked me if I was okay," I said, rubbing my wrist.

Grandma drew her hand to her mouth and gasped. "Has the baby moved today?"

I shrugged. "No." I frowned at her, mainly because I was ashamed of not responding to my baby's lack of movement. I felt abashed because even my dead mother knew enough to break through the boundaries of life and death to check on her unborn grandson's status, and here I was acting nonchalant.

The next few minutes were a blur. Before I could do or say anything, Grandma had woken my grandfather from his nap, rushed us all into the car, and commanded my grandfather to "hightail it" to the hospital.

The visit at the hospital was also a haze of events after the initial tests of heart rate, reflex and breathing were done on the baby. A team of doctors and nurses raced to revitalize my lethargic son. After a whirlwind of injections, probing, more testing and monitoring, the doctors finally gave the baby a thumbs-up. They released me later that night, telling me that if I had arrived just a few minutes later the baby might have died.

During the car ride home Grandma scolded me for allowing a whole day to go by without movement from the baby. "Lucky for you your mama was there. Lucky for you she is still looking out for you."

The next week Brandon was born a strong and healthy boy. On the night of his birth, I held my newborn in my arms and cried for my mother in ways I had refused to the past three years. I cried because I loved her. I cried because I missed her. I cried because even in death she had not betrayed me. I also asked God's forgiveness for ever doubting His provisions and I thanked Him for my son and my mama, the angel who never stopped watching over me.

~Kathryn Y. Pollard

Night Visit

Earth has no sorrow that Heaven cannot heal.
~Author Unknown

Daddy stood at the foot of my bed. "Don't cry, Jeanie girl, I'm fine. It's wonderful here. Don't cry."

I stared at him while wiping tears from my face. "Okay," I whispered.

After a few moments, he was gone. I lay there for a long time. Was it a dream? No, I wasn't asleep. I saw him, heard him, I was sure of it. I knew what he told me, and it made me feel better. Even though I was filled with sorrow, my father's visit left me with a sense of peace. It was the night before his funeral.

I stayed in bed until light began to shine through the windows, then rose to make coffee. My mother and young brother would soon be awake and our dreaded day would begin. I wouldn't tell them about my visit from Daddy. It would upset them, whether they believed me or not.

Mother dragged into the kitchen and with shaking hands poured coffee into her mug. I knew she was thinking, as I was, that Daddy always delivered her coffee each morning to her bedside as her "wake up call." We just couldn't imagine life without him.

I had asked all the "why" questions: Why Daddy? Why such a godly man? Why, when he was only forty-four? Now I was resigned to the reality since I could do nothing to change it, only be changed by it.

It was going to be hot as only August in Atlanta can be. I looked in on my brother and he was still lying on his bed, staring at the ceiling. "You awake? Time to think about moving."

"I'm not going."

"You have to, Steve." I struggled to keep my voice calm and low when I really wanted to scream. None of us wanted to go through the ordeal of this funeral. I finally hit upon the words I knew would move him. "Daddy would want you to be there."

He nodded, then grimaced to hide the tears in his eyes and threw his legs over the side of the bed. I realized then that this was perhaps harder for him than any of us. He was thirteen years old.

Daddy's words helped me through the funeral service: the music and flowers, the weeping crowd of family and friends who poured out of the chapel doors and stood on the sidewalk and grassy lawn, the faces of my mother and brother. I kept thinking about how my father was at peace and no longer in pain, and how he glowed when he told me not to cry for him. It helped. It didn't take away all of my grief but it helped. I felt he was with us, or at least with me.

I realized that grieving was for us, not for him. He was fine. It was those of us left to live without him who would struggle and weep—for ourselves and the years ahead, for events in our lives that would have a big hole in them because he wasn't there.

One such important time was my wedding the following year when my brother reluctantly walked me down the aisle. Only on reflection years later did I realize that my leaving was yet another blow in his young life. My husband's career as a Navy pilot took us away from all things familiar as we traveled across the country and then to Japan. We were away for over three years before being able to return home.

Sitting with my family around the old maple kitchen table one evening after dinner, we began to talk about how Daddy had been cheated out of so much life. My husband suddenly blurted out, "You know he came to see Jeanie the night before his funeral."

They stared at him and then at me for confirmation. I explained how he stood at the foot of my bed and reassured me that everything was wonderful and he was happy and I shouldn't cry for him. Steve then softly told us that Daddy had also come to see him that night, but he had convinced himself he must have been dreaming. Then Mother wiped her eyes and revealed to us that he had come to her too, to tell her of his love for her and that he'd be waiting but she had work yet to do raising their children, especially my brother.

We all talked at once, eager to finally share with each other. We'd always been afraid we wouldn't be believed and worried that telling about Daddy's visit would cause pain. We stayed up until the wee hours of the morning recalling every detail and the wonder of it. What joy to be able to talk about those night visits and how comforting to know we shared something so rare and beautiful.

It's been more than fifty years now, yet I can relive those moments as if they happened minutes ago. His angelic visit was my father's greatest gift to me. I carry it with me always.

~Jean Haynie Stewart

73

How Did He Know?

While we are mourning the loss of our friend,
others are rejoicing to meet him behind the veil.
~John Taylor

I was on a cruise in another land, far from the accident, when it happened. My cousin and I had just disembarked at our second port of call and stood waiting on the dock for my father and brother. They were right behind us, but were not permitted to disembark. An overseas phone call had been placed to our room. My father had to collect the message from the front desk before he could go ashore so my cousin and I waited on the dock for them to return.

We sat down and chatted about the places we would visit that day. Twenty minutes passed and still my father and brother did not return. My cousin asked, "Do you think something is wrong? They've been gone a long time." I didn't hesitate in saying, "Of course not. It is probably something to do with Dad's work." My cousin nodded and we continued chatting. Five more minutes passed. At last we spotted them coming off the ship.

I knew by the looks on their faces that something had happened. My brother and father emerged wearing the same expression, one of worry and disbelief. I ran to them and asked with fear mounting, "What's happened? What's wrong?" My brother pulled me aside. Dad went to Jenny and took her in his arms. We begged to know what was wrong, panic in our voices.

"You're scaring me. What is it?" I asked.

My brother lowered his voice and said, "It's Terry. He's been killed." I looked at Jenny. She was still pleading with my father to tell her what had happened. He was trying to gently lead her back inside the ship, to a private room where we could tell her what had happened to her brother. I looked at my own brother and neither of us knew what to say or do.

We got Jenny to a private area, sat her down, and told her that her brother had been killed. He had been a young police officer, thirty-two years old, with a wife, a three-year-old boy and a newborn baby girl. I assumed, at first, that he had been killed while on duty, but then we learned it was a car accident that had happened early in the morning on his way to work, just down the road from his home. Jenny's cries filled the room. I held her and tried to calm her.

What do you say to somebody who has been told such horrible news? So we sat in silence, her crying and my arm around her, giving her what human warmth I could.

We left the cruise and flew home on the next flight out. As the plane began its descent, Jenny, who had been silent the entire flight, began to quietly sob to herself. I looked at my cousin and wanted to help her, but didn't know how. I learned that sometimes words are not needed. I hugged her close and cried silently with her.

Our arrival in Toronto made the tragedy suddenly real. Being told about the accident while so far away made it seem like a horrible nightmare. Landing in Toronto brought us back to reality. We were no longer on a cruise, enjoying the weather and eating wonderful food, instead we had returned home for a funeral.

Several months later, I was traveling in England. The tragedy was still with me and I often found myself thinking of the day we were told about Terry's death. On the streets of Windsor I recalled my last conversation with him. Terry was quite a bit older than me, so we hadn't spoken much growing up. The one lengthy conversation I had ever had with Terry happened just a few days before the accident. I was at Jenny's house. Jenny was busy in the kitchen cooking, and Terry and I were deep in conversation in the living room. Our topic of discussion was the afterlife. Terry believed in it. He believed that there was a place we would go after death. We would see loved ones there once more. He firmly believed this, although I expressed my doubts. Some days I believed and some days I didn't. I found it chilling that Terry's last conversation with me was about the afterlife and his belief in its existence.

Still thinking about Terry and our conversation, I found myself in front of a church. I entered and sat down in one of the pews. As I sat with my thoughts, a man approached me. He was an elderly man, perhaps in his seventies, named Stan. He asked if he might sit with me. I smiled and nodded. He began to tell me stories of the church and the spirits that were believed to haunt it. When he finished, he looked earnestly into my eyes and said, "Forgive me, but I can see that you are sad. Someone has died in your family?" I was a bit taken aback at this blunt question, but I answered in the affirmative.

"It was a man and he died young, in a car accident, didn't he?"

I looked at this man and wondered how he knew what he did. Confused, I nodded and said nothing, unnerved at how much this stranger knew.

"You wish you had said more to him the day you last saw him and you wish you had let him know that you loved him," he said.

I started to cry. The stranger took my hands gently and said, "Your cousin knows you loved him and he wants you to know that he is happy and is working with children who have entered heaven. He loves the children and is very content where he is now."

I sat there, holding the hands of a stranger, and cried. I am not a person who cries easily. I'm always the "strong one" for others to lean on, but that day I was leaning on a complete stranger for emotional support. I left Stan that day only knowing his first name.

Months later Jenny was telling me about a dream Terry's wife had had. It had been so vivid that she felt as though Terry truly visited her. Terry told her not to be sad anymore, that he was happy because he was doing something he loved. He was working with children in heaven.

I had not told anyone about the conversation I'd had in Windsor,

England, in a quiet church, with an old man named Stan. I had kept everything to myself and this is the first time that I am writing of it. It was as though Stan had truly spoken with Terry. How else could he have known what he did? The eerie coincidence of the dream and Stan's reassuring words about Terry's "new life" chilled me.

Years have passed since that day, yet I still find myself thinking about Stan. Was he an angel? I wish I could meet him again and let him know how much his words consoled me.

~Laurie Ann Mangru

74

Some Angels Wear Hats

Angels are speaking to all of us... some of us are only listening better.
~Author Unknown

"I can talk to dead people." For most folks that statement alone would be evidence enough of a mental illness. But rest assured my mental health is intact. I've simply had experiences I can't explain any other way, or believe me I would. Who wouldn't want to avoid those worried looks from family and friends?

My encounters are nothing like the frightening experiences the little boy, Cole Sear, had in the movie *The Sixth Sense*. Instead my conversations unfold as I write and the dialogue occurs in my head—thoughts ping pong back and forth like the quick banter in a Hepburn/Tracy movie—except one of the people lobbing back responses isn't me.

I discovered my skill by accident years ago. I used to journal before I'd go to bed and on those pages I'd wrestle with my life's problems. After a while I not only wrote down my issues but I started to write down some pretty great solutions too. For quite some time, problems and resolutions blended well in the privacy of my journal, and then one night I was so impressed with a response, I read it to my partner, Ann.

"That answer doesn't even sound like your voice," she said. "You'd say it differently—use other words and phrases."

That got us thinking. What if all the great answers were coming from someone or something other than me? We decided I should explore the possibility and the next night while I was journaling I explicitly asked, "Who am I speaking to?"

I didn't know then that the response would change my life.

"I'm your Grandpa Art, the one who wore hats."

Now my hat-wearing grandfather died roughly seven years before I was even born. We'd never had any kind of relationship. I didn't know what his voice sounded like, not to mention he was… dead! I'd been having conversations and getting great advice, but I was still uncertain of the true source.

"Prove it," I said, certain it had to be my own imagination or subconscious.

The voice replied, "Okay. I'll tell you a story and you can verify it with someone you trust."

"Fair enough," I said as I wondered how in the world I would ever be able to verify anything. I'd never admit, except to Ann, that I thought I was talking to my dead grandfather.

He went on. "Years ago, when we lived on our farm in Wisconsin, there was a lamb. Its mother died giving birth. Your mom and Toots had to take care of it. They fed it with a nipple bottle until it was old enough to be on its own."

I had never heard that story before and since my mom had passed away when I was a teenager, there was only one living person who could confirm the tale: my Aunt Vi.

Toots, as her father had called her, was my mother's only sister. She had stepped up to fill the motherly void left after Mom's death and I trusted her implicitly.

"Go ahead and ask her about it. Better yet, I'll have Toots call you tomorrow," he said confidently.

Exhausted and unsettled by my experience, I went to bed. I woke up the next morning and told Ann about my writing. We were both fascinated by the conversation but uncertain about what would come next, and then we were swept away by the demands of our busy Saturday.

Later that same day, I returned home for only an hour to shower and change clothes. The phone rang and Ann answered it. I could hear her footsteps as she approached our bedroom. She handed me the cordless phone and whispered, "It's your Aunt Vi."

My face mirrored Ann's—a pop-eyed, heebie-jeebies expression. The sound track from *The Twilight Zone* blared in my mind as I remembered my grandfather's promise.

I raised the receiver to my ear and said, "Hi Vi, how are you?"

"I'm good. I was just sitting here thinking about you and feeling a little lonesome for you, so I thought I'd call and see how things are."

"That was sweet of you," I said.

After a few minutes of catching up on family news I steered her towards reminiscing about when she and my mom were young. I didn't want to come right out and tell her about the night before. My rational left brain didn't want to sound like a wacko, so I said, "Tell me about growing up on the farm. Did you and Mom have pets?"

"Well, we had a German Sheppard named Bruno. During thunderstorms he was always afraid. He'd hide in the barn or the outhouse. Afterwards we'd have a hard time finding him, to say nothing of having to clean him up."

"That sounds awful," I said.

I had heard that story before, so I tried to steer her in another direction.

"Did you have farm animals too?"

"Dad raised a few cows and an occasional pig to butcher. Sometimes he'd bring me with him to the stockyard in St. Paul and buy me lunch. When I was ten I wanted to grow up to be a waitress at that restaurant; I loved their white uniforms. Can you imagine?"

We both laughed. I wanted to keep her on the subject so I asked, "Did you ever have any sheep on the farm?"

"I think we did, but I don't remember for sure."

I was quietly disappointed. Then Vi continued, "Oh, we did have sheep! I remember one time there was a little lamb that had lost its mother and your mom and I fed it with a nipple bottle. One night we snuck the lamb into our bedroom and Dad pretended he didn't see us doing it."

My hands began to shake and my throat tightened as tears began to run down my cheeks. I couldn't talk, and Vi seemed to sense that something was happening on my end of the line.

"Kris, are you alright?" she asked.

I finally gathered enough composure to speak and told her everything that had happened the night before. When I was done with my jumbled, tear-filled account of my late night conversation with her father, Vi's end of the line was as silent as mine had been only moments before. I was certain she thought I was crazy. After what seems like forever she finally said, "Well, tell Dad that Toots said hi… and I miss him."

All I could say was, "I will."

That was my first experience with talking to an "angel," although there have been countless others. Maybe there's another explanation for it, but for me my experiences speak for themselves. I'll just keep writing down the conversations while I work to get more comfortable sharing them with people, and I'll leave the more rational explanation to those who will always remain skeptics.

~Kris Flaa

75

Bandit's Run

Dogs are miracles with paws.
~Susan Ariel Rainbow Kennedy

I was fourteen years old and lost in the woods. My hand gripped the steel handle of my father's pistol and I shivered from the cool of the coming night. I had fallen down a rocky ridge about fifteen feet above a deep valley and rolled into a dry creek bed below. I had a deep cut on my left arm and I was bleeding heavily. I didn't think too much of it, as I had cut myself on the sharp rocks many times before. I sat down hard on the stump of an old cottonwood tree and wondered what to do next.

Our family had been coming to the backwoods of Ozark country since I was born; my two older sisters, mom and dad, and now a baby brother. The little cabin sat against the hills near Lake of the Ozarks, and we would drive down from Kansas City, Missouri and spend every weekend fishing, swimming, hunting, and walking through the deep woods and rocky ravines that formed the landscape. This time, I had gone out alone. My father had given me the gun for squirrel hunting, or maybe a rabbit if one happened by, but now it felt like its purpose had become much more sinister.

Beyond the grove of dead elms, I heard the snapping of brush and the familiar low grunting sounds of wild boars. My father had warned me about them. He had come across a herd of them years before and barely escaped with his life. Now, here I was, lost, cold, alone. The sun had just gone down over the farthest hill and the woods were getting dark.

I pointed the gun in front of me and got to my knees. There was a pack of them, circling. Their yellow eyes cut a path in the darkness. The blood on my arm was thick and dry but they must have smelled it. There are too many of them, I thought, but I was suddenly unafraid as I heard my father's words: "If you ever get into trouble out there, stay calm and do what I've taught you to do. Survive."

The largest of the group charged me first, missing my arm by inches.

I rose to my feet, gun in hand.

They were all growling and grunting now, snorting and biting at each other.

I could barely see the coarse, wiry hair on their backs standing straight up, all the way to the dark red skin of their necks. I kicked at them and shouted.

I had three bullets in the gun. How many of the boars were there? Maybe six.

From behind me came a rattle of brush and then, one of the boars was on me, aiming for my neck. I fell back, and dropped the gun.

I brought my feet up to my chest and prepared to fight for my life.

Then suddenly, there was another growl. But it was a much different sound this time. It was lower than the excited half-squeals of the wild boar and it froze us all. I saw my chance and got to my feet, spotting the gun a few feet away.

As I went for it, I saw him. It was Bandit, my father's old coonhound. He lurched through the forest, his teeth all fury, showing no fear.

I picked up the gun and ran to him.

Two boars leapt on the dog's back, their golden eyes now green and focused. Bandit rolled, as he was taught to do.

They fell from his back and the dog was on his feet again, positioned in front of me.

I leveled the gun and aimed. I fired.

The shot was deafening in the still of night and roared up the sides of the hills, echoing through the ravine. The whole herd took off running with Bandit in hot pursuit. I called after him as I ran blindly through the woods, following the loud bawl of the old hound. I was up and over a small hill, into the next ravine. Bandit was getting farther and farther away but I kept on running, trying to keep up. Before I knew it I was in the clearing where I had first started the day, only about 100 yards from the cabin. I could hear my mother's voice calling for me and I ran to her.

My father was at her side, already putting on his jacket to come and search for me. I hugged my mother and burst out crying, trying to explain what had happened. I could feel my father's hand on my shoulder, he was telling me to calm down, everything was all right. I looked at him and said, "It was Bandit, Dad. He saved me. He came out of the woods, full speed, he..."

"Bandit?" my father asked. The look on his face was one of confusion and wonder. "David, Bandit's been dead for two years now, remember? We buried him up past those two hills, by that creek bed in the ravine. It must have been another dog, son."

I was going to tell him, tell them both, that I saw his face, I knew it was him, but something told me not to. As we all walked into the cabin together, I could hear a wail in the distance, coming from over the hills and down in a small ravine.

Or it could have been the wind.

~David Magill

76

A Mysterious Dancer

Dancers are the messengers of the gods.
~Martha Graham

A few months after my mother's surgery and treatment for breast cancer, she was feeling well enough to return to our beloved dance classes at our local gym. But she still had to go through a number of tests, one of which had her very worried. I figured that going to our usual class on Wednesday night would calm her nerves but I could sense her anxiety as we stood in the crowded room waiting for class to begin.

I took my usual spot in the second row while my mother stood in front of me. Suddenly someone stepped between us. I was a little frustrated that someone had cut in front of me, especially this woman, who I hadn't seen before. She was obviously a newcomer. I could sense that it was going to be a bad night. What could be worse than having someone new in front of you the entire time, stumbling over herself because she doesn't know any of the moves?

Our instructor stepped onto the small wooden stage in the front of the room, asking if there was anyone new to the class that night. A few people in the back raised their hands, but oddly, the woman in front of me didn't raise hers. It was then that I noticed something else out of the ordinary. This woman definitely had a sense of fashion that I had never seen before! From her fluffy brown hair to her big glasses and patterned shorts, this woman was dressed like she had stepped right out of the 1980s!

The volume of the stereo was cranked up, and we began our dances. To my surprise, the mysterious woman in front of me knew all of the moves to each and every song. She didn't make a single mistake! Our instructor must have noticed her as well. Usually, students will get invited up on the stage to dance. For one song, she made what I thought was a very interesting choice: my mother and the mysterious woman!

After a long, exhausting hour, Mom and I were back in the car heading home. "Did you see that woman?" my mother marveled, beaming with excitement.

"Yes," I answered. "Who could miss that crazy woman in her disco clothing?"

"Jess," my mother exclaimed. "That woman looked just like my Aunt Pam!"

Then Mom started to explain how every detail about this woman reminded her of her very special aunt who had passed on years before. It sounded like this woman and Aunt Pam were exactly the same. Her clothes, her hair, even the mysterious woman's perfect teeth — it was as if my mother's aunt was actually standing beside her the whole time. My mother and her Aunt Pam had been very close throughout my mother's childhood. They had always lived under the same roof, and Pam was like a second mother. Pam would always give my mother make-up tips before dates and was a key provider of other advice.

Sadly, Aunt Pam had passed away after a brave two-year fight. My mother had been one of her main caregivers, driving her to doctor appointments and chemotherapy, along with staying by her bedside in the hospital. Although it had been many years since Aunt Pam's passing, the two had something very special in common: breast cancer.

Suddenly, Mom's eyes grew wide. "Do you think it could have been an angel?"

That question had me feeling a bit lost. My mother had always been fascinated by stories about angels, but I wasn't quite the believer. The whole thing just had to be a coincidence, I mused. An angel coming in the form of my mother's aunt, in the middle of a workout class of all places! It seemed a little too far-fetched for a skeptic like me.

While I had my doubts, I replied with a "Maybe, Mom." She seemed so encouraged by this reminder of her aunt; I just couldn't break her spirit, especially since she had been so distraught over the upcoming tests. Surely, I thought, the woman in the patterned shorts would be back, and not suddenly vanish like all the angels in the stories I'd been told.

The weeks passed, and I could see a new, more positive attitude in my mother. One by one, her test results came back "normal" and, needless to say, our family was overjoyed. Life's routines went on as before, and together, Mom and I continued to attend our weekly dance class. Every Wednesday night, we looked around the room before class started, waiting to see if the mysterious woman would appear. Yet we never saw her again.

Could an angel really have come to comfort my mother in the form of a mysterious brown-haired woman in a Wednesday night dance class? I'm not so sure. After all, I was a skeptic. But now, I guess you could say I'm starting to believe.

~Jess Forte

77

The Visit

Hark! the music of the angels
Floating onward still we hear;
Blessed music, sweetest chorus
Ever sung to mortal ear.
~Fanny Crosby, "Music of the Angels"

M y mom Eva died eight years ago. I tried to dream about her for years, but my efforts were in vain. Many nights I would thumb through photographs of our annual holiday gatherings, I would sing her favorite songs, and I would cry and beg while saying my evening prayers. Nothing I tried could bring her image into my sleep.

My mom and I were very close. Our homes were back-to-back and our lives were interwoven from my birth until her death. We shared a beautiful, loving mother-daughter relationship, primarily because we shared the same principles and values on church, children, family and self-respect. She was my confidante and best friend. She could be brutally honest and frank when asked her opinion, but she always said her piece nicely.

There was nothing unusual about the early evening of January 6th—dinner with my two-year-old grandson, the "play at bath time" ritual, and finally sitting in my favorite chair to watch a few TV programs. I watched the 11:00 p.m. news as usual and at 11:30 decided to go to bed.

I walked into my bedroom to pull down the bed covers and set the alarm for morning. As I reached across the bed to flip the comforter I felt the warm presence of my mother in the room. I immediately recognized the visitor and smiled.

"Mom, you're here," I said. "I love you. I feel you here. I love you." For some reason, I sensed it was going to be a brief visit. I did not feel the need for words. I only felt a sense of acceptance and contentment. Then she was gone.

The visit left me giddy.

The following morning, I described the evening "visit" to my daughter, who also missed her grandmother very much. Grandma had always been there for her.

I drove to school that morning totally preoccupied with the experience. My classes went well all day and I kept that warm feeling from the visit. However, when I returned home in the late afternoon, I received a disturbing phone call from Marie, my close friend of forty-five years. She told me that her dad had died the previous evening.

In my effort to console her, I briefly shared my previous night's visit from my mother. We reminisced about our parents' longtime friendship, a friendship our parents shared since Marie and I were freshmen in high school. Both of our fathers belonged to the St. Theresa chapter of the Knights of Columbus, and our parents enjoyed the social dinners and dancing events.

When I hung up the phone I could not stop thinking about the coincidence of my mom's visit on the very night that Marie's dad died. I pictured my mother and Marie's dad dancing together on the Knights of Columbus dance floor.

The following day I attended the wake for Marie's dad and offered my condolences to her and her family. It was not until I spoke to Marie's daughter that I had the courage to ask the time of her grandfather's death. With tears, she answered, "Grandpa passed last night between 11:30 and 11:45 p.m." I anticipated her reply; I knew in my heart that it was at the time of my mother's visit. I knew that my mom was the angel chosen to usher Marie's father into Eternity.

~Roberta Cioppa

A Message from Heaven

Around our pillows golden ladders rise,
And up and down the skies,
With winged sandals shod,
The angels come, and go, the Messengers of God!
~Richard Henry Stoddard

"There's an assortment of refreshments," our hostess, Connie Bender, announced. "So feel free to help yourselves." People were commenting on how relaxed they felt after just experiencing a spiritual hands-on healing.

I was sitting across from a woman named Betty, talking about the morning news. Suddenly, a white light materialized behind Betty and an angel appeared. I looked around the table where ten people were seated in this Manitowoc, Wisconsin farmhouse to see if anyone else saw the angel. They did not. They were absorbed in socializing.

I tried to get Connie's attention by waving my hand. If anyone had knowledge of this type of phenomenon, she would. Connie has had these open-door Reiki healings at her house for twenty-five years, with people coming from throughout our state and the states surrounding ours. But my hostess, so preoccupied with the dialogue at the table, didn't notice my signaling.

Returning my attention to Betty, I noticed the angel was still standing there. This time, however, I clearly saw a physical form. The angel's wings were on what appeared to be a male from seventeen

266   Love from Beyond : A Message from Heaven

to nineteen years of age. He stood about five-foot-eight, with black, softly waved hair. His belted white robe sported a gold braided tie at the waist, accenting his slender build. His arched wings were magnificent. They were huge, pearly white layers of satiny feathers. Emanating from this winged messenger was a golden beam of light. Absorbed in this glowing vision before me, I faintly heard someone say, "I beg your pardon, is something wrong?"

Shaken from what I had observed, I blurted, "I'm sorry, Betty, I wasn't staring at you. I was staring at a glorious angel standing behind you, and I couldn't take my eyes off it."

Surprisingly, she said, "An angel! With wings and all? I love angels. What did it look like?"

While I described what I saw (with the angel slowly fading away), Betty covered her face with her hands and began to cry.

"I'm really sorry, Betty," I said, feeling remorseful for having mentioned it. "I didn't mean to distress you."

She looked up, reached across the table, taking my hand in hers, and said, "Oh honey, there's no need to apologize. I'm ever so happy you shared this with me. You see, the angel apparition you just described was my eighteen-year-old son who died in a motorcycle accident last year. And I have been asking him to give me a sign that he's all right. And you just did. So thank you for the message."

~Sylvia Bright-Green

My Little Girl's Angel

*I am convinced that these heavenly beings exist
and that they provide unseen aid on our behalf.*
~Billy Graham

Nothing could have shocked me more than the look on Tim's face when I opened the door so early that May morning. "What is it? What's wrong?" But he didn't speak. I shook his arms and started to cry, only from the look of pain on his face. There was something that hurt too much for him to say, that was going to hurt too much for me to hear.

"Kim is dead," he said, and fell toward me in tears.

Kim was the kind of friend who could always make you smile. She was kind to everyone, funny, and game for anything. I always knew that her personality would bring her great things in life because you couldn't know her and not love her.

I couldn't make sense of it that day, that week, that year. She was only nineteen. I spent a lot of time in the chapel at the college, sitting by myself crying gently. They knew just to leave me there — in time I would walk out and move on with my day. Slowly, I found strength to move forward with my life. Each of us did, in our own ways.

I thought about Kim through each milestone of my life: graduating college, getting my first real job, getting married. She never got the chance to do any of those things. The unfairness of it stung me.

And then I got pregnant with my first child. Kim would have been a great mother. She would never get the chance. As soon as

I found out the baby was a girl, I knew. She would be named after Kim.

Our beautiful baby girl was born on an early summer night when all of the flowers were blooming, just like the night Kim had died. She was perfect, and we gave her Kim's name. After all the nurses left for the night, and the room was quiet, I whispered to our baby and told her all about Kim. She listened intently, and we both fell asleep with her swaddled in my arms.

Sometime during the night, I felt a hand on my shoulder shaking me awake. I was tired from the labor and had been sleeping peacefully. I didn't want to wake up. But the hand squeezed my shoulder, so I could no longer ignore it. Thinking it was one of the nurses there to check on me, I slowly opened my eyes.

Kim was standing by the bed. Not Kim, really, it was more of a mist, but in it, I could see Kim's face. I knew it was her immediately. There was a sense of calm and peace in the room. No words were spoken. In my head, I heard Kim's voice, and she told me she loved this child and that she would always watch over her. My baby, in my arms, felt washed in peace. I could feel the love and peace coming from Kim. And I knew that she understood that this was my way of honoring all of the things she never got to do on Earth.

And then she was gone.

Fifteen years have passed. My daughter loves her name. There have been many times people have said, and we have thought, "She has a guardian angel watching over her." And she does.

~Sarah Clark Monagle

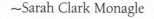

A Message from Mom

Music is well said to be the speech of angels.
~Thomas Carlyle

After my mother died at age sixty-two, following a long illness, I was left with a powerful, aching sense of loss. I desperately wanted her back. She was my biggest fan and no one could ever love me as much as she did. "You're so lovely," she'd tell me over and over again. My mother bore a strong resemblance in her younger days to actress Rita Hayworth. She was truly gorgeous. I'd reply: "Not as lovely as you, Mom!" The feeling of loss was especially strong because her death from an incurable cancer came too soon. I learned that you can never be ready for a parent's death. It was a terrible shock, and the memory of her suffering still overwhelms me.

But it wasn't her nature to complain, and she didn't focus on her pain and fear. She wasn't in denial either. "Your grandmother always told me to never worry, that she would always be watching over me," she said. "Don't worry about me. Just be happy in your own life, and follow your dreams!" She'd smile at me, a small, sad smile, and then let me know that our bond would also last through years of separation. "I'll always be with you, watching over you," she said.

When she was first diagnosed with ovarian cancer, I left my job and home in Florida to help my family care for her in her home. It was difficult, but she had, in fact, lived two years longer than the "within six months" her doctor predicted when he told her, "It's in

God's hands!" During this time we had some great times together. We went shopping, planted flowers, shared secrets and recounted adventures. On a summer day, weeks before she died, as we sat near a flower-bordered garden on a lake, she put her soft hand in mind and whispered, "I don't want to leave this—or you."

Although devastated, we still held onto hope. We prayed often for courage, and so did our family, friends, and church. There were also prayer chains of people we didn't know. I knew going through grueling chemotherapy treatments wasn't easy for her and I did my best to comfort her. She was very brave, even though the treatments wore her down. At that time, the hospital I took her to for chemotherapy sessions was not a very pleasant place to visit. It was dark and dreary, many of the employees were unfriendly and doctors had no empathy for the cancer patients. No one smiled or spoke to the people in the small, crowded waiting rooms, and patients were treated more like numbers than people.

Recently I visited a friend at that same hospital. It had been renovated and it felt completely different. Opening the front door was like pulling the ribbon off an unexpected gift. A beautiful bright building, it welcomed anyone who walked through the doors. The staff, employees, and volunteers were courteous and helpful.

As I was leaving the hospital that day, a young, dark-haired girl playing the piano in the lobby caught my eye. She was so engrossed in her music that one could tell she played from her heart. I was deeply moved. Many other people also stopped to listen.

"Isn't it lovely?" said a lady with silver hair that contrasted with her pretty pink T-shirt.

"Oh, yes," I replied, surprised at her soothing, familiar voice, and remembering how my mother, who loved pink, often said that same phrase.

"She plays by memory," the woman added, smiling.

I wanted to ask her how she knew, but tears welled up in my eyes. I turned away from the lady for a moment and when I turned back she was gone. I looked all over for her, even asking some people around me who were listening to the piano player.

"There was no one here in a pink T-shirt," a lady told me.

"No one was standing next to you," another said.

"But I was talking to her," I responded.

"No," a young man said. "You were talking to yourself."

Just then, that same soothing voice seemed to speak from deep within: "It's an angel sign—a reminder that you are always connected to those you love, and your loved ones are always with you." Suddenly, all the errands I had to do that day were no longer important. I sat down on a bench and thanked God not only for all my blessings, but for the angels who shower us with love.

~Kathryn Radeff

Biking Haleakala

Ever felt an angel's breath in the gentle breeze? A teardrop in the falling
rain? Hear a whisper amongst the rustle of leaves? Or been kissed by a lone
snowflake? Nature is an angel's favorite hiding place.
~Terri Guillemets

I couldn't sleep for excitement and jumped out of bed when 2:00 a.m. finally glowed on my travel clock. I pulled on shorts and a T-shirt, plenty for the warm weather that we'd enjoyed for six days on Maui. But the temperature at the summit of the Haleakala volcano would be much colder, so I stuffed a long-sleeved shirt, tights, and a jacket into a daypack and slung it over my shoulder.

I crept down the stairs of our condo's loft, but a stair squeaked. My two-year-old granddaughter in one of the bedrooms whimpered and was quiet again. My daughter, curled on the couch like she was still a young child, opened one eye. "Have fun, Mama," she said and turned over to go back to sleep. I'd hoped she or one of my two sons would join me for my sunrise trip to Haleakala, driving up to the rim and biking down. But they figured I was safe on a tour and didn't want to get up in the middle of the night for anything.

Ordinarily my husband would have gone with me, but business had prevented him from joining the family for our week on Maui.

Friends had ordered me to see the sunrise over Mt. Haleakala. I figured biking down the mountain afterward with a small group of adventurers would be fun. I ran a comb through my hair, added a touch of lipstick, and headed out to meet the van, my stomach just a bit queasy.

The parking lot had fewer lights on than I'd expected, but the office was lit and I headed there to wait. A security guard joined me and we chatted for a few minutes. Then he moved on. I sat on a bench and took a deep breath of humid, salty air, the sound of tumbling ocean waters soothing me. So I'd be on a strange bike with people I didn't know, biking down a mountain in the dusky light. So what? I'd be fine.

A twelve-passenger van drove up, pulling a trailer filled with bicycles, and the driver jumped out, hand extended "Hi. I'm Aaron," he said and slid open a door for me. I settled into the middle seat, my pack on my lap, and we headed out to pick up the other passengers.

A mother and daughter boarded at one hotel. "I'm glad there's someone else over fifty," the mother said with a warm smile.

It did seem to be a tour for young people. My chest tightened. Maybe the bike ride was more difficult than I had anticipated. I usually had an easy time meeting new people, but now I felt oddly alone.

Aaron picked up a second tour guide, Manny, and in about an hour and a half we arrived at the summit of Haleakala. We buttoned and zipped into our warm layers of clothing and followed our guides across a lava field. I stumbled on the black rocks that littered the hillside in the wake of the volcano's many eruptions, and thought of my family tucked into bed in the condo. They'd miss the sunrise, I reminded myself. And the bike ride.

We settled onto the flattest rocks we could find and waited for the sunrise. People leaned in to chat in groups of twos and threes, and again a feeling of being entirely alone swept through me. Voices dropped to whispers as the sky lightened and gauzy pink streamers spread slowly across the sky. Soon orange hues added their splash of color to the sunrise. We sat on top of the world, and put on sunglasses as the sun rose into view with a startling intensity. My friends had been right. The magnificent sight was unforgettable.

When the sun had cleared the horizon Aaron asked us if we

were ready to go. I shivered more from anxious anticipation than the cold.

After a short ride in the van partway down the mountain, we all clambered out and Aaron and Manny unloaded the bikes. The bicycles were heavy black things with thick, knobby tires and seats three times the size of my bicycle seat back home. When Aaron pushed a bike toward me, I climbed on. "It's very short," I told him.

"They should be that way so you can stand up easy," he explained, but I felt awkward and off balance with my knees bent at such an angle. "Peddle backwards to slow or stop," Aaron directed. No hand-brakes? I rode with footbrakes when I was a little girl, I reassured myself. But I wobbled as we set out and a biking accident I'd had a few years before came to mind. In dim light I'd hit a curb and fallen hard. The emergency room doctor had feared I'd broken my hip. I hadn't, but would I hurt myself today? I said a quick prayer for God to be with me and kept pedaling.

Manny rode sideways on his bike, one foot on the far pedal, as though riding a horse sidesaddle, and watched our little group. Over and over he had us pull to the side of the road to let a motorized vehicle pass, then start out again. One woman asked to get back in the van, the ride too difficult for her. Although I knew I should be confident, fear built inside me. I prayed again for God's help. My heart pounded and I gripped the handlebars as though my bike would turn into a bucking bronco.

Then I glanced beside me, and glanced again. There was Annie, my Golden Retriever, galloping beside me. We'd lovingly buried her in our yard two months earlier. She ran easily by my side, here in Maui, tongue lolling, ears windswept, paws just skimming the ground.

"Annie," I breathed. "It's you." Tears flowed down my cheeks.

Annie had been my best friend for thirteen years, accompanying me everywhere. When she could no longer jump in the car, I learned to lift her in so we could still be together. She'd seen me through adjustments to a new marriage and six stepchildren, and through the launching of my writing career. She'd kept vigil by my bed as I healed from a ski accident that badly injured my left knee. Most of all, she'd taught me about courage, struggling with arthritis from a very early age but still pulling herself to her feet right to the end to follow me everywhere.

How like her to be here now, as visible to me as the other tourists on their bicycles, reminding me to take heart and know that I would be safe biking down the mountain.

All fear drained out of me.

Then I could no longer see Annie, but sensed her beside me a little longer. Our group biked through Maui's upcountry, the fertile slopes of Haleakala where farms grew Maui's freshest produce. I'd never before seen mango trees or pineapple fields. My chest swelled with peace and joy. I wasn't alone after all. I never would be. "Thank you Annie," I murmured out loud. "Thank you God."

~Samantha Ducloux Waltz

Angels in Heaven
and on Earth

If I have freedom in my love,
And in my soul am free,
Angels alone that soar above,
Enjoy such liberty.
~Richard Lovelace

I was alone in the room where my older brother had just passed away. Hundreds of miles away, Nancy was alone in the room where her older sister had just passed away. We didn't know each other.

The ocean roared outside my beach cottage for days after the death of my brother Timothy. As I took an early morning walk, my thoughts turned to him and to the motorcycle crash that ended his life. I wondered if this tragedy had really been an accident.

My mind turned to Rebecca. Rebecca had been Timothy's greatest love. They met in their first year of college; then Rebecca turned ill and was forced to move away in hopes of a miraculous cure. For reasons only they knew, Timothy did not go with her. Though they remained devoted in their love, Timothy and Rebecca were never with one another again. I believe Timothy was thinking of Rebecca and not the road when he had his fatal crash.

As the sands of the beach curled around my feet, I remembered the times when my brother and I would walk for hours along this same terrain. Most of our conversations had been about love. Timothy would often refer to me as "his romantic and loving kid brother who would someday find his special angel on earth." I delighted when he read the love letters that he and Rebecca had shared. Through their love, I thrilled to the day when I would find "a Rebecca of my very own."

I remember Rebecca mentioning her younger, nameless sister whom she also described as "that romantic and loving kid sister of hers."

As I wandered through these memories, the first miracle of my day occurred. In the midst of my grief, I heard Timothy's voice merge with the ocean in inspiring words that whispered, "Angels create our most beautiful relationships… in heaven and on earth!" I stopped in my tracks. I looked up to the sky, a tear rolled down my cheek, and I knew that my brother had now become an angel! An angel to guide both of us to our own special angels in heaven and on earth.

I felt uplifted! I lay on the beach, my mind drifting. Who was my angel on earth? Was she linked somehow to Timothy's angel, Rebecca? I would have to wait. These revelations had wonderfully exhausted me. I walked back silently to my cottage and fell asleep.

Sleep came easily. But in what seemed like minutes, I awoke to a gentle knock on my door. Who could it be? The second miracle of my day was about to begin.

At my doorway was the most beautiful woman I had ever seen, a woman who radiated beauty from the inside out. She had a lovely, unassuming look about her as she swept back her long dark hair and spoke. "My name is Nancy Lopez. I'm Rebecca Lopez's sister. I was hoping to speak with Timothy." I couldn't believe what I was hearing, and seeing.

"Please forgive me for just popping in like this," she continued.

"No, not at all," I interjected. "I'm Timothy's brother. Please sit down. What a pleasure it is to meet you, Nancy. Rebecca and Timothy shared so much in their brief time together."

"Yes. Yes they did," she said a bit shyly. "Is Timothy here?"

I was thrown off balance. "N-no, no he isn't… that is…"

Nancy made it easy for me. She drew a step nearer, as if drawing me into her confidence. "I have bad news," she said. I couldn't imagine what she was going to tell me. I stood there motionless, breathless. "My sister Rebecca, Timothy's dearest love, has passed away."

I was in shock. I took a deep breath. Tears streamed down my face. Nancy must have felt the words I couldn't say, for immediately her shoulder was my salvation. I heard her lightly sobbing as she comforted me.

She whispered, "Rebecca told me that she had some desperately needed work to complete, and it would have to be done on June 23rd, at 8 p.m. I had no idea what she meant, but now I know... I know because that's the day and time that my sister Rebecca died!"

My mouth went dry and I wanted to faint. I whispered, "June 23rd at 8 p.m., did you say? Timothy died that very day, that very same hour!"

Nancy was frozen. "Oh my God, you mean they're both gone?" Her face now gave into the strain of the last few days, and she again burst into tears.

I suddenly felt myself of two minds—one of grief for Timothy and Rebecca, and one to reach out to Nancy. My arms reached out to comfort her. She sobbed in my arms.

"Yes, they're both gone, Nancy... but together, at last, I know it." My words needed no reply. Nancy's eyes revealed that she had understood.

We had lived a lifetime together in a matter of minutes, but the most miraculous was yet to come.

In a flash, and with the intensity of the moment, I suddenly heard Timothy's strong, inspiring voice embrace me with these words: "Angels can be with their angels, on earth or in heaven. I have found my angel, Rebecca, in all of her heavenly radiance! You too can have your chance of heaven on earth with your angel!"

I was overwhelmed, exalted. My eyes, welling up with tears, connected with Nancy's eyes. I knew that she too had been moved by something as wonderful and as unearthly as I had just experienced. As I drew nearer and shared with her Timothy's beautiful words about angels, to my amazement I heard Nancy exclaim, "I heard the same words! At the very same time, in Rebecca's voice!"

"Oh my God!" Nancy and I had the same stunning, lifetime revelation! And in the space of just a few short minutes, Nancy and I were no longer strangers. Does it really matter whether we find love in heaven or on earth? The most important thing is that we lavish in the love that we do find, and never let it leave us. As we felt these words together, Nancy and I walked hand in hand along the beach.... somehow knowing that Timothy and Rebecca were walking hand in hand alongside us!

~Al Cole

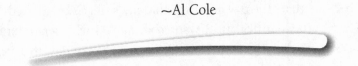

Chapter
9

Angels Among Us

Angel Guides

Leader of the Pack

We trust in plumed procession
For such the angels go—
Rank after Rank, with even feet—
And uniforms of Snow.
~Emily Dickinson

Night was quickly descending upon the mountains of North Carolina and rain was coming down in buckets when Danny, the lead rider in our group of five motorcyclists, signaled that he was turning. Thank goodness, I thought. A rookie biker, I had no experience riding in conditions like these. I was wet, cold, exhausted and—yes—more than a little frightened. But Danny's turn signal almost certainly meant we had reached the exit from the Blue Ridge Parkway that led to our motel. A warm shower, dry clothes, and a hearty supper were only minutes away.

But no. Instead of a bustling four-lane highway, we found ourselves in a deserted picnic area. We parked our bikes, made our way through the mud to a covered shelter, and pulled off our helmets.

"Sorry, guys," Danny said, looking embarrassed. "It was raining so hard I guess I missed the exit."

He pulled a soggy map from his jacket pocket and shined a pen light on it. Sure enough, we'd gone almost fifteen miles beyond the spot where we were supposed to get off. It was all I could do not to cry. Traveling this steep, curvy segment of the parkway would have been slow going even on a sunny day. On a rainy night, fifteen miles would take at least another hour.

"That's okay," we assured him. "Visibility is practically zero. It could have happened to anyone."

"Does somebody else want to lead?" Danny asked.

"Nope," my husband George assured him. "You're doing great. Let's stay in the same order as before. You, Jennie, me, Tim. Keith, you still okay with riding sweep?"

Keith nodded.

"Let's take a restroom break before we get back on the road," George said. "If we get separated at the exit, remember that our Hampton Inn is half a mile down on the right."

The guys were suited up and ready by the time I came out of the ladies room. I pulled on my helmet and gloves and whispered a little prayer as I cranked my bike. "Please, Lord, guide us on this treacherous journey."

I could see the lights of Danny's motorcycle at the end of the parking lot. I pulled in behind him and watched in my mirrors as the other three took their places behind me. We all gave the thumbs up sign and then slowly eased back onto the parkway. It was now pitch black. The rain was coming down even harder than before. It ran in rivulets down my windshield and splattered against my helmet's face shield. Fifteen more miles in this! Fifteen miles that we'd already covered once. But I couldn't fret about that now.

All I could do was concentrate on Danny's red taillight in front of me.

The road seemed curvier and the pavement slicker than it had just a few minutes ago. Back then, in the gray dusk, I had marveled at the sheer rock walls next to the inside lane. And gasped at the sheer drop-offs beyond the outside lane, the one we were traveling in now. A careless mistake could easily plunge a biker to her death.

"Stop it!" I scolded myself. "Don't think. Just relax and focus on Danny's taillight."

That single red taillight guided me down fifteen of the longest miles I'd ever traveled until, at last, we reached our exit. Danny turned on his blinker and I breathed a sigh of relief. Our motel was only a stone's throw away. "Thank you, God!" I said as I goosed the throttle, trying to stay close to the motorcycle in front of me as it merged onto a busy four-lane highway. Up ahead on the right, just as George had promised, was the bright blue sign of the Hampton Inn.

I downshifted and prepared to turn. But as I did, I could see that the bike ahead of me hadn't slowed. It kept right on going, past the entrance to the motel and down the highway, picking up speed as it went. I pulled under the covered parking area in front of the motel lobby, flipped up my face shield, and watched my companions roll in. George. Tim. Keith. Danny. What? How could Danny be last in line? I'd just followed him for the past fifteen and a half miles.

We pulled off our helmets and gazed, wide-eyed, at one another.

Finally, George spoke. "How'd you get back there, Leader of the Pack?"

"I couldn't get my bike to crank when we were ready to leave the picnic area," Danny said. "I honked and yelled but nobody noticed. I've been about ten minutes behind y'all until we turned onto this highway."

Now everybody was staring at the rookie rider. Me. "So you led us all this way?" Keith asked. "In the dark and the rain?"

"No way," I said, slowly shaking my head. "I wasn't in the lead. But I know who was."

~Jennie Ivey

What Can You Do?

Cast all your anxiety on him because he cares about you.
~1 Peter 5:7

I do believe in angels, but I do not believe they hover around our heads watching our every step like the one in the famous Guardian Angel painting. I was hesitant then to join my three sisters-in-law for a spiritual workshop where having "angel readings" was part of the process. In the end, I decided to go, just to be part of the family.

When the readings began, I rolled my eyes as the reader told everyone what they wanted to hear. Who wouldn't want an extraterrestrial guardian who had God's ear and our best interests at heart? It all just seemed too phony to me. I came up with a convenient headache and left early.

A year later I joined the same sisters-in-law for a course in meditation, which I do believe in. The instructor had bona fide credentials and a wealth of teaching and clinical counseling experience. In fact, one doctor I was seeing even mentioned her by name. I really wanted to experience the otherworldly feeling of escaping into meditation. Meditation, we're told, is when we are quiet enough in our minds to allow God to talk to us.

The sessions were thought provoking, and when Nancy, our instructor, "led us into meditation," I could feel the pull of the peaceful process.

By the third session, Nancy had us working at ever deepening meditation. "This afternoon," she began, "we are going to look for our spiritual guides."

Oh no, I thought. Here we go taking a left turn into the world of wacky!

Nancy began her monologue taking us into the meditation. We drifted; we relaxed; we were on a beach; our bodies became lighter. "Look for your spiritual guides. They will be here somewhere. It may be someone you love dearly who has passed away." Her voice was soft, mellifluous, seductive.

I was on that beach she described. I felt the breeze and smelled the salt air. There was someone I truly hoped to see. I looked for my father. When she said to look far down the beach, I scanned the expanse, willing myself to see him. He had been the giant of my life, and I missed him and his advice terribly. I wanted to tell him about my son, who was struggling with job difficulties. No matter how far I looked down that beautiful beach, it was empty. Tell me what to do, I prayed. How can I help my son?

Nancy's smooth voice interrupted my thoughts. "Look to your right," she instructed. I did as she asked, and there... was an angel. An angel! I was so startled that I almost cried out, but the beauty and calm of the lovely being before me drew me in. I couldn't tell if the figure was male or female; it seemed to consist entirely of color and light: masses of golden hair and green robes. And the wings—the wings were white, folded tightly to the back of the miraculous creature. I never, never expected to see an angel, and wings, well, that was beyond the realm of logical thought. But at the same time, within the meditation, I wanted to embrace him—or her—but I was stupefied by the majesty of the apparition.

I knew without being told that this was my spiritual guide.

Nancy told us to lay our problems before our guide if we were lucky enough to see one. I wordlessly asked how I could help my son, and just as wordlessly the answer came back to me: "What can you do?" I didn't understand the question. There was no inflection at all. Each word was given the exact same expressionless emphasis.

Nancy brought us out of the meditation. I came reluctantly.

Standing on that beach before the angel was a bit of paradise I had never expected to experience, and I didn't want to leave.

Others in the class complained that they hadn't seen or felt anything; a few jabbered about a great session. I didn't want to share my experience with anyone. It had been too personal, too intimate, too miraculous. Who would believe me anyway?

I hugged my secret to myself till much later that night when I shared it with my husband, Bill. "What can I do?" I asked him. "How can I possibly help our son with his problems? He's on the other side of the country. I don't know anyone in his field. I know nothing about the kind of work he does. The angel asked me, what can I do?"

Bill looked at me and said, "Maybe you are putting the emphasis on the wrong word. It isn't 'What can YOU do?' but 'What CAN you do?' Sometimes you have to know the difference. You always think you can fix everything or at least you should be able to. You have to accept that sometimes there is nothing you can do and you have to give it to God. You shouldn't need an angel to tell you that."

Apparently I do. That one little question has since formed the basis of my own personal serenity prayer. "What can you do?" If there is something within my power to do to help someone, then I must do it. If I ask the question and there is nothing I can do, I must give it to God.

And as I thank my angel for such simple yet profound advice, I ask for the wisdom to know the difference.

~Rosemary McLaughlin

85

Angel in the Airport

Faith makes things possible, not easy.
~Author Unknown

I t was my first time flying by myself and I was a little nervous. I had two layovers, one in Phoenix and one in Houston, and they were both huge airports. I had little time between flights. My shuttle plane from Yuma, Arizona, landed in the Phoenix International Airport. I got off the plane and collected my baggage. I only had twenty minutes to get to the gate for my flight from Phoenix to Houston. I memorized the gate number, E-27, and stuck my ticket in my pocket as I had to use both hands to carry my purse, carry-on and suitcase.

In just a few minutes, I was hopelessly lost and starting to panic. Somehow, I ended up in the middle of a cavernous room with no one around me! As I whirled around to look for someone that could help me, I started praying.

"Please, Lord, I'm lost and I only have a few minutes to get to my plane. Please help me!"

I choked back a sob and whirled around again. There standing beside me was a tall, handsome, young man, with dark hair and dark eyes, dressed in a blue uniform. I hadn't seen him enter the room.

"Can I help you, ma'am?" he asked.

"Yes," I cried. "I'm lost and I only have a few minutes to get to my next flight."

He smiled. "Follow me."

He took me down a flight of stairs and out a door where he flagged down a shuttle bus.

When the bus driver opened the door, the gentleman told the driver.

"Take her to gate E-27 and hurry, she only has a few minutes."

I went up the steps of the bus and then stopped; I turned around to thank the young man. There was no one there!

I sat down and stared out the window. I couldn't see him anywhere.

I puzzled over this, but I was so anxious to get to my gate I didn't give it anymore thought.

I barely made it on time. As I took my ticket from my pocket to hand it to the man at the gate, it dawned on me that I hadn't shown my ticket or told the young man what gate I needed! But he had taken me to the right shuttle and had told the driver what gate to take me to.

I puzzled over this on the short flight to Houston. When I got off the plane in Houston, I noticed that this time I only had fifteen minutes to get to my next flight and the gate was twenty gates away!

"Oh, no," I moaned. "Not again!"

"May I help you, ma'am?" I heard a familiar voice.

Whirling around, there stood a tall, handsome young man with dark hair and eyes, wearing a blue uniform. I'm sure I must have stood there like a dummy with my mouth opened.

As he smiled at me, I stammered, "Yes, I need to catch a flight to Tulsa, Oklahoma and I only have about fifteen minutes to get there."

He went out into the wide aisle, flagged down a trolley, and told the driver, "Take her to gate 22. She only has a few minutes."

I got on the trolley, looked back and sure enough, he was nowhere in sight.

After I settled in my seat and the plane had lifted off, I puzzled over these two strange events. Either this young man had a twin or I had just been helped by an angel, the same angel in both airports. There was only one explanation. I had prayed and asked God for help. He sent an angel, disguised as a tall, handsome young man, to help me with my flight to Houston and that same angel was waiting for me in Houston to help me to my flight to Tulsa.

A feeling of such peace came over me as I realized God will always answer prayer and will send an angel or someone to help you on your way.

~Pat Kane

86

Chicken Soup for the Soul

An Angel in a Yellow Buick

Angels and ministers of grace defend us.
~William Shakespeare

I love my job working as a developmental therapist for toddlers with special needs. I engage the children with educational toys like puzzles and books, and I try to get them to speak, follow simple directions, and behave in more age-appropriate ways. The therapy sessions are usually more productive when the children are in their natural environments, which are, of course, their own homes. While I love my job, it sometimes takes me into some pretty rough neighborhoods.

One day I had just finished my last appointment and it was already dark outside. I walked to my car quickly, got in, and locked the doors. I wasn't all that comfortable in this neighborhood during the day, and now that it was dark I was even more uncomfortable. To make matters worse, this was my first visit to this particular house and I wasn't exactly sure how to get back onto the main road.

I drove away from the house, turned down a side street, and made a few more turns before realizing that I was hopelessly lost. And the neighborhood had gotten much worse.

I kept driving, hoping to see some kind of landmark that I recognized. But the more I drove, the more confused and lost I got. I turned down another street, realizing too late that it was a dead end.

I was trying to get my car turned around when several rough-looking teenagers began walking toward me. This part of the city was known for its gang activity and when they discussed violent crimes on the evening news, this was usually where they took place. As they came closer, the boys began shouting vulgar things at me.

"Please, God, please, show me how to get out of here," I prayed. "Protect me from those boys and just get me out of here."

By then, the boys had spread out across the road. The only way to get through would be to hit them. Then I spotted a flash of metal. I realized that one of the teens was carrying a gun or other weapon. The tears—and the praying—began in earnest then.

"I need Your help, God," I murmured as they walked closer.

Then out of nowhere, a car pulled out of a nearby driveway. The driver backed up in front of my car, positioning himself between me and the boys. He started driving, slowly at first and then speeding up a bit. I realized that the teens would have to move or risk being hit by his car. Without even thinking about it, I stepped on the gas and followed him closely. The boys moved out of the way and I sped past them.

While I was relieved to have escaped the teens on the dead end street, I was still lost in a rough neighborhood. The car was still ahead of me, and it was then that I noticed the sticker on its bumper that read, "God is my co-pilot."

Tears again filled my eyes as I realized that God was still answering my prayers. I murmured a quick word of thanks and decided to follow the car. He led me right out of the neighborhood and onto the main road I needed to take to get home. As soon as we were on that road, the car pulled onto the shoulder and the driver gave me a little wave. I waved back and drove home.

During my next home visit to that neighborhood, I mentioned to my student's family what had happened. "I thought something really bad was going to happen, but then this car—a bright yellow Buick—pulled out between the boys and me," I said.

"Where were you?" my student's father asked. "Because I've never seen a car like that in our neighborhood."

"Oh, well, he pulled out of one of the driveways on one of the dead end streets," I said.

But the father shook his head. "I don't think so, Diane. There's only one dead end street in this neighborhood, and most of the houses on that street are boarded up. No one lives over there because the gangs have gotten so bad."

"But the yellow Buick…" I said.

Finally, my student's father convinced me to ride over to the dead end street with him. I knew for certain that it was the same street I'd been on the previous week. But he was right. No one lived there. The houses, even the one I was certain the yellow Buick had come from, were boarded up. No one had lived there in quite some time.

"Then how…" I started to ask, but then I saw it.

Stuck on the house's dirty front door was a very familiar bumper sticker.

And it was then that I knew that the driver of that yellow Buick was no ordinary man. He'd been sent by God to protect me and lead me out of danger.

I bowed my head and thanked God for His love and protection, and for sending me an angel in a yellow Buick.

~Diane Stark

Go Home

For your Father knows the things you have need of before you ask Him.
~Matthew 6:8

"J im!" I yelped, terrified as I came around the corner into the kitchen just in time to see ferocious flames licking the bottom of the cabinets. "What are you doing?"

"I'm making toast, Mommy," he told me with pride. Unable to find the bread, he had stuffed the toaster with crackers instead.

With trembling hands I unplugged the toaster and swept it into the sink, flooding it with water. I had always dreaded kitchen fires. Now we almost had one.

Yet another disaster averted. My weak knees barely carried me to a chair, where I collapsed. Looking towards heaven I silently charged my recently deceased husband with abandoning his family and leaving me with all the responsibilities.

Of course that wasn't rational. His death by a habitually intoxicated driver hardly qualified his absence from our family as abandonment, but I wasn't rational these days. The responsibility of keeping this rambunctious three-year-old safe weighed heavily on me.

Only the week before I had shaken out his comforter, expecting to see it float over his bed, to see, instead, two raw eggs and an open can of chocolate syrup fly across the room. Ugh! The walls, baseboards and carpeting of his room required some serious cleaning from that escapade.

And then there was the anxious moment when I heard his dreaded asthmatic wheezing. Going to find him, I collided with him in the hall just in time to see foaming bathroom cleaner running down his forehead and approaching his eyes.

"I sprayed my hair like you do, Mommy!" he cheerfully informed me.

Was that the week before or after he had taken my bulky sewing scissors and, with them coming perilously close to his eyes, cut away the entire middle section of his beautiful pale blond bangs? I was fast losing track of all the crises he created.

Today, frankly, I was feeling overwhelmed. I missed adult conversation, company and predictable behavior. I found myself thinking, "All work and no play, makes me a dull girl!" I sank down into the sofa.

Listlessly I began flipping through channels on the TV. *Sesame Street* caught my attention. "Kim! Jim!" I called. "Come and see what Big Bird is up to." Maybe he would engage Jim's attention long enough for me to wash my car, another male duty that had become mine.

Once outside, I set to work on the car. After a few minutes I thought I heard the phone ringing and shut off the hose.

Five-year-old Kim called, "Mom, it's for you." It was a friend whom I hadn't seen for quite a while.

Would I like to meet him for dinner? Just to get out of the house for a while? Would I! I called the babysitter and spent the rest of the afternoon getting myself ready for my night out.

While I made their dinner, Jim raced around the house being Spider-Man and tormenting his sister with constant interruptions while she was trying to produce a work of art with crayons and paper. "Sometimes I wish I knew where Jim drew all his energy from," I thought, shaking my head. "I'd like to find the source!"

The babysitter arrived and, after giving the usual instructions parents give, I kissed Kim and Jim and left to meet my friend.

The restaurant seemed especially quaint. The candlelight gave the silver a warm glow. The bone china reminded me of moonlight painted on a plate. And the food was perfect.

We sat and talked. We moved from the table to the lounge where we talked some more. I felt myself relaxing. I really needed this....

And then, an intrusive thought. "Go home now. Jim needs you."

The thought flashed into my mind, jarring my comfortable mood. Was there something to that? I didn't believe I could know if Jim needed me from that distance. I shook off the idea and refocused my attention on the story my friend was telling.

"Jim needs you. Go home." There it was again. Was it me, I questioned, or someone else? Still the urgent feeling that unsettled me was more than I could tolerate and I said, "I'm sorry. I don't really understand this, but I think I have to go home. I think Jim needs me."

The drive to my house seemed to take forever. My friend, alarmed, came along. I hurried from the car to the house and entered to find the babysitter asleep on the sofa. Jim's room was empty.

I began searching for him and found him lying on my bed, his beautiful blond hair soaked with a feverish sweat. He obviously had come looking for me in his distress and, not finding me, sought comfort in my room.

Beneath his eyes and around his mouth, his skin was a sickening blue. A weak wheezing noise was coming from his mouth. He seemed to be making very little effort to breathe. Terrified, I picked him up and shook him, calling his name. His eyes briefly fluttered open and then closed again.

We raced him to the hospital, where the emergency room staff whisked him away and began working on him, leaving me to pace in the waiting room. When they finally let me join them, Jim was awake. He was wearing an oxygen mask and looked small, weak and helpless. The doctor told me that X-rays revealed Jim had pneumonia in both lungs. For much of the next week, he remained in an oxygen tent.

Then, finally, one afternoon when I arrived during visiting hours, I found him racing around the pediatric unit being Spider-Man again. In that moment I was never more certain that being a mom was the happiest occupation a woman could be privileged to have.

I will never understand how he went from being his active normal self, without any sign of illness, when I left to meet my friend, to being so near death when I came home and found him. But this I came to understand: I was never really raising my children alone, without help. I was never really carrying that burden alone as I believed. Now I know I had unseen help. I learned that when I heard my angel say, "Go home. Jim needs you."

~Carol A. Gibson

Finding My Way

We are never so lost our angels cannot find us.
~Stephanie Powers

Naiveté is sometimes essential for an adventure, because anyone with experience would know better. At nineteen, I was as green as a hayseed. I grew up in a small Oklahoma town with a population of 3,000 and seldom traveled as a child. I didn't see an ocean until I was seventeen. So when a European friend wrote that he had to have surgery and couldn't come to visit the States one December, I decided to visit him in Europe instead.

Alone.

I packed my bags—two huge suitcases and a carry-on, as that was what the airlines allowed back then—and set off on my adventure.

I flew to Germany, although Zurich, Switzerland was my destination. Flying to Germany was cheaper and I was a college student, so cheaper was always the deciding factor. I had a plane ticket, enough money for a round-trip train ticket between Frankfurt and Zurich and around $50 in spending money.

Arrangements were made with my cousin, who was serving in the Army, to meet me at the airport and get me to the train station. He did and everything was running according to plans. He pointed me toward my train, said goodbye and left.

There I stood with two huge suitcases and a carry-on bag. All of which had seemed a good idea when I was back in Oklahoma. Not such a great idea when I realized I had to carry them on and off the train and make a connection too.

I struggled down an escalator, while tying to balance what seemed like all my worldly goods, to the platform I thought my cousin had indicated and waited. No train came.

As I was standing there a man came up to me without asking where I was going or if I needed help, and said, in perfect English, "I believe you're on the wrong platform." Then he told me where to go. I thanked him and was on my way.

I caught the right train and made it successfully to Zurich.

It wasn't until later, when I was a much more seasoned traveler and a resident of Zurich (which is a story for another day) that I started to look back on this adventure and wonder. If he hadn't given me unsolicited advice I would have missed my train and I had no idea how I would have found another. Also, I had insufficient funds to buy another ticket or stay in a hotel. So who was that man? How had he known that I was at the wrong track? Why had he taken the time to approach me and send me to another platform? And strangest of all, without ever asking where I was going, how did he know which train I needed to catch?

We always hear of angels among us. That day, thankfully, it seems I had one to help an adventuresome but ill-prepared traveler find her way.

~C.D. Jarmola

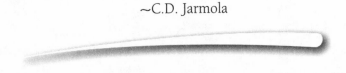

89

The Angel at Mile 25

We are each of us angels with only one wing,
and we can only fly by embracing one another.
~Luciano de Crescenzo

I was in the Yokayo Valley to compete in the Russian River Marathon, and to attempt my first sub-three-hour marathon. A sub-three-hour finish had eluded me in two previous races, but I was confident that the Russian River was about to change all that.

An amplified voice called us to the starting line. People stripped, stretched, and pinned on numbers. The first rays of sunlight caressed the morning sky as the final seconds ticked off the clock. The sharp crack of the starter's pistol pierced the air and the race was underway.

For a short time the large field of runners moved along in a tight knot. But the pack broke up quickly, the elite runners pulling away, the less-conditioned falling back and others simply maintaining. My breathing was labored for the first mile as my body adjusted to the pace. By mile two I began to loosen up. The going became fast and easy. My breathing settled out and my legs moved effortlessly beneath me. I allowed my mind to drift.

If someone asked you to sit down and design the perfect marathon course, you'd probably run it through the Yokayo Valley in Ukiah, California. As you move along the road, you pass endless rows of grapevines in the morning haze. You delight in a cluster of plum bushes. You marvel over the pink and white blossoms that adorn the fruit trees. The intense beauty of the 26.2-mile course remains etched in your mind.

Making marathon pace is much like making prose; it's an introspective business. A good marathoner always monitors body signals. Hydration and respiration are important. Heart rate and heaviness in the thighs and calves are to be noted. The internal questions never stop: What was my time on the last split? Should I take water at the next aid station? Should I back off on the pace slightly and save something for the end?

Unfortunately, I wasn't paying attention that day. I increased my speed, silently, confidently. The miles ticked off effortlessly. I had a vision spurring me on: It was the final mile of the race and I had taken the lead. There was one runner close, challenging me. He pulled alongside and it was a sprint to the finish. Spectators were cheering and shouting my name. I made a heroic surge, broke the tape and won!

My fantasy was transforming my reality. Or at least it was trying to. Oblivious to the miles that lay ahead, I sprinted, surged and passed more sensible competitors. I ran like a man possessed. It was a transcendental moment. My body became a machine. A sub-three-hour marathon suddenly became a piece of cake. I would knock thirty—no, forty-five minutes—off my best time.

But a problem developed late in the race. I ran out of energy before I ran out of miles. My legs suddenly felt numb and bloodless. My body began to quiver with fatigue, like a top that's begun to wobble. In marathoning they call it "The Wall," that unmarked spot in the road where familiar ends and unfamiliar rushes in. The wall is a threshold of pain few care to traverse.

A serious runner comes to think of fatigue as city residents do car alarms. You know it's supposed to signify that something bad is going on, but you've heard it so many times, you disregard its warning. My decision was to finish. The burning sensation in my legs would just have to be endured. I continued. Over the next mile, the stinging sensation that had started in my legs worked itself up through the rest of my body. I began to lose the ability to concentrate. My stomach was cramping badly, too, and I ran along clutching, grimacing and bending.

I invented a mental ploy to keep myself moving. I would imagine the finish line one mile away. When I completed that mile, I would try for another. Before long, though, I was in the grip of inexpressible fatigue. As I stumbled through the last aid station at mile 25, there was a sense of impending doom. I took water; I heard voices. The world went black and I fell to the side of the road.

I awoke slowly, gazing up into a gentle blue sky, still alive and intent on staying that way. Now there was no shame attached to dropping out of the race. I had earned my ride to the finish. I waited patiently for the paramedics to swoop in and carry me off.

Then I heard a command, "Come on, get up!" I remember being perfectly dazed, first by the demand, and then by how unhappy the whole prospect of getting to my feet made me feel. I turned my head toward the road. There stood a runner, bent over, hands on his knees. "Come on," he said. "We'll finish together." As he spoke, his body weaved to and fro.

What powerful forces reignited a fire that was extinguished by massive doses of agony and fatigue, I'll never understand. I knew only that his words were a healing salve, his determination a shot of adrenaline. He pulled me to my feet and together, like Napoleon's numbed, dog-weary soldiers, we jogged, walked and ultimately dragged ourselves down the road. When I spotted the finish I felt a surge of energy. I took off running, leaving my companion behind, and stumbled across the line overjoyed, astonished and exhausted all at once.

I stood there, waiting for my friend. I wanted to offer my thanks. I wanted to share a cold beer and a laugh and relive the race with him. But no one crossed the line behind me. I checked the finish chute, searched the crowd and scanned the parking lot. I went onto the course searching for him. Nothing. It was as though my running partner had simply vanished into thin air. An angel sent to rescue me.

I've competed in many marathons since then, but nothing has given me such a deep awareness of my physical and emotional limits. More importantly, thanks to the angel at mile 25 I learned an invaluable lesson about friendship and camaraderie. One that I continue to pass onto others.

~Timothy Martin

90

Lost

Then you will call, and the Lord will answer; you will cry for help,
and he will say: Here am I.
~Isaiah 58:9

The Friday night movie drew to a close and I smiled. The glow from the television flickered over the faces of my friends, and I could tell they had enjoyed the movie as much as I had. As a seventeen-year-old girl, there was nothing better than hanging out with good friends and cute guys.

"Ahhh! That was good!" Jake said.

Laughter and conversation filled the room. I looked at my watch. 12:30 a.m. I needed to get home.

Jake ambled over and sank onto the couch next to me. "Hey, can I get a ride home?" My heart beat faster. Although I was a very safe driver, and had been driving for at least six months, I still had no sense of direction. I had followed detailed, printed instructions to get to this house, and I was counting on my second, opposite set of instructions to get me home.

"I don't know," I hedged. "I'm not the best with directions."

"It's super easy," he said. "I live right off the highway."

Holding my breath, I searched the faces of people gathering their things. Who else could do it? I would seem like a jerk if I refused a ride to big, innocent, loveable Jake. No one would understand my fear of getting lost.

I looked back at Jake and his hopeful smile. He really was the sweetest guy there. How hard could it be?

"Okay," I said.

Jake's beefy, freckled arm clamped my body to his.

"Thank you Jenny! It's no big deal. You'll see."

The small crowd dispersed, and Jake and I climbed into my parents' car. I drove him to his house, which, thankfully, was within sight of the highway. After letting him off at the curb, I requested a run-through of the directions back to my house.

"Just make a U-turn and you'll be headed straight home," he said.

"There won't be any splits or forks where I have to choose a side?"

"None."

"You're positive?"

"Absolutely."

"Okay. Goodnight." I watched him walk to his house, took a deep "you can do this" breath, and made my U-turn to get back on the highway. After driving a while without recognizing a thing, an anxious glance at the dashboard clock told me it was 1:15 a.m. I focused on the road and studied every single sign and landmark, desperately hoping to see something I recognized. My sights locked on two big, green signs approaching rapidly. Oh no. Oh no.

A fork.

121 North or 121 South? 183 East or 820 West?

The names were familiar, but for the life of me, I had no idea which way to go. My heart was racing. "You can do this," I told myself. "Pick one. If it's not right, turn around and try the other."

I chose a path.

I was going south. Or was it west? I concentrated on breathing steadily and continued, still looking for a landmark I might know. Finally, I couldn't deny it. I had chosen the wrong path.

"Okay. Okay. Just turn around." I looked ahead to the next exit and wondered what my parents were doing. Were they freaking out? Or had they gone to bed hours ago, thinking that I would come home on time like I always did? With no cell phone, I had no way to find out.

I took the next exit. The road veered sharply to the right, and something was terribly wrong. Another mistake. A big one. A frightened cry escaped as I realized that I had not taken an exit, but some kind of loop!

My cries turned into loud, desperate prayers. As soon as I exited the ramp, I pulled over and looked behind me to where I had just been. I quieted as my eyes took in the maze of highways and signs all converging and circling each other with bridges and overpasses.

God, help me.

I studied my surroundings. There were hardly any streetlights. I rechecked my doors to make sure they were locked. Every building was shrouded in darkness. Except one.

Scenes from every scary movie I had ever seen flashed through my mind, but I knew what I had to do. "Okay, God," I prayed. "I put my trust in you. I know I can't sit here on the side of the road all night. Please protect me. I trust you. No matter what happens, I trust you."

Breathing shakily, I pulled into the small, dingy parking lot of the twenty-four-hour diner. The view through the smoky windows showed only swarthy, formidable-looking men.

Not a woman in sight.

Determined, I parked the car and opened the door. Legs trembling, I breathed another prayer and managed to walk toward the entrance. As I reached it, the door opened, and a man dressed all in white stepped out of the building.

His eyes met mine, and I was struck by the kindness of his gaze. He did not look surprised to find me there, but seemed already aware of my situation.

"Can I help you?"

His face was open and caring, and he had a calm, capable demeanor. As I stood there studying him, I realized my fear had disappeared.

"I'm lost, and I need a phone to call my parents."

"Where do you need to go?"

"The Hurst-Euless-Bedford area."

"Oh, well, I'm on my way home right now and I live right by Euless. Would you like to follow me until you know where you are?"

I stared at him and contemplated his comforting presence, his white clothing, his perfectly timed appearance, and the likelihood of running into someone that just happened to live in my neighborhood when I was so far from home. I desperately wanted to ask, "Are you an angel?" But all I said was, "Okay, thanks. That sounds good."

I followed him for quite some time as the scenery changed from foreign, to vaguely familiar, to "I know where I am." I thanked God over and over and enjoyed the wonderful feeling of relief.

When my exit came, I left the highway and soon locked the front door behind me as I breathed in the familiar scent of home.

I knew I would have a scary story for my parents in the morning, and I knew a cell phone would soon be coming my way.

And I will always wonder…. Did I see an angel?

~Jenny Snow

"Step Back!"

It comes down to whether you believe in
seven miraculous escapes a week or one guardian angel.
~Robert Brault

My son Ryan was a ten-year-old soccer whiz kid, rarely without a ball at his feet.

I came to pick him up from practice one evening. It was dark, and the bright lights cast large shadows on the field.

Wind started to blow in from the southeast. One of our not-infrequent, Central Florida thunderstorms was brewing.

Ryan stood in front of the goal mouth, blocking final shots from his remaining teammates waiting for their rides, when I saw a gust of wind lift the back end of the goal. No sandbags, no anchors held it down.

The solid, wooden four-by-fours of the goal mouth's frame fell forward, the crossbar rushing straight toward Ryan's head.

Ryan and the other kids didn't notice.

I didn't know what to do. If I called Ryan's name, he might turn to look at me but not move, or move toward me and remain in jeopardy. I wanted him to run fast, away from the goal, but didn't think he could outpace the falling frame.

I felt powerless and said nothing, but my heart screamed out to God.

All of a sudden, Ryan, still facing forward and seemingly oblivious to the impending danger, took a step backward, deeper into the goal, a fraction of a second before the heavy frame fell around him. It missed his head by mere inches, coming down right where he had stood the moment before.

I ran over to him.

"Are you okay? I'm so glad you stepped back into the goal. What made you do that? It was the only safe thing you could have done," I said, realizing the truth of those words as I helped him scramble out from under the net.

"I heard you yell, 'Step back!' so I did," he said.

"I didn't say anything," I said. "No one here did. It happened so fast, I didn't even know what to tell you to do."

We looked at each other, the same thought forming.

"Do you think it was my guardian angel?" he asked.

"I'm sure it was," I said, and I thanked God for sparing my son.

~Barbara Routen

Chapter
10

Angels Among Us

Angel Protection

Whispered Warning in the City of Angels

Put your ear down close to your soul and listen hard.
~Anne Sexton

"Don't stop." No kidding. There was no way, in any scenario, I'd stop.

I had just navigated Sunset Boulevard, after emerging from one of the many rock clubs peppering that stretch of the Sunset Strip. It was the late 1980s. Big hair and heavy metal had their black-nail-polished grip on the nation.

As the manager of a variety of bands and musical acts, the company for which I worked was a bicoastal one—and an international one—based in Tokyo. We had an office in New York City's hip SoHo (before big business muscled its way in and turned unique into uniform) and two offices in LA: one just off Sunset Boulevard and another in residential Coldwater Canyon, a part of Beverly Hills (yes, it really was the 90210 area code). It was heady stuff for a twenty-something girl living her rock-n-roll dream. I was young and totally into the fact that I worked in New York City and travelled to work in LA—not to mention around the world.

I was by myself in the crummy little company car. Exiting the clubs before closing time did not help me beat the traffic. Even at 1:30 in the morning, the Strip was rocking with Spandexed and eye-linered fans, lipstick-pouting wannabes and other assorted musical misfits swarming the Strip, spilling out from places like the Whisky, The Roxy and the Rainbow.

I hated to cut out "early," but in reality, I was drained. Too many meetings and too much band insanity had left me so tired that not even a night of heavy metal clubbing could energize me. A full schedule of record company appointments and meetings with promoters loomed large in a few hours. I needed to be sharp. As much as I loved to squeeze every last second out of my LA experience, I could no longer string a sentence together out of sheer exhaustion.

My destination was a double dead-end road snaking amongst the hills, with a brooding, romantic-sounding name: Gloaming Way. No more than fifteen minutes from the Strip in theory. In practice, with traffic, it could take up to twenty-five minutes to get back to the Gloaming house. But to get to there, I needed to traverse Coldwater Canyon Drive.

How I hated that. In the daylight, it was bad enough. In the dead of night? Even worse.

Scary and treacherous, Coldwater Canyon Drive always freaked me out. As it ascended into the mountains, it merged with Mulholland — another winding road of white-knuckle driving. Thank goodness my turnoff was before that nightmare of a road.

From off Sunset, I'd take two quick right-hand turns, one onto N. Rexford and another onto N. Beverly, which dovetailed into the long stretch of Coldwater Canyon Drive.

My hearing still muffled from a night of volume ten music, I cranked the radio and cracked the window for fresh air. The stench of cigarettes clung to my clothes and hair.

As I turned right onto N. Rexford, I noticed headlights in my rearview mirror, coming up fast. My first inclination was to speed up, but then I thought, "Why should I? They can just slow down."

A stop sign was ahead so I started to slow down. The car behind me hit my bumper, lightly.

"Don't stop."

I was alone in the car, but a voice had just whispered the order: "Don't stop."

It was not the announcer on the radio.

It was not the song.

It was not a voice in my head.

During the past few months, there had been several news stories about rear-ending accidents. When the driver would get out of the car to check damage or trade insurance information, the person in the car behind them would rob them — or worse.

It was nearly two in the morning. No way was I getting out of the car. Besides, if there was any damage, it would be to my car and at that moment, I couldn't care less. So, I listened to that breathy yet commanding voice in my ear.

I had no time to freak out about that voice, no time to think about what it might be.

I continued down N. Rexford with the same car tailgating me, beams on high. It tapped my rear bumper again and again until I knew this was no innocent accident.

"Don't stop."

It was that voice again, but louder and clearer. There was no one else on the road. No cars, no pedestrians. I drove the speed limit until I came to N. Beverly and another stop sign. The car hit me again, so hard this time it pushed me through the stop sign into the intersection.

"DO NOT STOP."

This time, the voice reverberated through my entire body.

Four things I knew for certain in a split second: stopping on N. Beverly wouldn't happen; the car behind me wanted to hurt me; I wasn't driving to the house; and although I was alone in the car, I wasn't.

What happened next, I can't explain, even over twenty years later.

An overwhelming urge to get to the police station took hold of me. The thing was, I had no idea where it was — at least no conscious idea, anyway. I was flooded with warmth, and it felt like another pair of hands laid over mine. I jerked the wheel to the left, U-turning in the intersection, backtracking the way I came, down N. Beverly and onto N. Rexford, going beyond my starting point, towards Santa Monica Boulevard.

I couldn't see the car in my rearview mirror, but that didn't mean it wasn't there. I'm not sure how fast I was going, but it wasn't the speed limit anymore.

And there it was. Not the car, but the Beverly Hills Police Station. I cut into the parking lot of the station. The car that had followed me? Gone.

At that point, I turned off the ignition and flopped my forehead against the steering wheel. Then the uncontrollable shaking started. The sensible thing to do would have been to exit the car and report everything to the police. I couldn't.

Amazingly enough, my muffled hearing from my musical evening was gone. It was clear.

Playing on the radio?

"Angel" by Aerosmith.

"Listen to the lyrics."

I did.

I sat in the car and cried.

Alone—but not alone.

When I tell people the story of what happened, many try to explain it away—probably to make rational sense of it. "You were prepared. You heard the bump and rob story, so you didn't stop." "Oh, it was your subconscious talking or the radio."

But it wasn't.

What I didn't tell them is: This wasn't the first time I'd been saved by my guardian angel.

And it wasn't my last.

~Syndee A. Barwick

Saved by the Voice

Leave sooner, drive slower, live longer.
~Author Unknown

After teaching high school classes all day, I spent the late afternoon and evening correcting senior research papers. Successful completion of a perfectly typed and formatted eight- to ten-page paper, complete with proper attribution of works cited, was a requirement for graduation.

I'd skipped dinner and worked well past my normal bedtime, but I was proud of the fact that I'd finished the entire stack of twenty-five papers. Tomorrow, the students and I could talk about the changes they needed to make.

My route home was along acres of cranberry bogs, and the wispy "bog fog" illuminated by my headlights danced across the pavement. Low beam or high beam, I couldn't see very far in front of my car.

I just wanted to get home and go to bed. I'd driven this road every workday for nearly thirty years. Despite the fog, I was speeding right along, anxious to call it a day.

"Slow down," a stern voice implored me.

Startled, I lifted my foot from the gas pedal and looked quickly in the rearview mirror to see if perhaps a male student had stowed away in my back seat.

"Stop!"

I heard the shouted command, clear and strong. I slammed on the brake, totally unnerved and shaking head to toe.

Still, I saw nothing in the roadway in front of me, and no cause for alarm.

With my car completely stopped, I sat there for a moment with the engine idling, telling myself I was being silly, that I was just too tired, or too hungry, and my imagination was playing tricks on me.

I took a deep breath and started inching forward again at a very slow crawl.

A scant few seconds later, an enormous bull elk loomed out of the fog, standing directly in my path. I stepped on the brake again, stopped, and breathed a very deep sigh of relief.

Never in thirty years had I seen an elk in this area. They are huge animals. This fellow had antlers that spread almost as wide as my car, and I'm sure it weighed more than 1,000 pounds.

There is no doubt in my mind that if I had not heeded the mysterious warning, I would have collided with this woodland monster and died right there that night.

"You have a guardian angel," said a colleague the next day when I related my tale in the faculty room.

"Good thing," said my principal. "We need you to help these kids get their diplomas."

His was not the most compassionate of statements, but perhaps he hit the nail on the head. Perhaps I was spared because I still had work here to do. Perhaps I was still needed on the planet.

I hung a small crystal angel on my rearview mirror to remind me to always listen well and respond immediately without question.

~Jan Bono

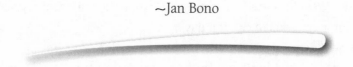

94

Learning to Listen

Angels are all around us, all the time, in the very air we breathe.
~Eileen Elias Freeman,
The Angels' Little Instruction Book

I always knew there was more to our world than what most people thought. I loved to read about ghosts and spirits, angels and beings of Light who are there to help us and guide us. But they never really made their presence known in a big way until after our baby girl was born.

Jim and I bought our first house a year before Eryn was born. We were so proud of that place even though it had no running water, plastic sheeting for windows, and a homemade door that we held closed with a butter knife. During the day you could see outside through the space between the walls and the ceiling. But we had a house and twelve acres that we could call our own. We had some great parties in that house and it became a gathering place for all our friends.

We had a really cold winter when Eryn was just over one year old. Our only heat was a fireplace with glass doors and a built-in fan at the top. Jim had a job as a welder at the place they were built. The fireplace heated the main living area but the rest of the house stayed quite cool thanks to all the holes between the walls and ceilings. We never could find and patch all of them.

One day I had set Eryn down on her blanket in just her diaper, surrounded her with her favorite toys and curled up on the couch to read where I could keep an eye on her. The fire was blazing and life felt very cozy and complete.

I suddenly felt like there was a presence beside Eryn and a thought flashed through my mind.

"Move her to the other side of the room."

"That's weird," I thought. "She is really happy where she is. Why would I think that?"

After looking around a bit I couldn't see anything that could hurt her so I went back to my book.

A few minutes later I felt the presence again and this time it seemed bigger, as though it needed to get my attention. But again I put it down to imagination.

This time I heard the words in my head as though they did not come from me but were spoken by someone else.

"Move her to the other side of the room."

Again, I looked around the area and couldn't see anything.

"It must be my imagination," I thought. "There is just no sensible reason for me to move her."

As I turned my eyes back to my book, the skin on my arms prickled. The presence became unmistakable.

"Vicky! Move her now!"

Well, they called me by my name. Before I even had time to think, I had jumped up off the couch and grabbed little Eryn into my arms and pulled her blanket across the room. Not five seconds later, the glass from the fireplace blew out and super heated shards landed right where Eryn had been sitting, melting into the linoleum floor.

I held my baby and stood shaking and crying, staring in disbelief at the glass embedded in the floor where Eryn had been sitting only seconds before. I felt waves of gratitude to this incredible being, whose presence I could feel in the room, that came to us and saved our little girl from harm.

Even though I had always believed that angels visit regular people, I never, in my wildest dreams, thought that one would find its way to my door.

I believe that this was Eryn's guardian angel and he had come to keep her safe and protect her.

Throughout her life I called on that angel to be with her. During her teen years, I know that her angel kept her from being injured in a terrible accident when the driver of the truck she was in lost control and went over a steep embankment. I believe that same angel also kept our other daughter, Amy, and her friend from getting into the back of that pickup.

After the accident, which paralyzed a young man, Amy told me that she went to get into the back of the truck when she heard a voice.

"Get out of the truck, now!"

She was so surprised and shaken that she got out immediately and told her friend to stay behind with her. Amy is convinced that listening to that voice saved their lives.

I have learned to listen to those warning voices. They have helped me, my children, and my grandchildren many times over the years.

~Vicky Ford

95

Angel at the Wheel

Angels shine from without because their spirits
are lit from within by the light of God.
~Eileen Elias Freeman,
The Angels' Little Instruction Book

I n June of 1997 I was traveling to Montreal from my home in Toronto. Close friends had asked me to DJ for their wedding reception. Tight financial circumstances at that time compelled me to plan a quick trip, and I had other commitments the next day.

As I planned for the trip, I realized I needed to bring my equipment and travel the seven hours on the day of the wedding, then drive back immediately following the reception. It would take about fourteen hours of driving—a whirlwind twenty-four-hour experience. I was no longer a young man but I figured I could do it.

On Saturday morning I packed my van, kissed my family goodbye, as our infant daughter was too young for this journey, and left alone. The trip to Montreal was pleasant—a warm, late-spring day and a wonderful trip along one of Canada's most pleasant highways. I arrived in Montreal in the late afternoon, set up my equipment, and had about two hours to relax before the reception began. I wandered downtown Montreal and enjoyed being an observant tourist. I thought about sleeping in my van, but it was too hot in the parking lot.

The reception was held at one of Montreal's most splendid hotels.

Greek by descent, my friends' wedding featured many Greek customs and cuisine. I carefully avoided alcohol, as I faced a long drive home. A fun-filled celebration followed and I enjoyed playing a part in this wonderful experience. At 1 a.m. the music ended and I began packing and loading my equipment. At about 2 a.m. I departed the hotel for the long journey home.

It's a strange thing to travel a path by night that you only just travelled a few hours earlier in daylight. The lights, the shadows — they create an ethereal image that I find very poetic. It was just my radio, the scenery and me for the next seven hours. An hour after I departed, the deep night darkness replaced the scenery as I entered the rural stretch that made up about five and a half hours of my trip.

Canada's Highway 401 is similar to interstate highways throughout the U.S. — two lanes going in each direction, separated by a grassy median about 100 feet across. As I continued to drive, I fought my weariness. A trick I knew, from years on the road as a musician, was to wait as long as possible to consume coffee. That way the coffee had full effect. I had planned for a rest stop somewhat farther ahead.

At about 5 a.m., in the early stages of dawn, weariness won the battle. For most of my trip I had been the only vehicle visible. The last thing I clearly remembered was being on the highway. The next thing I realized was that I was parked at the left side of the median that divided the highway.

I'd had what I thought was a dream, and I was confused as to why I was stopped. I opened the door to get out. Standing beside the van, I looked behind me and observed the median. The grass, which was two- to three-feet high in places, showed a line of tire tracks nearly a quarter mile long. The tracks showed a vehicle leaving the highway and rolling down the slope to the bottom of the median, traveling over rocks and knolls, then turning back and ending at my van.

I had left the road and somehow come back to the highway and stopped safely, only striking one or two road markers that held reflective signs along the side of the highway.

I thought of the dream I had experienced only a moment before.

I was cognizant of being behind the wheel, but a bright white light had surrounded me and my arms so warmly—as if wrapped in warm blankets from my shoulders to my hands. I felt the steering wheel while immersed in what I could only describe as a blanket of peace. I felt so very peaceful, yet I was aware of bouncing and swerving jostling me.

Standing behind my van, aghast at the sight of the fresh wheel tracks, I began to realize that something or someone had played a role in my avoiding a complete catastrophe. Given the slope into the center of the median, I was shocked that I had not rolled over. I tried to imagine myself actually driving over this median, but I would not have chanced it. It was nearly impossible for even the most experienced stunt driver, so an overtired entertainer would be an instant casualty.

Tears rolled down my cheek. I thought of that warm feeling and bright light. I thought of my family. I walked around the van—I observed a slight dent from the reflectors I had knocked over. I walked back and righted the reflectors, then restarted the van and gingerly returned to the highway. Not one vehicle had passed me while stopped. I started driving and felt the warmth around me. I kept thinking, and asking myself, what happened? How did I not meet disaster?

It had to be an angel. A divine presence had wrapped around me and saved me from injury or death. The light, the warmth, and the calm that surrounded me remained with me for the entire trip home. I never saw an angel, per se. There was no winged figure that majestically stood before me. I definitely felt a presence, a power that guided my van back to the road safely.

The trip home was filled with awe, thanksgiving and peace. I remembered stories my mother told from World War II when she was a teenager in London, England. She told us there were stories of British fighter planes being flown by angels in the desperate struggle that thwarted the German Air attacks. "Figures of light" in the cockpit, she would say. If someone had observed my van that day, would they have seen a "figure of light" at the wheel? I keep reflecting on it and will never stop believing that an angel was at the wheel of my van.

Twice more in my life, I have faced near-disaster. Both times took place on commercial ships—once on Lake Ontario, and once in the coastal waters of the Pacific Ocean in British Columbia. Both were situations where the ship and people on board were in peril. And both times, I felt that warm presence. I visually saw nothing, but I was well aware that I was protected. I felt peace was always present.

Thank you to the angel that has never left my side, and sometimes takes the wheel. I always know you are there.

~Peter J. Green

96

Not Really Alone

When the Angels arrive, the devils leave.
~Egyptian Proverb

The day started out like so many others—a jump in the shower, a quick cup of coffee and a trip to the park for a walk with my dog. My life had become so mundane. I didn't have to think about what I was doing—I just did it. No surprises. No excitement. No joy.

I'd been widowed for several years; my parents were long gone; I had few friends. I felt alone and forgotten. Some days, it seemed the only thing I really had to look forward to was that daily dog walk.

My forty-pound Heinz 57 dog, Salsa, always liked to circle the park before being turned loose in the fenced "doggy" area. Just after rounding the second curve that morning, I noticed two white pit bulls racing toward the park. They were collarless, on their own, and didn't appear to be up to any good.

Knowing how protective and territorial my dog can be, I tugged on her leash and tried to pull her back to the safety of the fenced area where I hoped to escape the pit bulls. No such luck—Salsa stood her ground, fixated on the rapidly approaching marauders.

The pit bulls locked on their target and tore across the ballpark toward us. Visions of brutal carnage raced through my brain. One dog would jump me, the other my dog. Both dogs would attack Salsa and rip her apart. Salsa would try to protect me and end up getting us both torn to ribbons. No matter what happened—it wasn't going to be pretty.

Trying to remain calm, I quickly considered my options. My walking stick wouldn't be much protection against two seventy-five-pound behemoths, and the pepper spray I carried around since I rescued Salsa ten years earlier had probably dried up. Not knowing what else to do, I threw myself on top of my fearless dog, tried to bury her head beneath my body, and said a desperate prayer.

All of a sudden, a teenage boy appeared and started batting at the pit bulls with the skateboard he was carrying. Where had he come from? I hadn't noticed him when I entered the park and I'd never seen him around the neighborhood. Why was he there? There was only one sidewalk in the park and it didn't look challenging enough to attract a skateboarder—even a beginner. Wasn't he afraid the dogs would turn on him? They didn't appear to be particularly pleased about being beaten with a piece of wood.

The larger of the two dogs bared its teeth and tried to devour the skateboard in one toothy chomp. Undaunted, the boy yanked the board from the dog's powerful grip and used it to whack the dog. The dog yelped and attempted to get away from the teenager's swinging skateboard. Obviously fearing similar punishment, the second dog turned tail and headed out of the park. Seeing the wisdom of its partner's departure, the first dog followed suit, with the teenager and his skateboard close behind.

Still lying on the ground, I looked around. The dogs were definitely gone but so was the boy. I wanted to thank him for coming to my rescue but I didn't know who he was, where he had come from, or what had happened to him. For months afterward, I asked everyone I met in the park if anyone knew or had seen the boy. No one had. He had mysteriously materialized and then, just as mysteriously, vanished. How did that happen?

And then it dawned on me. I hadn't been alone that day. I hadn't been forgotten. God had always been with me, watching over me, shedding His light on me. Maybe the teenage boy had been sent by God. Maybe not. Either way, I realized God had come to my rescue and sent a teenage guardian angel to protect me. From that point on, I knew I would never again feel alone or forgotten.

~Margaret Nava

The Angel in Red

Insight is better than eyesight when it comes to seeing an angel.
~Eileen Elias Freeman,
The Angels' Little Instruction Book

I'll never forget the day my one-year-old daughter Becky came down with what I thought was a terrible cold. We had been to the doctor's office a couple of days earlier, but she wasn't improving. It was a cold day in Georgia. We rarely had ice or snow, but we woke up that morning to a blanket of the white stuff on the rooftops, roads, and highways.

Over thirty years ago, we were not at all prepared for severe weather in Georgia. We could count on two things happening when it snowed. First, everyone stayed home. Second, the telephone lines would be busy. I was not a fan of ice or snow, but as long as we had electricity and I had food in the house, I was content to just watch it come down.

As the day progressed, however, Becky began running a high temperature and had a terrible cough. It took me quite a while to get a telephone line so that I could contact her doctor. But finally, a line was open and to my surprise our pediatrician answered my call. He happened to be in his office.

"Can you get her to my office?" he asked.

Fortunately, my husband Roy was home. When I told him that we had to take Becky to the doctor, he went outside and began shoveling the snow off the driveway. I wrapped our twin sons in coats, mittens and gloves. I grabbed the heaviest blanket I could find and wrapped Becky in it. Off we went, slipping and sliding, making our way to the pediatrician's office. Even thought it took three times longer than usual, we made it without any problems.

The doctor thought there was a possibility that Becky had pneumonia, so he instructed us to take her to the hospital for chest X-rays. Roy drove slowly toward the hospital. There were very few people on the road. He stopped at the foot of a hill where the driveway led to the entrance.

"I don't think I can make it up the hill in the car," Roy hesitantly explained.

"I'll get out and carry her up the driveway," I said with some trepidation. The driveway was covered in ice. As I gazed at the hill before me, I offered up a brief prayer and thought about how there was not a soul in sight.

Roy and the boys watched us as we started walking up the hill. I had only taken a few steps when my foot slipped. But by the grace of God, I caught myself. I started walking again when suddenly my other foot slipped and I knew that we were going down. There was absolutely nothing I could do. It seemed like we were going down in slow motion. Of course my first thought went to how I would protect my sick child.

Suddenly, I felt a pair of strong hands grab my arm and pull me up. A man had appeared from nowhere. The only thing I noticed about him was that on that freezing cold day he wasn't wearing a coat, mittens or a hat. I noticed he was wearing a red sweater.

"Hold on," he said. "I'll walk with you."

I was no longer afraid. Somehow, I knew I would make it with his help. We finally made it to the top of the hill. He reached out to open the door for me. I walked inside ahead of him and turned to say thank you, but he was gone. The man in the red sweater had vanished into thin air. I proceeded to the office where we were supposed to report. Shortly thereafter Roy, Brad and Chad joined me.

"Did you see us almost fall?" I asked Roy.

"Yes, I did," he said. "I wondered how on earth you were able to stay on your feet."

"That man helped me," I explained.

"Nancy, you and Becky were the only ones walking up the driveway," he explained. Neither he nor either of the twins saw the man who held us up on the ice and then opened the door for us to go inside.

Thirty-four years later, even though the hospital has been remodeled and expanded, I think of the angel that wore a red sweater who kept us from falling that cold and icy day.

"Why a red sweater?" I wondered later. Then one day it dawned on me. "Roy and the boys would have certainly seen someone wearing red if he had been a common man. But he wasn't. He was an angel that God sent in the nick of time to save us from a terrible accident. And I was the only one that would see him."

~Nancy B. Gibbs

A Lifesaving Angel

We should pray to the angels, for they are given to us as guardians.
~St. Ambrose

When my car careened out of control on a deserted road, I thought I was doomed. Then I heard a soft, calming voice and sensed a mysterious, kind presence. It was just after five o'clock on a snowy November afternoon. I was on my way home from work and looking forward to a quiet evening. As I rounded the corner, a raccoon darted in front of my car. Swerving to avoid it, I bounced onto the shoulder. But just as I pulled back onto the road, the steering wheel locked. I panicked and jammed my foot on the brake, but the car wouldn't stop and I plowed into a tree. Glass shattered and metal crunched. I felt my head slam forward. My torso was crushed. Then everything went black.

When my eyes fluttered open, I could smell smoke and gasoline. I fought to regain consciousness. Although groggy and confused, I realized that I was trapped. But then I looked to my window and saw a handsome, kind-faced man with dark hair and brown eyes. He was dressed in a white shirt and wore no jacket.

"Am I dead?" I asked him. The man smiled and shook his head.

"No, you're alive," he said gently. And with a single pull, he wrenched open the mangled passenger door. Then reached across the seat and undid my seatbelt, scooping me into his arms. I could almost feel myself floating as he lifted me from the car and carried me a dozen yards from the wreck, tenderly placing me on the ground. Shaking with shock and relief, I touched my aching head and felt blood. He knelt by my side, and comforted me, dabbing my head with a cloth. He then covered me with a soft blanket.

"Help is on the way," he said. "You're going to be fine." He was so kind and his voice so gentle that I couldn't help relaxing. The next thing I knew, paramedics were loading me into an ambulance as firemen hosed down my flaming car. "Wait!" I cried. "I have to thank him!"

"Thank who?" a paramedic asked. But when I told him the story, he shook his head. "There was no one here when we arrived," he told me. "You were lying on the ground—alone."

"What about the blanket," I cried. "Where's the blanket he covered me with?"

"There was no blanket," he said. At first authorities suspected that I had hallucinated my rescuer. But someone had called 911—though the call was untraceable—and everyone agreed that I couldn't have climbed out of the wreck on my own. "Another few minutes and the car would have exploded with you in it," a mechanic determined.

Despite weeks of searching, I could never find the man who pulled me from my wrecked car. I can still see his face every time I close my eyes.

~Kathryn Radeff

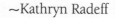

Team Angel

For every soul, there is a guardian watching it.
~The Koran

My mother has always joked that I don't have one guardian angel—I have a team. "One angel can't handle you," she laughs. It certainly made sense to me when I was a child, and as an adult, it seems to be equally true. I'm not exactly low-maintenance. I imagine that my angels have to work in teams to keep up with me. Perhaps there's one who handles all the things I lose, another for health, another for safety.

Team Angel makes itself known to me in small, yet significant ways: impossible situations seem to work themselves out, and assistance appears from unlikely sources when I need it. When I'm feeling low, I'll often come across random references to Michael, the Archangel who resonates most with me. I will be in a museum and suddenly see a painting of Michael, for instance. I'll be walking down the street and I'll see a poster of him in a store. It happens way too often to be coincidental. Every now and then, however, Team Angel has to take more drastic measures to keep me safe.

When I was in my mid-twenties, just going to work every day was an ordeal for me. It wasn't the job, so much; it was getting there. My workplace was in the middle of Times Square, which was arguably one of the most popular tourist destinations in New York City. The crowds were always dense. Street vendors lined the sidewalks. I never knew when a tourist was going to stop abruptly right in front of me, hit me with a knapsack, or block the sidewalk. Navigating Times Square required nimble feet, quick reflexes and a knack for defensive walking. When I crossed the street I had to be especially vigilant: taxis and buses were often reckless, despite the hordes of people.

One afternoon, I stood impatiently at 47th Street and waited to cross Seventh Avenue. Behind me, a serpentine line for the half-price Broadway ticket booth, men handing out restaurant menus and street vendors clogged most of the available sidewalk space. As usual, I hovered on the very edge of the curb as I waited for the light to change.

As I stepped into the street, a cab hurtled toward me. It took me completely off-guard, as the vehicle seemed to have come from nowhere. I always looked both ways and crossed with the light, but it seemed to be a moot point. The cab was following its own set of rules. It happened so quickly that I didn't even have time to realize that the taxi was going to hit me dead on.

Someone roughly grabbed me by the elbow and pulled me backward, out of harm's way. As I stumbled back to the curb, I could feel the wind from the cab as it sped past. I exhaled and shuddered as I realize how close I had come to a complete disaster, but my heart warmed to realize that a complete stranger had saved my life by reacting so quickly.

"Thank you…" I said, and turned to my rescuer. The only problem was that nobody was standing next to me. The sidewalk in my immediate area was empty, and the tourists at the discount ticket booth were too far away to have offered any assistance. I looked to my left. The space there was empty, too. I examined my elbow. Whoever saved me had pulled me back very abruptly, but oddly enough, there wasn't any pain in my arm or bruising on the skin.

Who pulled me out of the street? Say what you will, but I think Team Angel was in Times Square that day.

~Denise Reich

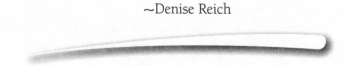

Saved by an Angel

But even now I know that whatever you ask of God, God will give you.
~John 11:22

Our wonderful day at the lake turned into a tragedy as a car came over the yellow line into our lane at full speed, hitting us head-on. After the impact I only remember bits and pieces: the rancid smell of leaking anti-freeze and burned rubber; the loud whir of the Jaws of Life, and my two young daughters screaming and crying. My husband was told by one of the paramedics on the scene that I only had about three minutes to live when they got to me. I was bleeding to death.

My injuries were devastating. My body was crushed from the waist down. I went from being a healthy twenty-four-year-old woman to a bruised and broken accident victim with a life full of limited mobility, pain, and multiple surgeries. But our blessings were beyond measure! Our accident happened in front of a volunteer fire station. Both of my daughters, Tiffini who was six, and Krista who was ten months old, had bruises, but would heal completely. My husband walked away from a head-on collision with nothing more than a scratch on his stomach and a strained hand from holding onto the steering wheel. Even with my injuries, I had survived this horrific event with no major head trauma.

I spent three days in the ICU, and a month in the hospital's trauma unit. While there I had three surgeries: a ten-hour emergency surgery when I first arrived, then two four-hour surgeries on my shattered right ankle. I cannot begin to express the amount of physical pain I was in. When I was finally released from the hospital, on a stretcher in an ambulance, I needed twenty-four-hour care. Not to mention the care needed for my two young daughters. My parents turned their living room into a makeshift rehabilitation room. I spent six months totally bedridden in a hospital bed set up in that room. My body was broken, but my spirit was not.

As I slowly healed and my pain was brought under control, I had more time to think about what had happened to us. Doctors, nurses, family and friends all called it a miracle. How I survived a 110 mph impact was something many could not understand. This was always a topic in every conversation of every person that came to visit me. The picture of my mangled car only heightened their amazement. I always believed in miracles but never thought I would experience one.

My faith is what kept me strong during this difficult time, and I knew that I needed to share this with my impressionable six-year-old daughter. I wanted her to know that I did not blame God for what had happened, and that God is still with us even when we have bad times. I called her to my bedside and began to talk with her. As I began to explain how I felt, she cut me off in mid-sentence and said, "I know that, Mommy. I saw the angel move in front of you just before the car hit us."

I stared at her. "You saw an angel?"

"Yes, he moved in front of you to protect you."

It was always puzzling to me how my upper body had been so protected from the slivers of broken glass and mangled metal. The dashboard had me trapped so tightly that it took thirty minutes to be extracted from it. Now, without a doubt, I understood. An angel saved me.

"Did she have wings?" I asked, curious.

"No," Tiffini told me without hesitation.

"Then what did she look like?" I asked.

"It wasn't a she angel, Mommy, it was a he angel, and he had long blond hair and a white robe."

I was stunned. It wasn't because I didn't believe her, but it was the matter-of-fact way she talked about it and how she corrected me when I kept referring to the angel as a she. When I think of angels, I always think of them as female. Most likely because of how often they are portrayed that way in art. This was a conversation I will never forget.

How humbling it is to me to have been saved by an angel. Not only did it save my physical life on this earth, but it made me realize that I do matter. That was something I struggled with most of my life. It has been seventeen years since my accident, and I have learned to appreciate each day, and take the hard times as life lessons and grow from them. And I have learned to not only cherish my family and friends, but let them know that I do. I hope that the angel who saved me is pleased with how I am living my second chance.

~Anna M. Jones

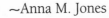

Who Was that Woman?

The most tangible of all visible mysteries—fire.
~Leigh Hunt

In 1991, my first husband and I lived in a small condominium in the suburbs of Denver. The condo had two bedrooms, one bathroom, a kitchen, living room and dining room. The kitchen was like a hallway with doorways at both ends and a breakfast bar that opened into the living room. The refrigerator, sink, oven and stove were all on one side and it was just countertop on the living room side. On this countertop were all of the appliances—blender, coffee pot, toaster oven, and toaster—all the major cooking utensils, and the roll of paper towels.

One evening, my husband had gone out with his friends. I enjoyed some quiet time to myself, being in complete control of the remote, watching television and making myself a fabulous dinner of tater tots and fish sticks in the toaster oven. I read while having a glass of wine, then turned off all the lights, except the small one over the stove, and went to bed around 10 p.m. I fell into a fast and deep sleep.

I was woken about an hour later when a woman came running into my bedroom screaming, "The house is on fire!" and then vanished. I woke with a start, not quite sure what had just happened, and bolted upright in the dark bedroom. I quickly looked behind me to my husband's side of the bed, which still lay empty, and surmised he was not home yet. The entire condo was still dark and very quiet.

I slid out of bed slowly, with my adrenaline rushing and my heart racing. I peeked out the bedroom door and up the hallway that led to the living room and the kitchen. I saw nothing in the darkness except the glow in the living room from the small light over the stove. I slowly made my way up the hall, and immediately smelled smoke. I looked to the breakfast bar opening, where I saw smoke coming from the top of the toaster oven. Not able to discern what was burning, I raced into the kitchen and flipped on the light.

I discovered the end of a paper towel roll had unwound a sheet or two, and the corner of the roll was closed in the toaster oven that I had, apparently, forgotten to turn off. Flames were shooting out all sides of the toaster oven. I grabbed the smoldering roll and, when I pulled on it, the portion closed in the toaster oven yanked the door open. A billow of smoke filled the area. I tossed the paper towel roll into the kitchen sink and slapped the faucet on with one fell swoop. I grabbed the largest cup I could find and started heaving cups full of water over the top of the toaster oven.

I launched cup after cup of water onto the appliance while sparks flew, the metal sizzled, and smoke filled the room. For one fleeting second I started to think that the whole place was going to burn down. I had a sudden memory flash of my mother telling me that you put out a grease fire with salt. So I grabbed the container of salt and shook it wildly over the toaster oven. The flames mostly diminished now, I grabbed a tea towel, dunked it into the sink—now full and overflowing with paper towel water—and threw it over what appeared to be the last of the flames and spark. Then time froze. After at least a minute of my standing there panting, huffing, puffing, and kind of crying, I turned off the water in the sink behind me. Then, I slowly lifted the wet tea towel and peered into the toaster oven to make sure nothing else was burning. Everything was smoky but nothing was burning. I spun the power dial to "OFF" using the tea towel, as if that mattered at this point, and fanned the air with my hand.

I realized that, when I served myself dinner, I had grabbed a paper towel for a napkin and had inadvertently closed the end of the roll into the toaster oven. It had been smoldering for about two hours and all the leftover grease and crumbs in the toaster oven had ignited.

It was only after I processed the cause of the fire that I recalled the woman had run into my bedroom to tell me the house was on fire. This realization made me weak in the knees. I wasn't sure what I had seen or who the woman was. I spent several minutes walking through the condo, now turning on all the lights and looking in every room and every cupboard and every closet. I was genuinely home alone and everything was closed and locked and exactly as it should have been—except of course for the kitchen and the toaster oven. The singed toaster oven sat on the damaged countertop in a pile of salt and a pool of water while water still dripped onto the floor from where the sink had overflowed.

I had no idea who the woman was or what she was doing in my house. Would I have been seriously injured in a devastating house fire that night? Thanks to whoever she was, I will never know.

~Sheryl Ricigliano

Meet Our Contributors

Debbie Acklin is a frequent contributor to the *Chicken Soup for the Soul* series. She lives in Alabama with her husband, two children, and Duchess the cat. She loves travel, photography, and, of course, writing. In the process of writing her first book, she hopes to also become a successful fiction writer. E-mail her at d_acklin@hotmail. com.

Monica A. Andermann lives and writes on Long Island, where she shares her home with her husband Bill and their cat Charley. In addition to several other credits in the *Chicken Soup for the Soul* books, her written work has been included in such publications as *Sasee*, *The Secret Place*, and *Woman's World*.

Beth Arvin is pleased to be a repeat contributor to the *Chicken Soup for the Soul* series. She writes a daily blog, betharvin365.livejournal. com, and a blog, "I Think So," for the *Kent Reporter*. Contact her via e-mail at betharvin@gmail.com.

Dana J. Barnett is a writer and English teacher. Her favorite things to do are writing, reading, hiking, watching movies, junking, and doting on her cats. Currently, among other projects, Dana is working on a children's book. Please send good thoughts her way. E-mail her at dbarnett25@gmail.com.

Syndee Barwick is a believer in the unseen. As an ordained interfaith minister, freelance writer and contributor to other *Chicken Soup for* *the Soul* anthologies, she knows from experience that the Universe is full of everyday miracles. E-mail her at thestoryshaman@gmail.com.

Irene Bastian farms with her husband in the foothills of Alberta, south of Calgary. Irene writes of God's handiwork in nature, the lessons it teaches and her family's faith walk as her daughter copes with a severe epilepsy disorder, which has totally changed the family's life focus. E-mail her at ibastian@platinum.ca.

Patty Beaumont received her Bachelor of Arts degree, with high honors, from Carlow University in 2000. She has been a professional grant writer for ten years in Pittsburgh, PA. In addition to writing for nonprofit organizations, she hopes to devote more time to writing inspirational stories in the future.

Glynis Belec celebrates life after cancer with her family in Ontario, Canada and counts her blessings daily. She is a freelance writer, a children's author and a tutor to some fabulous students. Check out her webpage at www.glynisbelec.com.

Sherry A. Bentley is a fourth grade teacher in central Ohio. She has a master's degree in literacy from Ashland University and is a National Writing Project Teacher Consultant. She is an avid reader who enjoys inspiring a love for both reading and writing in her students.

Susan Boles lives with her husband of thirty-six years and their three spoiled dogs in Tyler, TX. Originally from the Pacific Northwest, she has enjoyed a lifetime of traveling and journaling all the stories of the treasures and lives she's met along the road—true stories of life and love.

Retired teacher **Jan Bono** has been published in magazines ranging from *Guideposts* to *Woman's World*. She wrote a humorous personal experience newspaper column for over ten years, and has penned five humorous short story collections and a dozen one-act plays. Check out her work at www.JanBonoBooks.com.

Jo Brielyn is an author, poet, and health writer. She is also a singer/keyboardist with the band 24:Seven, an Air Force veteran, former youth leader, owner of CreativeKidsIdeas.com, and self-proclaimed coffee addict. Jo resides in Central Florida with her husband and their two daughters. E-mail her at jo@jobrielyn.com.

In **Sylvia Bright-Green's** thirty-three-year writing career, she has been published in twelve books, sold hundreds of manuscripts to newspapers and magazines and has written columns for local and national publications. Being a metaphysician/teacher, she also assists others to love and believe in themselves. E-mail her at bright-green@att.net.

Debra Ayers Brown is a freelance writer, humorist, blogger, magazine columnist, and award-winning marketing professional. A University of Georgia graduate, she earned her MBA degree from The Citadel. Debbie loves spending time with family and friends on the Georgia coast. Visit www.DebraAyersBrown.com and connect with her via www.About.Me/DebraAyersBrown.

Minnie Browne is active in her church, a court appointed Child Advocate/Guardian ad Litem, an artist, retired schoolteacher, and a freelance writer. She has been published in the *Chicken Soup for the Soul* series, *The Ultimate Mom*, the *Granbury Showcase Magazine*, and the *Langdon Review of the Arts in Texas*.

John P. Buentello writes essays, fiction, and nonfiction for adults and children. He is at work on a new novel and a picture book for children. E-mail him at jakkhakk@yahoo.com.

Trish Castro is retired and a full-time caregiver to her older sister who has COPD. She enjoys gardening, crafting, cooking and writing short stories and song lyrics. Although not famous, she is working on her autobiography simply because her life has been rather unusual and colorful!

Cindy Charlton is a published author and professional speaker using her own life experiences to bring hope and inspiration to everyone. She is the proud mom of two sons, and considers her dog to be an "angel with paws." E-mail her at cindycharlsky@gmail.com.

Melissa G. Christensen earned her Bachelor of Arts degree and Teacher Certification in English. She is a stay-at-home mom to her two energetic young children. Melissa spends her rare quiet moments cooking, reading, and pursuing her dream of writing children's stories.

Roberta Cioppa is an artist, sculptor and educator. She received her BFA and master's degrees from the University of Bridgeport and a CAS from Fairfield University. Roberta's paintings and sculptures are in numerous public and private collections, and can be viewed on the Internet.

Al Cole, from CBS Radio, is host of the syndicated show *People of Distinction*. He is also a singer and sought after motivational speaker. Al is also Communications Director for the World Green Energy Symposium in New York. Nancy is Al's lovely and talented fiancé. E-mail him at alcole2817@gmail.com.

Pam Depoyan holds a B.A. degree in English from Loyola Marymount University, Los Angeles, CA. Working in corporate communications, she also writes freelance and has been published in *Highlights for Children* and *Pray!* She enjoys creating "word-photo stories" that inspire and encourage. Read more or e-mail her at www.wordglow. wordpress.com.

Deborah Durbin is a British journalist and author of eleven nonfiction books. Her debut novel, *Oh Great, Now I Can Hear Dead People*, is now available from Amazon. Deborah is married, with three daughters, and resides in the UK. E-mail Deborah at deborah.durbin@talktalk.net.

Kris Flaa obtained her Master of Arts degree in gerontology before she left corporate management to write, see the National Parks, and spend more time with her family and friends. She's completed her first novel and is working on a second. She lives near Minneapolis with her partner and their charming Westie. E-mail her at kflaa@msn.com.

Vicky Ford lives in rural British Columbia, enjoying life with family and friends. She sees life as a spiritual journey and plans on presenting spiritual workshops in the future. Vicky loves travel, cooking, entertaining and playing with her grandchildren, and plans to write all about it. E-mail her at vickyf333@gmail.com.

Jess Forte is a new college student in Florida. She has recently self-published one of her stories and hopes to have many more published. When not writing, she enjoys spending time with her friends and family. Her goal is to leave an impact on the world as an author.

Ken Freebairn loves to write and had been married for over forty years to his childhood sweetheart. They have two wonderful children and three of the cutest grandchildren you have ever seen.

Nancy B. Gibbs is a pastor's wife, mother and grandmother. She is the author of eight books and a Christian speaker. She has been published in numerous *Chicken Soup for the Soul* books, other anthologies, newspapers, magazines and devotional guides. E-mail her at Nancybgibbs@aol.com.

Carol A. Gibson's work has been published in the *Chicken Soup for the Soul* series, *Parables for Today* 2012, *God Still Meets Needs* devotional and Downey Christian School reading textbooks. Her devotional, *Walking as Children of Light*, will be available through WestBow Press in December 2012.

Peter J. Green has become a "professional storyteller" in the tourism industry around Niagara Falls and southern Ontario. From a career in music and entertainment, Peter now lives in western New York with his wife, Danielle, and daughter (and up-and-coming storyteller) Maddie. Visit the family at www.encounterniagara.com.

Sheryl Grey lives with her husband and their four foster-adopted children in Indiana. Her writing has also appeared in *Adoptive Families* magazine and on the Midlife Collage website. She is currently working on her first novel.

Judy Gyde is a nurse and freelance writer from Toledo, OH. She and her husband of forty-two years help pastor a church and enjoy traveling. Her daughter, Christine, who the story was written about, has been married twelve years, is the mother of four children and is a schoolteacher.

Wendy Hobday Haugh is a freelance writer and piano teacher in Burnt Hills, NY. Her stories and nonfiction articles for adults and children have appeared in dozens of national and regional magazines, including *Woman's World*, *Highlights for Children*, and *Saratoga Living*. E-mail her at whhaugh@nycap.rr.com.

Morgan Hill is a former TV ad executive, now inner-city high school teacher and writer. Her B.A. degree is in TV-Radio-Film, with an M.S. degree in Special Education. She hopes her personal stories will inspire students' efforts toward landing their first job and making positive plans after graduation. E-mail her at mhwriter5@gmail.com.

Gary R. Hoffman taught school for twenty-five years. He has published or won prizes for over 325 short stories, poems, and essays. His short story collection, *I Haven't Lost My Marbles: They Just All Rolled to One Side*, will be published this fall by Mockingbird Lane Press. Learn more at www.authorgaryrhoffman.com.

Carol Huff, owner of Sudie Belle Animal Sanctuary in northeast Georgia, is a frequent contributor to the *Chicken Soup for the Soul* series, as well as a freelance writer for other well-known magazines. Aside from writing, she enjoys horseback riding and spending time with the animals. E-mail her at herbiemakow@gmail.com.

Jennie Ivey lives in Tennessee. She is a newspaper columnist and the author of numerous works of fiction and nonfiction, including stories in several *Chicken Soup for the Soul* anthologies. Visit her website at www.jennieivey.com.

JP Jackson observes and records the daily absurdities of life. Kids and dogs keep her humble, as well as providing poignant material. Part-time nursing helps to support her writing habit… soon to be a collection of humorous short stories! E-mail her at jpoi@live.com.

C.D. Jarmola, author of *Murder Goes to Church*, works as theatrical director at Oklahoma Wesleyan University when she's not busy writing books or taking care of her family: the Theologian, the DJ and the Diva. Read more about her life and her upcoming books on her blog devotionsfromtheresidentheretic.blogspot.com.

Anna Jones lives in central Kentucky with her husband and two daughters. She enjoys traveling, reading, and spending time with family and friends. Writing is her passion and she has published short stories in multiple anthologies. E-mail her at AJCaywood1@ yahoo.com.

Tom Kaden is counselor at Someone To Tell It To—www. someonetotellitto.org. He is a graduate of Messiah College and Asbury Theological Seminary. Tom and his wife Sarah and their four children live in Carlisle, PA.

Pat Kane, who resides in Joplin, MO with her husband Walter and their three dogs, is a published author who enjoys writing stories and novels for children and inspirational stories of real-life events. She's a member of the Society of Children's Book Writers and Illustrators and the Missouri Writer's Guild.

L.A. Kennedy is a writer and an artist. She began journaling when she was twelve. Her unusual and humorous experiences are the source for many of her short stories. Her works in progress include two novels. She also sculpts and creates folk art. E-mail her at elkaynca@aol.com.

Mary Potter Kenyon has had over 300 articles and essays published in newspapers, magazines and anthologies, including four *Chicken Soup for the Soul* books. She conducts couponing and writing workshops for local colleges and writes a weekly column for Dubuque's *Telegraph Herald*. She blogs at marypotterkenyon.com. Learn more at marypotterkenyon.writersresidence.com.

Cathi LaMarche is the author of the novel *While the Daffodils Danced* and has contributed to over a dozen anthologies. She currently teaches composition and literature in a Catholic school in St. Louis. She shares her home with her husband, two children, and three dogs.

Lisa Leshaw has created a new "bucket list" that includes writing for a major magazine. Until then she is thrilled to spend her days on frog hunts with Mush and Gab and walks in the park with Stu (and eating tons of chocolate when no one is looking).

Donna Lowich works as an information specialist, providing information to people affected by paralysis. She enjoys writing about her family and personal experiences. Other hobbies include reading and counted cross-stitch. She lives with her husband in New Jersey. E-mail Donna at DonnaLowich@aol.com.

Thomas J. Lumbrazo has lived in Northern California for forty-seven years with his wife Carol. He was a city planner and now is an author, artist, and photographer. If you wish to see the Archangel Michael cloud from Sedona, visit his website at www.whenangelstouch.com.

David Magill lives with his wife Patti in Minnesota. He enjoys writing, reading, and exploring life through a literary lens. David is currently writing many short stories, mostly real life events as relayed to him through his friends and family, or recalled from his own memory. E-mail him at dpmagill@yahoo.com.

Laurie Mangru completed a double major program at the University of Toronto in English literature and Spanish. After, she moved to Japan where she has taught English for nine years. Laurie is a world traveler and has enjoyed writing short stories and poems since she was a child. E-mail her at laurieloveswriting@gmail.com.

Donna L. Martin splits her time between running a Taekwondo school, where she is a Fourth Degree Black Belt, and writing children's picture books, middle grade and young adult novels. You can contact her on her blog at www.donasdays.blogspot.com or her website at www.donnalmartin.com.

Tim Martin is the author of numerous young adult novels, including *Summer With Dad*, *Rez Rock* and *Wimps Like Me*. He is a contributing author to over a dozen *Chicken Soup for the Soul* books. E-mail Tim at tmartin@northcoast.com.

Dennis McCloskey has a journalism degree from Ryerson University in Toronto. He has been a full-time freelance writer since 1980 and is the author of several books, including the 2008 award-winning biography, *My Favorite American*. He lives in Richmond Hill, ON, with his wife Kris. E-mail his at dmcclos@rogers.com.

Rosemary McLaughlin was a teacher of English and writing for thirty-five years. In retirement, she has been writing, traveling and enjoying her home and family. E-mail her at rosemarymclaugh@gmail.com.

Michelle Close Mills' poetry and short stories have appeared in many poetry and short story anthologies including several in the *Chicken Soup for the Soul* series. Michelle resides in Central Florida with her husband, two kids, two meowing furbabies, and three chirping featherbabies. Learn more at www.authorsden.com/michelleclosemills.

Sandy Moffett is a poet and inspirational author. She and her husband Greg live in Bakersfield, CA, and have four children and six grandchildren. Sandy works in her family's funeral business and strives to bring comfort through her writings. E-mail Sandy at sm@sandymoffett.com.

Sarah Clark Monagle is an educator, mother, writer, photographer and brain tumor survivor. Her work has been published in poetry reviews, and she is a regular contributor to the *Chicken Soup for the Soul* series. She is currently working on a poetry collection and a novel. You can follow her at www.sarahmonagle.wordpress.com.

Marya Morin has been freelancing for many years and writes custom poetry on commission. She lives in the country, where she is retired and has plenty of time to pursue her most favorite hobbies of all, taking care of her family, reading and writing.

When **Gail Molsbee Morris** isn't chasing after God's heart, she chases rare birds across America. She can be reached through her nature blog at godgirlgail.wordpress.com or Twitter at @godgirlgail.

Nell Musolf lives in Minnesota with her husband and two sons, and is always on the lookout for more angels in her life. E-mail Nell at nellmus@aol.com.

Before retiring to New Mexico, **Margaret Nava** spent twenty years traveling throughout the Southwest, researching and writing short stories about nature, spirituality, and Native American traditions. Since then, she has written two New Mexico travel guides and three lady-lit novels. E-mail her at angeladunn08@aol.com.

Linda Rhinehart Neas is a teacher, poet, and writer. She has two books, *Winter of the Soul* (2008) and *Gogo's Dream: Swaziland Discovered* (2010). She teaches ESL, writing and poetry throughout New England. Ms. Neas lives in an enchanted cottage with her beloved husband, where her muses are her daughters and grandchildren.

Susana Nevarez-Marquez is a lifelong observer of spiritual events. The sense of wonder that the Blue Bug incident provoked sparked an urge to write. Currently, she writes ethnic and romantic fiction, all with a supernatural element inspired by true events. E-mail her at NevMarWrite@gmail.com.

Linda Newton is a counselor in California, and a popular speaker at women's events. Visit her online at www.LindaNewtonSpeaks.com. She is author of *12 Ways to Turn Your Pain Into Praise*, and *Better Than Jewels*.

Susan Allen Panzica is a graduate of Montclair State University who interrupted a career in New York City to marry her chiropractor husband, manage his office, and raise a family. Susan is a speaker, women and children's Bible teacher and writer of the devotional blog Eternity Café. Learn more at www.susanpanzica.com.

Vi Parsons is a genealogy researcher, teacher and author. Her books, *Jacob Dragoo and our Susanna Bright Side* and *The Dragoo Cemetery: Marion County, West Virginia*, document her ancestry. She also co-authored *Double Take*, which offers a glimpse of her childhood memories growing up with her twin. Visit her website at www.carrtwins.com.

Andrea Peebles lives with her husband of thirty-five years in Rockmart, GA. She is a frequent contributor to the *Chicken Soup for the Soul* series and enjoys cooking, reading, writing, travel, photography and spending time with family. E-mail her at aanddpeebles@aol.com.

Kristine Peebles has a Bachelor of Arts degree in English from Duquesne University in Pittsburgh, PA. She lives with her two sons, two cats, two tortoises and a host of angels. E-mail her at rosecourt710@gmail.com.

Dr. Debra Peppers, troubled teen to Teacher of the Year, inducted into the National Teachers Hall of Fame upon retirement, is a member of the National Speakers Association, an Emmy Award-winning playwright, author, radio and television host. She has traveled the world speaking. Contact Dr. Peppers at www.pepperseed.org.

Novelist, blogger, and award-winning food writer, **Perry P. Perkins** is a work-at-home dad, and the owner of hautemealz.com. Perry has written for hundreds of magazines including *Writer's Digest*, *American Hunter*, and *Guideposts*. His inspirational stories have been included in many *Chicken Soup for the Soul* anthologies.

Karen (Kandy) Petillo received a Bachelor of Arts degree in journalism and a master's degree in American History and European History from California State University, Fullerton. She enjoys traveling and adores her five grandchildren. She is a Realtor in Newport Beach, CA. E-mail her at kandypetillo@cox.net.

Pamela Millwood Pettyjohn, a Berry College graduate, is a teacher, musician, and writer at church. She participates in the North Georgia Group of the Chattanooga Writers' Guild. Pamela and her husband Charles enjoy volunteering in a nursing home, music ministry, hiking, photography, and being with Cole, their dog.

Lori Phillips is a writer, author and editor residing in Orange, CA.

She has a Bachelor of Arts degree and Master of Education. In addition to being the Marriage and Dreams editor for BellaOnline.com, she owns reallifehelpbooks.com and the-dream-collective.com.

Christine Pincombe-DeCaen previously worked as a chef. Now she takes care of her young daughter full-time. Christine enjoys writing, painting, making and selling her jewelry. She is working on her first fiction novel. E-mail her at sarahkayday@hotmail.ca.

Kathryn Y. Pollard grew up in Oklahoma spending most of her time locked inside her bedroom writing stories and poems. She resides in Georgia. She is a published author of one novel and several short stories. She loves to teach the Bible and encourage people to enjoy life.

Reverend Anthony D. Powell resides in California. He started writing about his life-changing experiences due to an unexpected death of a close friend. It was at that moment God gave him a vision that would change his life forever. May this story bless and encourage you in your time of need.

Kathryn Radeff is a writer and educator. She teaches writing workshops in western New York and Southwest Florida, and as a teacher gives inspiration and instruction students need to achieve success. Kathryn enjoys traveling, swimming and spending time with her adorable dog, Remington. E-mail her at kradef1@msn.com.

Denise Reich practices aerial arts, dances, takes photos and paints. She writes regularly for the Canadian magazine *Shameless*; other recent credits include WritersWeekly.com and *The Pet Press*. Denise is pleased to have contributed to numerous *Chicken Soup for the Soul* books. Visit her website at www.freewebs.com/denisenox.

Sheryl Ricigliano works as a tax accountant in Wheat Ridge, CO. She and her husband enjoy walking, hiking, baseball games and spending time with their three children.

Cindy Rodberg is a Utah native who grew up close to the Wasatch Mountains. Cindy feels an open mind to the unseen world enhances the physical world. She co-authored *Medicine Wheel Ceremonies*, a book detailing the creation and use of self-created prayer circles.

Catherine Rossi adds creative flair to everything she touches. She loves cooking, floral arranging and cake decorating. This is her first writing adventure. She has also just illustrated her first children's book called *Katie's Smile*.

Freelance writer, columnist, correspondent and songwriter **Barbara Routen's** mission is telling the stories of unsung heroes in forums like *The Tampa Tribune*, *Family Digest* and *Pen Woman Magazine*. She also shares encouragement through live performance, teaching music and speaking to civic and religious groups. E-mail her at Barbara. Routen@gmail.com.

Ruth Ann Roy is a wife and proud mother of three children: Nathan, Nolan, and Rachel. She teaches second grade in Midwest City, OK. Her son Nathan wrote a story for *Chicken Soup for the Christian Teenage Soul* entitled "A Divine Purpose." Ruth's goal is to continue writing stories and eventually a series of children's books.

Sara Schafer is an ordinary woman who has had extraordinary events (miracles) throughout her life. She is a two-time cancer survivor. She is married with two children and a grandson. She writes nonfiction inspirational stories and daily devotionals. E-mail her at sara757s@ aol.com.

Diane Marie Shaw served eleven years as Executive Secretary to a Colorado Springs pastor; she now spends her time writing. Diane has been published in other *Chicken Soup for the Soul* anthologies and her church publication. Active in the writers' guild Words for the Journey, you can visit her blog at needmorewordscs.blogspot.com.

Shirley Nordeck Short has been published in previous *Chicken Soup for the Soul* editions, *Guideposts*, *Reader's Digest* and local publications. She combines her two great loves by writing about the guinea pigs she rescues, and assures you if her guinea pigs could talk they'd have lots of angel stories to tell. E-mail her at shirleynshort@gmail.com.

Penny Smith, a seminary graduate and teaching elder in the church she attends, is also active in missions. Her writings cover a variety of genres, and appear in numerous Christian periodicals. She authored *Gateways to Growth and Maturity Through the Life of Esther*. E-mail Penny at psmithgtg@verizon.net.

Jenny Snow is a happily married wife and a mother of two wonderful boys. She is an elementary math tutor in North Texas. Jenny loves God, time with family and friends, the outdoors, and reading (or writing!) a great story. E-mail her at write4you22@yahoo.com.

Diane Stark is a former teacher turned stay-at-home mom and freelance writer. She is a frequent contributor to the *Chicken Soup for the Soul* series and the author of *Teachers' Devotions to Go*. She loves to write about the important things in life: her family and her faith. E-mail Diane at DianeStark19@yahoo.com.

Jean Haynie Stewart writes and edits in Mission Viejo, CA, with her husband of fifty-two years. Her stories can be found in *Chicken Soup for the Soul* books for True Love, Beach Lover's, Twins and More, Father & Daughter, Brothers & Sisters, Horse Lover's II, and more, as well as newspaper and magazine articles and other anthologies.

Kamia Taylor has been writing published stories since the age of six, and currently spends her time on a small organic farm rescuing dogs, recovering from her disability and helping others to do so too.

Christine Trollinger is from Kansas City, MO. Her stories have been published in several *Chicken Soup for the Soul* books over the years as well as many other publications.

Kristen Nicole Velasquez is a childhood cancer survivor. She graduated with a Bachelor of Science degree in elementary education. She loves helping children and is an active advocate for pediatric cancers. Her current projects include building and writing cancer prevention and awareness material. E-mail Kristen at childhoodcancersurvivor@yahoo.com.

John P. Walker is the Senior Pastor of Fairview Avenue BIC Church in Waynesboro, PA. His writing has appeared in books and other publications in the United States and Canada including several stories in the bestselling *Chicken Soup for the Soul* series. E-mail John at RevJohnnyWalker@aol.com.

Samantha Ducloux Waltz is an award-winning freelance writer in Portland, OR. Her personal stories appear in the *Chicken Soup for the Soul* series, numerous other anthologies, *The Christian Science Monitor* and *Redbook*. She has also written fiction and nonfiction under the name Samellyn Wood. Learn more at www.pathsofthought.com.

Christy Westbrook enjoys writing inspirational stories about everyday life. She loves spending time outdoors with her family and friends. She lives in Lexington, SC with her husband Thad and their four children: Abby, Katie, Marc and Matthew.

Elisa Yager is a regular contributor to the *Chicken Soup for the Soul* series. When she's not writing, Elisa can be found doing something involving history, human resources, music or something in her church. Elisa would love to hear from you! E-mail her at author_ElisaYager@yahoo.com.

Nancy Zeider, grandmother and retired registered nurse, lives in Southern California with her husband, son, and many pets. Her close friend, Heidi Gaul, wrote this story for her.

Meet Our Authors

Jack Canfield is the co-creator of the *Chicken Soup for the Soul* series, which *Time* magazine has called "the publishing phenomenon of the decade." Jack is also the co-author of many other bestselling books.

Jack is the CEO of the Canfield Training Group in Santa Barbara, California, and founder of the Foundation for Self-Esteem in Culver City, California. He has conducted intensive personal and professional development seminars on the principles of success for more than a million people in twenty-three countries, has spoken to hundreds of thousands of people at more than 1,000 corporations, universities, professional conferences and conventions, and has been seen by millions more on national television shows.

Jack has received many awards and honors, including three honorary doctorates and a Guinness World Records Certificate for having seven books from the *Chicken Soup for the Soul* series appearing on the New York Times bestseller list on May 24, 1998.

You can reach Jack at www.jackcanfield.com.

Mark Victor Hansen is the co-founder of Chicken Soup for the Soul, along with Jack Canfield. He is a sought-after keynote speaker, bestselling author, and marketing maven. Mark's powerful messages of possibility, opportunity, and action have created powerful change in thousands of organizations and millions of individuals worldwide.

Mark is a prolific writer with many bestselling books in addition to the *Chicken Soup for the Soul* series. Mark has had a profound influence in the field of human potential through his library of audios, videos, and articles in the areas of big thinking, sales achievement, wealth building, publishing success, and personal and professional development. He is also the founder of the MEGA Seminar Series.

Mark has received numerous awards that honor his entrepreneurial spirit, philanthropic heart, and business acumen. He is a lifetime member of the Horatio Alger Association of Distinguished Americans.

You can reach Mark at www.markvictorhansen.com.

Amy Newmark is Chicken Soup for the Soul's publisher and editor-in-chief, after a thirty-year career as a writer, speaker, financial analyst, and business executive in the worlds of finance and telecommunications. Amy is a *magna cum laude* graduate of Harvard College, where she majored in Portuguese, minored in French, and traveled extensively. She and her husband have four grown children.

After a long career writing books on telecommunications, voluminous financial reports, business plans, and corporate press releases, Chicken Soup for the Soul is a breath of fresh air for Amy. She has fallen in love with Chicken Soup for the Soul and its life-changing books, and really enjoys putting these books together for Chicken Soup for the Soul's wonderful readers. She has co-authored more than four dozen *Chicken Soup for the Soul* books and has edited another three dozen.

You can reach Amy with any questions or comments through webmaster@chickensoupforthesoul.com and you can follow her on Twitter @amynewmark.

Thank You

We owe huge thanks to all of our contributors. We know that you poured your hearts and souls into the thousands of stories that you shared with us. We appreciate your willingness to open up your lives to other Chicken Soup for the Soul readers and share your own experiences, no matter how personal. As I read and edited these truly awe-inspiring stories, I was excited by the potential of this book to inspire people, and impressed by your unselfish willingness to share your stories. Many of you said this was the first time you were sharing your angel story, so we thank you for letting our readers be your confidants. This was a great read for all of us at Chicken Soup for the Soul, and we commented to each other on how much we enjoyed working on this title.

We could only publish a small percentage of the stories that were submitted, but every single one was read and even the ones that do not appear in the book had an influence on us and on the final manuscript. Our editor Kristiana Pastir read every submission and pared the list down to several hundred semi-finalists. After I chose the 101 stories, Kristi chose many of the wonderful quotations that were inserted at the beginning of each story, which we think add so much richness to the reading experience. Our assistant publisher D'ette Corona worked with all the contributors to make sure they approved our edits, and she and editor Barbara LoMonaco performed their normal masterful proofreading job.

We also owe a very special thanks to our creative director and book producer, Brian Taylor at Pneuma Books, for his brilliant vision for our covers and interiors.

~Amy Newmark

Improving Your Life
Every Day

Real people sharing real stories—for twenty years. Now, Chicken Soup for the Soul has gone beyond the bookstore to become a world leader in life improvement. Through books, movies, DVDs, online resources and other partnerships, we bring hope, courage, inspiration and love to hundreds of millions of people around the world. Chicken Soup for the Soul's writers and readers belong to a one-of-a-kind global community, sharing advice, support, guidance, comfort, and knowledge.

Chicken Soup for the Soul stories have been translated into more than forty languages and can be found in more than one hundred countries. Every day, millions of people experience a Chicken Soup for the Soul story in a book, magazine, newspaper or online. As we share our life experiences through these stories, we offer hope, comfort and inspiration to one another. The stories travel from person to person, and from country to country, helping to improve lives everywhere.

Share with Us

We all have had Chicken Soup for the Soul moments in our lives. If you would like to share your story or poem with millions of people around the world, go to chickensoup.com and click on "Submit Your Story." You may be able to help another reader, and become a published author at the same time. Some of our past contributors have launched writing and speaking careers from the publication of their stories in our books!

Our submission volume has been increasing steadily—the quality and quantity of your submissions has been fabulous. We only accept story submissions via our website. They are no longer accepted via mail or fax.

To contact us regarding other matters, please send us an e-mail through webmaster@chickensoupforthesoul.com, or fax or write us at:

Chicken Soup for the Soul
P.O. Box 700
Cos Cob, CT 06807-0700
Fax: 203-861-7194

One more note from your friends at Chicken Soup for the Soul: Occasionally, we receive an unsolicited book manuscript from one of our readers, and we would like to respectfully inform you that we do not accept unsolicited manuscripts and we must discard the ones that appear.

The National Bestseller with Real Stories from Real People

Chicken Soup for the Soul.

Messages from Heaven

101 Miraculous Stories of Signs from Beyond,
Amazing Connections, and Love that Doesn't Die

Jack Canfield,
Mark Victor Hansen,
and Amy Newmark

When our loved ones leave this world, our connection with them does not end. Sometimes when we see or hear from them, they give us signs and messages. Sometimes they speak to us in dreams or they appear in different forms. The stories in this book, both religious and secular, will amaze you, giving you new knowledge, insight and awareness about the connection and communication we have with those who have passed on or those who have experienced dying and coming back.

978-1-935096-91-7

Chicken Soup for the Soul

for the Soul ®

Think Positive

101 Inspirational
Stories about
Counting Your Blessings and
Having a Positive Attitude

Jack Canfield,
Mark Victor Hansen & Amy Newmark
Foreword by Deborah Norville

Every cloud has a silver lining. Readers will be inspired by these 101 real-life stories from people just like them, taking a positive attitude to the ups and downs of life, and remembering to be grateful and count their blessings. This book continues Chicken Soup for the Soul's focus on inspiration and hope, and its stories of optimism and faith will encourage readers to stay positive during challenging times and in their everyday lives.

978-1-935096-56-6

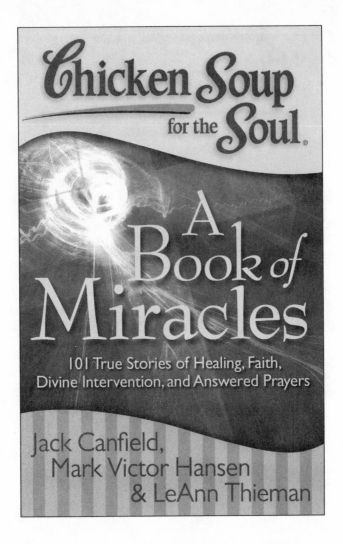

Chicken Soup for the Soul

for the Soul

A Book of Miracles

101 True Stories of Healing, Faith, Divine Intervention, and Answered Prayers

Jack Canfield,
Mark Victor Hansen
& LeAnn Thieman

Everyone loves a good miracle story, and this book provides 101 true stories of healing, divine intervention, and answered prayers. These amazing, personal stories prove that God is alive and active in the world today, working miracles on our behalf. The incredible accounts show His love and involvement in our lives. This book of miracles will encourage, uplift, and recharge the faith of Catholics and all Christian readers.

978-1-935096-51-1

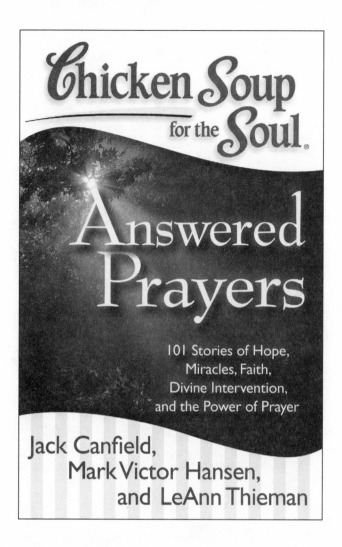

Chicken Soup for the Soul®

Answered Prayers

101 Stories of Hope,
Miracles, Faith,
Divine Intervention,
and the Power of Prayer

Jack Canfield,
Mark Victor Hansen,
and LeAnn Thieman

We all need help from time to time, and these 101 true stories of answered prayers show a higher power at work in our lives. Regular people share their personal, touching stories of God's Divine intervention, healing power, and communication. Filled with stories about the power of prayer, miracles, and hope, this book will inspire anyone looking to boost his or her faith and read some amazing stories.

978-1-935096-76-4

Chicken Soup

www.chickensoup.com

for the Soul